Ethnicity, Race and Education: An Introduction

Also available from Continuum

Anti-Discriminatory Practice (3rd edition),
  Rosalind Millam

Meeting the Needs of Students with Diverse Backgrounds,
  edited by Rosemary Sage

Multiculturalism and Education,
  edited by Richard Race

Perspectives on Participation and Inclusion,
  edited by Suanne Gibson and Joanna Haynes

Ethnicity, Race and Education: An Introduction

Sue Walters

continuum

Continuum International Publishing Group

The Tower Building	80 Maiden Lane
11 York Road	Suite 704
London SE1 7NX	New York NY 10038

www.continuumbooks.com

British Library Cataloguing-in-Publication Data
A catalogue record for this book is available from the British Library.

ISBN: 978-1-8470-6232-1 (paperback)
        978-1-4411-7673-8 (hardcover)

Library of Congress Cataloging-in-Publication Data
Walters, Sue, 1958-
Ethnicity, race and education : an introduction / Sue Walters.
    p. cm.
  Summary: "An introduction to the key issues underlying contemporary research and practice around ethnicity, inclusion, 'race' and education in relation to curriculum, teaching and school policy" – Provided by publisher.
  Includes bibliographical references and index.
    ISBN 978-1-8470-6232-1 (pbk.) – ISBN 978-1-4411-7673-8 ()
1. Multicultural education–United States. 2. Education–Social aspects–United States.
3. Minorities–Education–United States. 4. Academic achievement–United States.
5. Discrimination in education–United States. 6. Educational equalization–United States.
7. Education and state–United States. 8. Curriculum change–United States. I. Title.

LC1099.3.W35 2012
370.1170973—dc23

                                                                                2011017070

Typeset by Newgen Imaging Systems Pvt Ltd, Chennai, India
Printed and bound in India

To Jill and Bryce for giving me a home when I needed one . . .

To Mum for everything . . .

To Alisdair and Cameron for introducing me to a teenage perspective . . .

To Findlay for great conversation (the best) . . .

To Jon for the shared pints . . .

To Dad, often missed . . .

Contents

Acknowledgements

Writing, I have discovered, is a very solitary activity. My thanks therefore go to everyone who has provided distraction, companionship and supportive words. I am also indebted to all of those friends who have let me talk to them about 'the book' and put up with my absence from ordinary life for longer than I would wish. I fear I have been a rather dull and boring friend for rather too long. Special thanks go to Jeremy Kingston for listening and helping me get started with the first chapter as well as for being an excellent friend and helping me take time out. I am also indebted to Jane and Frank Ellis for getting me through a week when both writing and life seemed particularly impossible. Thanks to both Michael Alway and Annie Hay for listening and for their guidance when it was needed.

There are also friends who have been supportive with all those other things that threatened to get in the way of writing – Em and Robin Chittenden, Penny Edwards, Shahina Choudury, George Middleton, Sharon Davis, Elfie and Peter Martin to name but a few. I would also like to acknowledge a debt to those friends who have provided academic stimulation and support through the process of studying for a DPhil and starting to work in Higher Education: Lynn Erler, Christian Grieffenhagen, Ben Fuller, Mohammed Naciri, Felix Kullchen, Lynsey Emmett, Jim Williamson, Peter Smith, Viv Ellis, Helen Fisher, Ruth Forecast and Joy Ann McInnes. Ally Baker has been a very supportive and encouraging editor for which I am very grateful.

The other debt is to my family, particularly to Jill and Bryce for letting me live with them for a year and a half while writing most of this book. I am sorry that I didn't do more of the cooking. The biggest thank you must go to my mum for just being there and for all the support and encouragement over the years.

Introduction: Why Do 'Race' and Ethnicity Matter?

Do 'race' and ethnicity make a difference to your experience of education? Does your 'race' and ethnicity make a difference to your achievement in school? Does education reproduce ethnic differences and racial inequalities or can it challenge and change them?

Why does an understanding of the role that ethnicity and 'race' play in education matter?

This book addresses these issues through an examination of current research, debate, policy and practice across mainstream and non-mainstream educational settings.

The central purpose of this book is to introduce the key issues underlying contemporary work, thinking and practice around ethnicity, 'race' and education in the British context. It is intended as an introduction, a road map if you will, to what has been said, researched, argued over and acted upon over the past 30 years. It is intended to inform those who want to know about these issues and who are looking for an introductory guide: you might be a teacher, school governor, head teacher or senior manager in a school, or an undergraduate or postgraduate student or a researcher setting off to study this field. This book is intended to offer you an account of research as well as of debates and policy. It is thus able to contribute to evidence-based practice and critical reflection with regard to diversity, inclusion, racism and anti-racism in educational settings. It will provide an answer to the questions posed above and make a case for why ethnicity and 'race' matter when we consider education and its processes and outcomes.

Reflection activity

Did your 'race' or ethnicity make a difference to your experience of school?
How? How much?

Make a record of your responses to these questions.
You might want to write about your responses, draw a picture or make a diagram of the ways in which you feel your 'race' or ethnicity made a difference. You can also record any questions that emerge as you undertake this task.

The approach adopted in this book stresses the social, historical and political aspects of ethnicity and 'race' as concepts and emphasizes the importance of power and identity in any discussion of ethnicity and 'race' and their effects. The account is careful to include in its analysis majority ethnic identities, thereby emphasizing that ethnicity and 'race' are not just possessed by recent migrants or people of non-white skin colour but are possessed by all. Other axes of social differentiation such as class and gender, and how they mesh with ethnicity and 'race', are also included in what is presented. Readers are offered the opportunity to see how ethnicity is interwoven with gender, language, class and religion in influencing educational experiences, opportunities and outcomes.

In this way in your response to the reflective task above you may have mentioned your gender, your age, your socio-economic background, your language and/or your religion as being important in someway, alongside your 'race' or ethnic identity, during your school days. If you are a White, English-speaking, British-born person you may have responded to the task by writing about other non-white, non-British-born or English pupils in your school as issues of 'race' and ethnicity do not seem to be relevant to you. You may have not yet considered how your own ethnicity has a powerful impact on your educational experiences and outcomes. Some of you may have noted an experience where you felt treated differently, with negative or positive outcomes, because of your 'race' or ethnic identity while others may have noted how their 'race' or ethnic identity affected some of the choices they made while at school. It might also be the case that some of you wondered what exactly was meant by 'race' and ethnicity, and why the term 'race' appears in speech marks in this text.

This book touches on all of these issues and is organized in the following way. You might want to think of this as the story that the book tells or use this outline as a way of finding the particular issues that you want to explore or develop your knowledge of. The various chapters of the book can be used to develop and deepen your initial responses to the reflective task posed above so that by the time you have worked through the book you have a much deeper insight into how your ethnicity and/or 'race' affected your educational experiences and those of the other pupils (and teachers and parents) around you.

Chapter 1 considers how we categorize and name groups of people according to some notion of 'race' and/or ethnicity and the implications of this. This necessitates a consideration of what is meant by the terms race, 'race', ethnicity and ethnic group, as well as an examination of ethnic monitoring and its uses and potential abuses. An explanation of why 'race' is very often written with inverted commas around it is offered in this chapter.

Chapter 2 then looks at the quantitative research that has explored the school achievement of different minority ethnic groups. The quantitative research conducted in the 1970s and 1980s established that some minority ethnic groups were underachieving in school. Chapter 2 sets out this work, describes who was achieving and who was underachieving in school according to the statistics and discusses the limitations of this work. It also considers the debates about how achievement should be measured and conceived of and some of the dangers of conceiving of learners and achievement in this way. Debates about how differences in achievement between groups should be presented and how policy makers have talked about these differences are also discussed. The studies presented in this chapter cover a period of 35 years. The later studies, those conducted in the past 20 years, are more sophisticated in their methodology and analysis. One of the things highlighted is the dynamic, shifting nature of who is doing well in school and who is not and the difficulties inherent in measuring and talking about this.

Chapter 3 moves us on to consider qualitative studies of minority ethnic pupils' school experience. These studies, unlike the studies outlines in Chapter 2, were able to explore what was happening inside (and in some cases outside) schools. They were able to begin to explore what some of the explanations might be for the poor achievement (and high achievement) of some ethnic minority groups. The chapter outlines the findings of a series of qualitative studies that considered minority ethnic pupils' (and in some cases their teachers') experiences of school and in doing so shows how these experiences are structured according to the perceived ethnic identities of learners, the role that teacher expectation (or 'teacher racism') and action plays in creating or hindering school achievement for particular groups and how 'race'/ethnicity meshes with class, gender and other axes of social differentiation in order to position particular pupil groups in certain ways and how learners respond to these positionings. Chapter 3 can also be read as an account of developing theoretical approaches to understanding learners' identities, school experience and achievement and of the role of education in society in relation to the reproduction of social inequalities. The approaches utilized in the research presented mirror theoretical developments in the wider field of the sociology of education, namely the utilization of 'critical' approaches to understanding the social world (particularly the concept of 'resistance') and 'post-structuralist' approaches which focus on discourse, power and subjectivity. In this manner, the book, and particularly this chapter and Chapter 4, can be read as a specific and particular example of theoretical and methodological changes and developments in the field of the sociology of education.

Chapter 4 begins with a major critique mounted against the qualitative work that was outlined in Chapter 3. This critique became a major debate in the field of 'race'/ethnicity and education and mirrors a wider debate in sociology regarding objectivity, truth and the status of knowledge. The debate focused on claims in much of the qualitative work outlined in Chapter 3 that 'teacher racism' was a key factor in the underachievement of certain minority ethnic groups. The debate is fully explored as the issues raised are central to what we can claim to know about 'race'/ethnicity and education and the actions that we should take as practitioners, researchers and policy makers. The key issue at the heart of the debate is whether researchers and research should be, and can be, objective and what counts as evidence. The rest of Chapter 4 explores issues that arise when researching 'race'/ethnicity and education and how researchers can begin to think through these issues.

Finally, Chapter 5 considers the responses that have been made to the findings of research and to government inquiries that have explored 'race'/ethnicity and education and the kinds of actions that have been taken at national and local level by policy makers, schools, parents and pupils in order to address disadvantage. Government educational policy in relation to minority ethnic pupils is discussed as are critiques of these responses. The chapter also considers the phases that government policy can be said to have passed through, founded upon differing understandings or expectations about the relationship of minority ethnic groups to a notion of British society, namely assimilation, integration and cultural pluralism. The discussion of school responses considers debates regarding multicultural and anti-racist education, and critiques of both, as well as an examination of the kinds of initiatives undertaken in schools and the role of teachers (both as initiators of multicultural and anti-racist initiatives and hinderers of these initiatives). Minority ethnic parent and pupil responses, actions and initiatives are also discussed.

Having outlined what this book covers, it is worth returning to one of the questions posed at the beginning of this Introduction in order to set the context for the rest of your reading and the way in which you may choose to use this book. The question was: Why does an understanding of the role that ethnicity and 'race' play in education matter? The research outlined in this book indicates that 'race' and ethnicity do make a difference to people's experiences of education. This difference can be a difference to:

- your achievement in school, i.e. the outcomes of your schooling (see Chapter 2);
- your experience of being a pupil in school and the relationships you have with your teachers and peers (see Chapter 3);
- the expectations that your teachers have of you and the kind of support and resources they provide (see Chapter 3);
- the classes that you are allocated to (see Chapter 3);
- your chances of being excluded from school (see Chapter 3);
- whether (and when) you go into further and/or higher education and where you go (see Chapter 2);
- your chances of promotion if you are a teacher (see Chapter 3);
- your relationship with your child's school and teachers if you are a parent (see Chapter 3);
- as well as to conducting research in educational settings (see Chapter 4).

Thus, 'race' and ethnicity pervade education and all of our experiences of it, playing a part in positioning people differently in relation to resources, opportunities, identities and outcomes. It is for this reason that an understanding of 'race', ethnicity and education is important. Why it matters.

What Do We Mean by 'Race' and Ethnicity?

Introduction

This book is about 'race', ethnicity and education, so it seems important to start with a discussion of what race, 'race' and ethnicity are. This means starting with a discussion of what a number of words actually mean and how they are, or have been, used. I will start by discussing the terms race and 'race', and then consider the term ethnicity. This is because the terms often appear together in writing about race or racism, ethnic groups and ethnic minority experiences. This happens so often, in fact, that it is easy to think of race and ethnicity as referring to the same thing or of thinking of them as indivisible. Race also frequently appears with speech marks around it (as in 'race'). This section explains how this came about, what it means and how the terms race, 'race' and ethnicity come to be so frequently elided. This entails a brief examination of the history of these terms and concepts.

Race and 'race'

Race is actually a modern term. It only came to be widely used in the later part of the nineteenth century (Pilkington, 2003: 12). This was when it became a key term in the science of classifying people into physically defined groups or races. This 'race science' was based on the belief that it was possible to classify all humans into a small number of races based primarily on physical differences (Fenton, 2003: 19).

It was also posited that the people belonging to each race had different temperaments, abilities, intellectual capacities and moral qualities and that these physical, intellectual and moral qualities were passed on within races (Fenton, 2003: 19). In addition, and because of these supposed physical, intellectual and moral qualities (and the differing cultural achievements that arose from these), there was thought to be a hierarchy to the races (i.e. there were superior and inferior races) with Caucasians (White people) being the superior race (Pilkington, 2003: 3). It is no coincidence that this 'race science' came to prominence at the time of the European empires; it allowed such nations to uphold their sense of their own superiority and to deny the attributes of civilization to their subject peoples. Those at the top were there on merit because of their natural superiority and it was acceptable for them to exploit the labour and resources of those inferior to them.

According to Banton, by the end of the nineteenth century 'very many people identified themselves and others in racial terms' (Banton, 1997: 34 cited in Pilkington, 2003: 13) and this thinking was legitimized by Western science (Pilkington, 2003: 3).

Challenges to this 'race science' began to emerge in the first half of the twentieth century. Ideas about racial classification and the division of people into particular racial groups began to be seen as mistaken science. Scientific methods were not, in fact, able to divide people up into different races and to say that races existed became scientifically untenable. This was because it emerged that there were more differences between people who were purported to belong to the same racial group than there were between one racial group and another. When developments in genetics became more sophisticated this was confirmed (Pilkington, 2003: 3, 14).

> The visible differences between people are biologically trivial . . . there is far greater genetic variation within than between groups previously defined as races. (Jones, 1996 cited in Pilkington, 2003: 14)

Race as a concept, and as a classificatory system based on science, therefore had no credibility or scientific value (Pilkington, 2003: 14; Fenton, 2003: 20; Fenton, 1999: 4–5). At the same time, another challenge to the idea of race and of inherited fixed characteristics and temperaments came about through work in America in the 1930s. Boas showed how context and social environment were fundamental in the production of different ways of behaving and living (Fenton, 2003: 57). We did not behave in the ways in which we did or have fixed characteristics and tendencies because of what we inherited through our bloodline from our parents and their parents but because of how we were socialized by our families and communities in the environments in which we lived. However, while these challenges to 'race science' were mounting, they did not necessarily stop people continuing to take social and political action around the concept of race. For example, a key tenant of Nazi belief and political action in the 1930s and 1940s was the notion of the 'Aryan race' and the need to keep this race pure through the mobilization of anti-Slavic and anti-Semitic feeling and the extermination of Jews and Gypsy Roma.

So while race as a concept has been shown to be scientifically wrong and to have no intellectual credibility, it is a term that is still to be found in use politically and emotively. It is in use as an idea that people still take action around and a term used in policy discourses as well as in people's everyday ways of talking about the world. Ordinary people, writers, academics, politicians, political commentators and some institutions still use the term race. And as Pilkington notes, race still has real effects: people continue to be treated as belonging to a particular group because of their physical characteristics (particularly skin colour) and to suffer the particular disadvantages that fall to that perceived racial group (Pilkington, 2003: 3). W. I. Thomas is credited with expressing 'the first law of social constructivism' when he stated that 'if someone believes a thing, it will affect what he or she does, and will therefore be real in its consequences' (Jenkins, 2002: 21 cited in Karner, 2007: 17). This is a useful way of conceptualizing race – race may not be real according to science, but it is real in its consequences.

Many writers and commentators claim that race should be rejected as a term, especially in the social sciences. They feel very strongly that retaining the term lends credibility to it as a concept and perpetuates the idea that people can be divided into distinct races. Miles, for example, argues that it is a 'methodological error' to treat race as a reality in sociology (Pilkington, 2003: 17). On the other hand, Fenton, among others, argues that a discourse that contains race as an idea is a very powerful feature of many people's commonsense thinking and ways of relating to each other as has been indicated above. As a result he claims that we cannot simply abandon race as a term (Fenton, 1999: 4). This point is argued by many social scientists who believe that because race is such a feature of everyday discourses and the social relationships between people, the term race should be retained rather than discarded.

As a result of the above debate, many social scientists and writers prefer to place the term race in speech marks (as 'race') to signal that they are using the term knowing that it has no scientific validity, but that it is a term that has resonance and meaning for people in both their thinking and in their everyday practices. In this book, therefore, race and 'race' are used in this way. The term appears throughout the text of this book as 'race' to signal that the term has no scientific validity but that it is a term that is utilized and has meaning for people in their everyday practices and meaning-making. However, race is used when earlier writers and ideas are presented that did impute a scientific validity to the idea of 'race', when perceived biological/physical characteristics are utilized as the basis for differentiating people and when presenting the ideas of contemporary writers who chose not to use inverted commas in this way.

A key point to make before we move on to look at the concept of ethnicity is that whatever tactic is adopted by social scientists, it is accepted that biology and physical characteristics have little to do with race or 'race'. What is actually to be understood as race or 'race' is the **meanings** that people attach to colour and/or physical characteristics as they go about their everyday lives. The meanings, of course, will change according to time and according to place. What this means is that different meanings will be attributed to colour and physical differences in different places and at different times.

Fenton (2003: 26–33) gives a good account of this in discussing the way in which people have been and are categorized into races in America. He describes how these categories or labels came about and how they changed according to economic, political and historical processes/events.

Fenton begins with slavery, and how during slavery 'Negros' were seen as 'a race apart' and as low in the hierarchy of races and in civilization (Fenton, 2003: 26). This was used to justify slavery. Citizenship in America at this time was limited to 'White persons'. When slavery was abolished, White solidarity and political manoeuvring in order to protect employment opportunities combined to maintain the dominant position of Whites. 'White' and 'Black' people (the categories that were now in use) were kept very separate in people's understandings and daily actions and they were conceived of as different races. In the nineteenth century immigrants arrived in America from across Europe. While they were white (-skinned) they were not initially welcomed or accepted into the category 'White' as they were perceived to be of a lowly economic position and 'undesirable'. White Americans came to view themselves as Anglo-Saxon and Protestant (as the category White was no longer enough to differentiate them from these other white-skinned people) and to refer to these 'other' white-skinned people as Celts (Catholic), Teutons, Nordics, Jews and Slavs (Fenton, 2003: 28). When people arrived in America in the late twentieth century from East Asia, Latin America and the Caribbean, the classification roughly based on using the idea of 'White' and 'Black' races was disrupted again. Not only did many of these groups of people not fit into a simple dichotomy of 'White' and 'Black', but some, e.g. Puerto Ricans, revealed that they had a different way of conceptualizing race – they saw it as a cultural category connected to their Puerto Rican identity rather than a colour/racial category (Fenton, 2003: 26–33).

This account by Fenton, briefly indicated here, gives some sense of how the categories and labels that are on offer with which people are supposed to define themselves as belonging to a particular race are not the labels of some naturally given, always there, race but come about through history, economic events and politics. In this way we can see that races (and later ethnic groups) are socially constructed – they change according to time and place and the meanings that are given to particular physical markers also change according to time and place.

Ethnicity, ethnic groups and ethnic identity

During the past 50 years or so ethnicity has emerged as a key term in the social sciences as a way of talking about social groupings of people that are based on a notion of difference. One of the reasons for this is that the term does not suffer from the same 'historical association of error' as race does (Fenton, 1999: 6) and does not carry the same 'problematic connotations' (Pilkington, 2003: 3).

This adoption of the term occurred in both sociology and anthropology. The terms race and tribe had been used by anthropologists in the late nineteenth and early twentieth centuries in order to document peoples and cultures in places far away from the West. However, these terms began to acquire negative connotations – rather than reflect the distinctive, rich, complex systems and organizations of other groups and societies of people. The terms became associated with a notion of primitive backwardness, with a lack of technological development and with a pre-literate state in the people so described (Barot et al., 1999: 2). (Just as indicated above in the discussion of the term race, it is no coincidence that these studies of races and tribes were conducted in colonial Africa.) Anthropologists, and later sociologists turned to the terms 'ethnic group' and later 'ethnicity' as ways of avoiding these negative connotations as well as to suggest ways in which people organize themselves around notions of identity and belonging to specific groups rather than having these ascribed to them (Barot et al., 1999: 2). In addition, rather than focusing solely on the lives and cultures of some 'exotic others' living far away, there was a move to begin looking at people's lives and cultures in the West. For instance, in the 1960s, Cohen used the concepts of ethnic groups and ethnicity to study and analyse British stockbrokers and the Notting Hill Carnival in London (Cohen 1969 cited in Barot et al. 1999: 2).

So how can we define ethnicity? The terms ethnic and ethnicity come from the Greek 'ethnos', meaning people (Pilkington, 2003: 18). In their current usage they retain the notion of belonging to a particular group of people, of a belief in having a shared ancestry and heritage with that group of people (Smith, 1986: 192 cited in Pilkington, 2003: 18) and of sharing some kind of cultural markers with that group, perhaps a shared language or dialect, or ways of dressing, or customs or religion. Anthias and Yuval-Davis refer to this as 'sharing (the group's) conditions of existence' (1992: 8 cited in Pilkington, 2003: 18). Thus ethnicity refers to a sense among a group of people of a shared culture and descent, a shared ancestry of some kind with a national or regional origin (Fenton 1999: 3–4). A focus on ethnicity implies a focus on cultural markers (for example, language, religion and/or shared customs) and descent. When we speak of ethnic groups we are talking of how a people's sense of a shared descent, belonging, culture, language, religion, clothing and shared customs makes them feel a member of, or places them within, a group of like people.

Reflection activity

How would you describe your ethnicity? What ethnic group do you see yourself as belonging to (if any)? Does this change according to where you are and who you are with?

If you do see yourself as belonging to an ethnic group, what is it that you feel you share with this group that gives you a sense of belonging to this group? What is it that makes you part of this ethnic group and not another one?

Is this ethnic identity an important identity for you? Is this the most important identity you have or are other identities more important? Does it make a difference where you are and who you are with? Do you feel that you chose this ethnic identity?

If you don't see yourself as belonging to an ethnic group why is this?

Do others see you as belonging to an ethnic group? What do you feel about this?

Take some time to write down your responses to these questions and then, as you read on, reflect on where you stand in relation to the issues and debates that are discussed in what follows.

There are two important points to pick up on here before we can move on to discuss the relationship between 'race' and ethnicity. First, we need to be mindful of the distinction touched on above between an ethnic identity, or membership of an ethnic group, being something that a person or group chooses for themselves or whether it is something that is ascribed to them. To what extent for Pakistanis in Britain has that ethnic identity been ascribed to that group of people and to what extent is it a label and identity claimed by the group itself? This question is posed at two levels. At one level it asks, is the ethnic group or label something that someone else, the state for example, decides about you and decides to use to describe you? Or, is it a label that the group uses to describe itself to denote that it is not the same as other ethnically perceived groups of people? At another level it asks, is this identity the most important identity for you and is it always the most important identity that you have?

Let us take the first level first. An ethnic group label can be created because a group of people claims that label or group identity for themselves or through the state, or one of its institutions, imposing this label upon a group. This is where we need to think about power and who has the power to do the naming. Fenton identifies the following as those who are most likely to do the naming – settler or ruling groups (e.g. in colonial situations they established names and created groups 'that came to take on . . . a distinct and actual character' Fenton, 2003: 10), the state or institutions of the state through laws or through policy initiatives that require the categorization of groups, or an elite within the group (Fenton, 2003: 10). He reminds us that, as we have seen above, classificatory systems are constructed (by rulers, the state, elites or groups themselves) in particular contexts (Fenton, 1999: 12). He also points out that if a label is applied to a group then that group can resist a label that they have been given. In this way ascribed categories/boundaries can be the basis of political action and solidarity for a group. He gives the example of African-Americans embracing the term 'Black', turning it from a term that had negative connotations to one that had a positive identity associated with it (e.g. 'Black is Beautiful') (Fenton, 1999: 18).

If we now look at the second level of my question which asked if ethnic group identity is the most important one that someone has, we will be touching on one of the key debates that has occupied social scientists working with the concepts of ethnicity and ethnic groups. This debate is focused on whether ethnic ties (our sense of belonging to an ethnic group arising from our ties and identifications with other people, and originating in our birth and socialization within a family and culture) remain deeply embedded in our sense of identity throughout life or whether such ties and a sense of belonging to an ethnic group only play an important role in our lives at certain times and places? A key distinction that is made between these two positions is that primordial ties, those that arise from our socialization and strong identifications within our family and culture, are affective ties and can be irrational and override rational choices while ethnic ties are understood from the other perspective: they only become important at times and in places where we make a rational choice to use an ethnic label and claim membership of an ethnic group. This position is referred to as an 'instrumentalist' understanding of ethnic grouping (or sometimes 'circumstantial' or 'situational'), while the other position is referred to as a 'primordialist' understanding. This debate has frequently been represented as an either/or debate. However, writers such as Fenton point out that this does not have to be so at all. 'Someone can have an ascribed ethnic identity that is deeply embedded in their personality and life experience (the primordialist view) yet still perceive the circumstances under which it may be instrumental to deploy it (instrumentalist view)' (Fenton 2003: 84).

The second thing that we need to discuss before moving on to look at the relationship between 'race' and ethnicity is an understanding of ethnic identities and ethnic group membership. If people can be considered to be members of ethnic groups then this implies that there must be some way of knowing who belongs to a particular ethnic group and who does not, i.e. who is included and who is excluded. Barth, in a frequently quoted essay, posited the view that ethnic identities are sustained by the maintenance of the boundaries that separated one ethnic group from another rather than by a wider sense of cultural difference. That is, they are sustained by how one group recognizes its difference to another group. Ethnicity is defined by Barth as a form of social organization based on the drawing and reproduction of group boundaries. This 'boundary drawing' is a continuous social process, the identity and the continuation of the group only requires this maintenance of the boundary (Karner, 2007: 22. For Barth's essay see Barth, 1969). Fenton uses the example of 'A's being the people who speak language 'A'. ' "A"s are the people who are not the "B"s and speaking language "A" is the way of knowing and showing this' (Fenton, 2003: 106). The cultural items that mark one group from another may change but the most important thing according to Barth was 'the ethnic boundary that defines the group, not the cultural stuff which it encloses' (Barth, 1969: 15 cited in Fenton, 2003: 108).

Whereas the focus so far in our discussion has been on the concept of ethnicity and looking at ethnic groups and how they are distinguished and/or distinguish themselves from one another, more recent work on ethnicity has focused on ethnic identities – how people, and when people, call on an ethnic identity, how people may call on more than one identity as they move through their daily life and how they may weave together an ethnic identity from a range of sources. An influential writer in this area is Stuart Hall. Hall has challenged the notion that people only have one 'ethnic identity' and that they can be located only within one clearly bounded, discrete ethnic group. He posits instead that people have multiple identities which draw on the resources of language, history and culture in what Hall calls 'the process of becoming rather than being' (Karner, 2007: 71). Hall includes in his analysis a focus on how people may resist labels and categories that they are initially presented with. He challenges the idea of 'roots' as at the core of our ethnic identity (the idea that is at the heart of notions of ethnic groups as fixed) and suggests instead that it is our 'routes' through life that we should pay attention to.

Examples of research: K. Hall (1995) and Back (1996)

Pilkington provides us with some examples of research that demonstrates this understanding of ethnic identity.

K. Hall's research (1995) showed how young Asian people 'create(d) not one unitary cultural identity, but rather multiple identities' as they moved between their homes, the temple, the shopping centre, school and the disco. 'They were aware of moving between different worlds (Asian and British) and shifting identities accordingly, but in the process often produced new identities' (Pilkington, 2003: 119)

Back's study (1996) showed that young Caribbean people shared a common neighbourhood identity with their young White peers, yet in other contexts, where racism was more pronounced, they drew on a Black identity (Pilkington, 2003: 119).

In this we can see that there is a move among sociologists and cultural theorists to seeing ethnicity and our ethnic identity as something that shifts according to time and place and that there is a move to seeing people as not having just one given ethnic identity but seeing people as having multiple identities that are dependent on place, but which also take account of things such as class, gender, disability and so on. Other writers and researchers have also demonstrated how people pull together or call on elements of ethnic identity from two or more sources and refer to this as 'hybridity'/syncretism. By this they are referring to where 'different cultural traditions intersect, overlap, shape one another (and) are merged into new . . . identities' (Karner, 2007: 73). Thus recent developments in sociological and cultural theory present ethnic identity as something multiple, fluid and dynamic rather than singular and fixed. You might want to return to the notes that you made in response to the reflective task above and consider whether you presented yourself as having just one ethnic identity or whether, in what you wrote, there were tensions around this and you found your-self writing about how your ethnic identity depended on where you were or who you were with, or how your identity was something that was often changing and was influenced by other cultural traditions or sources.

Once we have reached this point in thinking about and understanding ethnic identity, ethnic groups and ethnicity we have to recognize that it is not so easy or straightforward to think of these things as somehow 'real' and out there, fixed givens of everyday, politi-cal and economic life. Instead we have reached a point where we can see that 'people . . . do not just possess cultures or share ancestry; they elaborate these into the idea of com-munity founded upon these attributes as they live their lives (Fenton, 2003: 3). As a result ethnicity and ethnic groups are differently constructed in different contexts. Of course people do not have the freedom to create any identity they wish. First, society and the state present certain recognized ethnic identities or categories/groups that people are asked to use or place themselves within. People will start with these categories/groups as options and although they may resist and challenge these categories and create new ones (as exemplified in our discussion of Hall above and in the concept of hybridity/syncretism), these are the categories that are most often recognized and have meaning in the socie-ties and communities within which people live. We will be looking some more at these categorizations or labels in the section below. Secondly, racism and racial discrimination severely restrict the possibilities for identity construction for people who are members of minority ethnic groups. We need to also recognize, according to Parekh, that even though we can conceive of people having multiple, shifting identities, this does not mean that within a particular moment in society we cannot recognize 'several cultural communi-ties with their overlapping but nonetheless distinct conceptions of the world, systems of meaning, values, forms of social organisation, histories, customs and practices' (Parekh, 1997: 166–7 cited in Pilkington, 2003: 119) i.e. we can, and do, recognize and use as part of our everyday way of thinking and talking about the world, certain ethnic groupings and ethnic identities that have a shared meaning for us living within a particular society at a particular time.

In looking at the history of the concept of ethnicity and ethnic groups, we can say that the problem with the early focus on ethnic groups in social anthropology and sociology was that it lent a sense of homogeneity and completeness to the idea of ethnic group and made invisible the differences that exist within a group and how groups are dynamic and always changing. It presented a simplistic version of the world in which people belonged to one eas-ily identifiable ethnic group and believed that what was to be studied was the relationship between these groups differentiated by ancestry and culture. Recent debates and research in sociology and anthropology have shifted our understanding away from this approach, away from an idea of ethnic groups and ethnicity being something that is a given and in some way 'real' to an understanding of ethnicity, ethnic groups and ethnic identity as always being shaped, reshaped and constructed (Barot et al., 1999: 6). In this way we can say that ethnicity, ethnic groups and ethnic identities are 'socially constructed' just as we identified earlier that 'race' is 'socially constructed' while at the same time not losing sight of the fact that both 'race' and ethnicity are 'real' in their consequences. By this I mean that both 'race' and 'ethnicity' have a reality in everyday life as well as in policy, politics, economics and history because people use these terms and give meaning to them in their everyday practices and in the actions they take as citizens.

'Race' and ethnicity

We have come a long way from our starting point which was to think about how we might understand the difference between the terms 'race' and ethnicity. We have looked briefly at some of the key understandings and debates about these terms and why 'race' frequently appears, as it does here, with speech marks around it. Despite looking at each term separately, describing how it has been, and is, used and putting forward how it differs from the other term, readers would have noticed that there is still a considerable overlap in how the terms 'race' and ethnicity are used and what they refer to. This is succinctly expressed by two key writers on ethnicity and what they say is reproduced here as they identify this problem well, but also go on to give what they think are the clearest, although very broad, delineations of 'race' and ethnicity as the terms are commonly used in popular, policy and academic discourses:

> The actual use of ethnic group and race in popular, political and administrative discourses gives no immediate guide to any analytic distinction since . . . the terms are frequently used interchangeably . . . but historical usage, and the legacy of now discredited theories of the division of humankind into fundamentally different 'types' link the term 'race' with physical or visible difference, and explicitly or implicitly convey the idea that populations marked by characteristic appearance are constitutionally or biologically different. By contrast the term 'ethnic' or 'ethnic group' is used primarily in contexts of cultural difference, where cultural difference is associated above all with an actual or commonly perceived shared ancestry, with language markers, and with national or regional origin. This reference to physical/biological (race) and the cultural/ancestral (ethnic) provides the reader with a broad guide to the centre of gravity of the two terms with respect to their place in popular, political and academic discourses. (Fenton, 1999: 3–4)

> Race entails distinguishing people on the basis of physical markers, such as skin pigmentation, hair texture, and facial features, and placing people into discrete categories. Ethnicity on the other hand entails distinguishing people on the basis of cultural markers, such as language, religion, shared customs, and identifying key social groups. While members of a purported race may not identify themselves as sharing a common racial identity, members of an ethnic group necessarily recognise that they share a common ethnic identity with other members of their ethnic group. (Pilkington, 2003: 2)

Pilkington makes a very interesting and insightful observation, however. In discussing the ethnic categories that we use in everyday life and in policy and academic discourses we actually use labels like 'White', 'Black British', 'Black Caribbean', and these labels of ethnicity and ethnic group (see below for a discussion of the categorization of ethnic groups and people's ethnicity) include in them a notion of race – they include skin colour and reference to biological/physical appearance (Pilkington, 2003: 25). In this way Pilkington makes the claim that ethnicity, in the way it is used, to some extent contains race. Similarly, other writers, following Miles (1989), use the term racialization to refer to the process by which people become defined 'according to apparent differences of skin colour, national origin or other attributes and positioned as different from the (usually White) majority' (Open University, 2010a). Here the idea of racialization contains ideas associated with both race and ethnicity.

'Race' and racism

While we might chose not to use the concept of race or 'race' in our writing and discussion we need to retain and use the concept of racism. Race might not be real but racism is. By racism we mean 'an ideology of innate superiority that (brings) about discrimination, exclusion and marginalising of particular categories of individuals' (Miles cited in Barot et al., 1999: 4). Simply put, we cannot substitute ethnicity for 'race' and racism.

There have been different, evolving ways of conceptualizing 'race' and racism. We have already touched on some aspects of this in relation to 'race' above, but it is worth giving a brief overview here of some of the main approaches to conceptualizing 'race' and racism.

'Race' has been debated about in relation to whether we can understand 'race' as operating as an autonomous (and the most significant) category when we think about how people organize themselves in society or whether 'race' should be seen as an aspect of class, and capitalist, relations. Writers that argue for the latter see 'race' as a means by which capitalism divides groups of workers from each other and reproduces a compliant but productive workforce. In this view 'race' is subsumed by, or seen as less significant in understanding society than class and is understood as an aspect of economic reproduction. At another level a distinction is made between conceptions of 'race' that see 'race' as operating autonomously and conceptions that understand 'race' to be operating alongside gender, class, sexuality and other social axes of differentiation. In this view, 'race' is to be considered alongside these other aspects of social identity in order to properly conceptualize and understand social and economic processes and differentiation. As we have seen above, a further debate has occurred around whether race is real, a biological fact or a socially constructed categorization of people.

Examples from research: Gillborn (2008) and Connolly (1998)

In terms of 'race' and education it is worth considering here how two of the commentators whose work will appear later in this book formulate 'race' in their work.

Gillborn has recently started to work using the approach of Critical Race Theory (CRT). Using CRT, Gillborn, in *Racism and Education: Coincidence or Conspiracy* (2008), argues that race issues are not peripheral and that 'race inequality should be placed centre-stage as a fundamental axis of oppression' (Gillborn, 2008: 1). In this work race and racism are foregrounded and set at the centre of the analysis and explanation of educational phenomena. There is a strong focus on how whiteness operates to exclude and the non-accidental ways education (and society) operates in order to reinforce White identities and interests. Other axes of differentiation are recognized although the focus is on how race and racism operates 'with, against, and through' these additional axes of gender, class, sexuality and disability (Gillborn, 2008: 36). There is something of a tension between this kind of analysis and that of a class-based analysis of race and racism (see Gillborn, 2008: 37; Cole, 2007, 2009).

Connolly (1998: 17) utilizes the theories of Bourdieu and Foucault in his work and posits 'race' as a discourse (a way of talking about the world, and therefore of representing the world), alongside gender and sexuality, that can be called upon, in this case by young children, in order to fashion a gender identity and to make sense of experiences in the context of the primary school. In this work, 'race' is not understood as a stand-alone category that dominates an explanation of social life, but as a category that operates alongside other discourses to produce particular identities and opportunities in school. Youdell (2003, 2006) also approaches 'race' in this way in her work.

Reflection activity

How do you define racism?

Give an example of racism occurring?

Make some notes and then refer to these as you read on. Think about the way in which you defined racism and your example of racism and how it fits with the issues and debates that are discussed below.

'Racism', like 'race', can also be understood and theorized in a number of ways. It can be understood as:

- Individual ignorance and prejudice. Arshad refers to this as 'personal racism' (Arshad, 2005: iv).
- Cultural superiority when one cultural group sees itself as superior to others and imposes 'its patterns, assumptions and values on others, often in a manner that many do not even notice' (Arshad, 2005: vii).
- Institutional, in that the institutions of society are seen to maintain inequality between different ethnically defined groups even though the individuals working within those institutions are not wittingly racist (see Chapter 5).

As we have seen above, racism can also be conceived of as fundamental to state power and/ or as a public discourse utilized in people's meaning-making everyday.

'New racism' is a term that has been utilized to suggest the ways in which the old biological, supposedly scientific, notion of race (now rejected) has been replaced by a new form of 'race' talk and racism. This 'new racism' focuses on 'culture' and 'difference', rather than supposed physical differences. It utilizes notions of Britishness, nation, national identity and belonging as a way of situating some members of society as British and part of the nation and others (those that have a 'different culture') as not belonging and not part of the nation. As Gillborn and Youdell note, 'new racism' 'has become an especially powerful force in contemporary politics and popular culture' (Gillborn and Youdell, 2000: 5).

Ethnic minority, ethnic majority, 'white' and whiteness

So far in this discussion of 'race' and ethnicity care has been taken to refer to ethnicity and ethnic groups and ethnic identity as something that is held by, or applies to, all of us. This is not what we always find in writing about these issues, however, and it is certainly not what is in many people's minds when they think about ethnicity, ethnic groups and ethnic identity. What most White people think of when they are reading or using the words 'ethnicity' or 'ethnic group' is people other than themselves. This is because the terms associated with ethnicity are usually used by the White majority in order to define people who are not like them, or they are used by people who are made to feel that they are not like the majority in the society they live in to describe themselves. It is also the case that most of the attention directed at ethnic groups and ethnicity has been about explaining or describing or documenting the lives or activities of people who are perceived as ethnically different to White people. In this way it is common in Britain to find the terms ethnicity, ethnic group and ethnic identity used to talk about Bangladeshis, African-Caribbeans, Pakistanis, Black Africans and so on rather than to talk about White people. This is one of the reasons why the use of the term 'ethnic minority' was changed to become 'minority ethnic' in policy documentation and academic writing. It was an attempt to flag up the fact that all of us have ethnicity and belong to an ethnic group. Some of us to a minority ethnic group (i.e. an ethnically defined group that is a minority in terms of both the number of people that belong to that group compared to the number that belong to the majority group and a minority in terms of their access to power and resources) and some of us to a majority ethnic group (i.e. the group that is the majority in terms of both the number of people that belong to that group compared with other groups and the majority in terms of access to power and resources in society). A capital letter is used for *White* in this book to emphasize that White people also have an ethnicity and belong to ethnic groups and in order to be consistent with the use of *Black*: Black is usually written with a capital letter when Black people are being discussed. As Fenton and many other commentators have noted, in Britain the ethnic majority, White British-born people, are scarcely conscious of themselves as 'ethnic' at all. The roots of this are to be found in British history and in colonialism in that Whites have been in a dominant position, first as settlers and colonial masters and then through the British state, and have therefore turned their gaze upon 'others' naming and categorizing subject and minority peoples and using the discourses of ethnicity to do this. In this process, whiteness becomes and remains 'the norm': White people are normal; it is other people who are different. We need to also appreciate that power is involved in this – when differences and fixed characteristics are assigned to 'other' groups of people they are being powerfully defined as different (as 'other') and this frequently involves seeing the 'other' as inferior in some way. Just as we have seen above, in the example Fenton provides of the changes in racial categorizing in America, being included or excluded from the category White is related to issues around access to employment, opportunities, resources and political power.

Ethnic monitoring

Above we have looked at the meaning and history of the terms ethnicity, race and 'race' as well as ethnic identity and ethnic groups. Now we turn to the issue of ethnic monitoring and its purposes.

Case study: A conversation

This conversation, or something very like it, took place in April 2007 as Ruth was applying for a job in Britain after many years working overseas.

Read through the conversation and think about these questions:

What issues emerge here concerning ethnic monitoring?

Do you agree with Ruth's decision? Why? Why not?

Ruth: I really don't feel comfortable about this.

Sue: About what?

Ruth: This ethnic monitoring form that I have to fill in with my job application.

Sue: Haven't you had to fill one in before when you have applied for a job?

Ruth: No I haven't. I've been living and working abroad for so long.

Sue: Why do you feel uncomfortable about it? It is so normal for me in Britain.

Ruth: Well I don't like the idea that I have to define myself like that, choose one of those labels. I don't want to be known in that way. And another thing is that I don't like the idea of anyone having that kind of information about me and it being something they want to know in order to decide if they are going to give me an interview.

Sue: Oh I don't think that will happen. The form doesn't go to the people who are deciding who to interview; it stays with the personnel people. They need it to see who gets the job so that they can check that they don't always appoint a nice White man or never appoint anyone from an ethnic minority.

Ruth: But I just don't like it. I don't like it that people you don't know use labels like this and ask you to define yourself in this way. It's too much like the Nazis in Germany and what happened to the Jews.

Sue: Well I don't think being asked to say what ethnic group you belong to is for the same reason as that. People ask for that information because they want to be able to monitor who they employ. They can look at the make-up of their labour force and who they have appointed and see if they are employing people that reflect the make-up of the population and if they are not then they can do something about it.

Ruth: Do they do that then?

Sue: Well I am probably being a bit naive but that is what companies and institutions say they do. Lots of organizations ask people to fill in ethnic monitoring forms so that they can see what is going on. I think that they have to. It is important. It's like in education, before they collected information about the ethnicity of pupils it was impossible to see whether the education system was working effectively for all pupils or whether some pupils were doing better than others. Without any data or actual figures people could just argue about this using anecdotes or their own opinion. If you start to monitor pupils using their ethnic group you can easily see that some ethnic groups do really well in exams at the end of schooling but some do really badly. Once you can show that then you can expect schools and policy makers to begin to do something about it rather than deny that there is a problem.

Ruth: But shouldn't that just be about some pupils are failing in school and we need to make sure that we provide support so that they don't? Why do pupils or their families, why do I as a teacher, have to give my ethnicity on one of these forms?

Sue: Well I think it is because ethnicity and the ethnic group you are seen to belong to might be part of the explanation for why those children are not doing well in school. At least it is one of the explanations that has to be explored. And they will want to know what your ethnicity is so that they can see clearly what ethnic groups teachers belong to. Back in the past, people wanted to know how many ethnic minority pupils there were in English schools, and by ethnic minority they meant not White – they meant immigrants, because there were concerns among white parents and politicians that the presence of non-White, immigrant children would affect the achievement of their children; it would hold them back. So I can see where your concern comes from about labelling people and getting them to define themselves as 'immigrant' or 'Asian' or 'Black'. At the same time though it also gave ammunition and power to the people who wanted to argue that having immigrant, non-White children in a school did not hold back White children – they could do research to show this but in order to do that research they had to define children in terms of ethnic groups. That's why I think it is OK to ask people to fill in those forms.

Ruth: I see what you mean but I am still uneasy. They are such limiting labels. What do they really mean? What am I supposed to put anyway. I am Jewish by birth but I am a Buddhist now, there's nowhere to put that. Am I just White then? White British? I think I am European, that is how I think of myself, not British or English. Even if I tick this box, which I am obviously supposed to do, the White British one, what does it really tell them about me? I am just fitting myself into their labels.

Sue: Yes, I see your point there. It is really difficult if you are mixed race or dual heritage as well. I always wonder what a lot of people actually put. When I worked in Norfolk in the 1990s, the box that most people ticked, when we were gathering data about the ethnic minority communities we were working with, was 'Other'. That didn't tell us very much at all. There is a long complicated history of how the labels, the boxes that you can tick on that page, came about and it is certainly the case that the labels and boxes are still changing.

Ruth: Well I will tick the box although I am still not happy about it. I feel reassured to know that the people selecting candidates and making the job offers don't actually see these forms. That makes me feel a bit better. I do see why for someone like you it is useful to be able to look at what happens in terms of the ethnic groups people say they belong to but I am still uneasy about it all.

This conversation touches on so many of the main issues and complexities that come up when we think about ethnic monitoring. These include the reasons why ethnic monitoring is undertaken, and the difficulties, limitations and dangers inherent in trying to use ethnic monitoring.

Let us look first at the reasons why ethnic monitoring is used. As Sue explains above, ethnic monitoring is used to monitor how different ethnically defined groups of people are doing in society. More specifically, it is used in order to identify, measure and monitor inequalities and patterns of discrimination in society. For example, in order to support the implementation of race equality legislation in the 1980s, the then Commission for Racial Equality (CRE) needed to have access to data in order to identify patterns of discrimination (Leech, 1989: 8). At the same time, for those with responsibility for the delivery of public services and resources, there is a need to gather data that show that this is being done equitably. Data collected through ethnic monitoring can be used to follow how particular groups of ethnically defined people are faring in society in comparison with other groups and in comparison with how things were in the past. Without the classification that ethnic monitoring requires, the labels that Ruth is so concerned about, 'no reliable data is possible about discrimination against minority ethnic people' (Gaine and Burch, 2004: 21) or about discrimination against majority ethnic people for that matter. Richardson rightly states that 'we need to collect and collate the information which policy-makers and decision-makers need . . . in order to create and maintain a more inclusive society' and 'so that provision can be more sensitive to need' (Richardson and Wood, 2000: 75). Ethnic monitoring is not only used to monitor and measure patterns of discrimination but also to identify how the provision of services can be more suited to people's particular needs. If it is found that Bangladeshi children are doing particularly badly in end of school exams, as was the case in Norfolk in the early 1990s, then the local education authority can target resources at this particular group of pupils, teachers, parents and families in order to address some of the barriers that exist to school success.

At this point in our discussion it is worth drawing attention to the following point that has been expressed very clearly by Pilkington (2003: 25). The reason for asking people to identify themselves by ticking a box that denotes their ethnicity is not to measure or describe ethnicity or the major ethnic groups that are to be found in society, it is done in order to monitor how non-White groups are faring, in other words to identify and monitor ethnic groups in order to monitor and measure inequalities pertaining to ethnic groups. It is also worth noting that while ethnic monitoring asks people to say what ethnic group they belong to, the categories and labels that people are usually offered with which to define themselves ('Black British', 'White') include and call on attributes that are linked to physical appearance and therefore 'race' as well as nation.

The history of ethnic monitoring

Thought was first given to including a question in the census in 1978 that asked people to say what ethnic group they belonged to. Before this date the census had asked for parents' place of birth, but the data gathered in response to this question were considered inadequate and unsatisfactory (Leech, 1989: 1). This was because many White British people had parents who were born oversees in British colonies and thus they appeared in the census results in the 'wrong' category. From 1971 the General Household Survey had asked people what their skin colour was and in 1977–8 the National Dwelling and Housing Survey began to offer 12 ethnically defined categories for people to choose from. The Labour Force Survey began to ask for race and ethnic origin in 1981 (Leech, 1989: 1). We have identified the reasons why this kind of information was suddenly wanted above. In addition we can note that significant numbers of people were coming to settle in Britain from the New Commonwealth and Pakistan at this point in time. This meant that there was an increasing wish to monitor this settlement and how immigrant groups were faring (again it was minority, non-white-skinned people who were under the focus of attention from the state). The discussion around whether to include an 'ethnic question' in the census of 1981 (the census is conducted in Britain every 10 years i.e. 1971, 1981 and so on) reveals the kinds of debates and concerns about asking an 'ethnic question' that Ruth identified above. With regard to the census the debate ranged around the questions of 'Can it be asked?' and 'Should it be asked?' (Leech, 1989: 1–2).

The ethnic question: Should it be asked?

Many thought that issues of race and ethnicity were so complex and imprecise that no suitable question could be formulated and that more damage would be caused socially than useful data be generated. There were vocal campaigns initiated around the whole issue with the CRE on one side arguing that there should be an 'ethnic question' in the census and various ethnic minority groups and anti-racist campaigners arguing against such an inclusion (Leech, 1989: 2) for the kinds of reasons identified by Ruth above.

The ethnic question: Can it be asked?

In addition to the debates about whether the question should be asked, there were considerable difficulties identified through a number of pilot tests in 1975, 1976 and 1977 with 'can it be asked?' Various formulations of an 'ethnic question' were tried, i.e. the people designing the question for the tests tried to identify both the groupings or categories of people that would provide the kinds of data and information that policy makers, institutions and public services wanted in order to properly monitor their activities and monitor for racial discrimination and inequality and, at the same time, come up with categories or labels that people completing the census would identify with **and be willing** to use to describe themselves with. This was, and still is, a very difficult task. (See Leech, 1989; The Runnymede Trust, 1994; Modood et al., 1997 for more on this.)

Ethnic monitoring: Issues, dangers and limitations

One of the key difficulties with ethnic monitoring is finding labels that fit how people wish to define themselves. As Ruth said above, one of the key ways she thinks about herself and her 'ethnic identity' is through religion. She was brought up Jewish and now sees herself as Buddhist, but religion is usually not included in the labels on offer. The same is true of language, and for some people the language that they speak is one of the key defining characteristics of their sense of ethnic identity. Gaine and Burch did some research into how young people describe themselves if they are asked to give an ethnic identity, the range of self-ascription was extremely wide (and included 'national origins, parental roots, geographical regions, religion, colour and . . . knowledge of how one is perceived by others' Gaine and Burch, 2004: 21), far wider than the categories on offer in the 2001 Census classifications. In the past 'Black' has been used as a label for all people of colour, yet this label, while acknowledging the similar experiences of discrimination that non-White people can experience in British society (and providing a sense of political solidarity in challenging that discrimination), was contested by Asian groups because it made them invisible. They did not wish to use this label to describe themselves. Now Asian (and within that grouping the labels of Bangladesh, Indian, Pakistani) is on offer as a category in nearly all ethnic monitoring.

Other categories and labels have also undergone these kinds of shifts because people have contested the label or the category, or refused/failed to recognize it as defining themselves. The label 'West Indian' has changed to 'Afro-Caribbean' and then to 'African-Caribbean' over the past 30 years. The label 'Black' has been challenged. For example, in Scotland, the label as used in the 2001 Census has been challenged by African communities as being divisive and unhelpful (Arshad et al., 2005: iv). The Race Equality Advisory Forum (REAF) in Scotland argues that the labels 'Black' or 'White' should not be used in ethnic monitoring at all as they lack clarity and reinforce racism, especially towards people with African backgrounds (Arshad et al., 2005: v). Within the UK, devolution has meant that changes have been made in what is offered to reflect the changing political and personal sources of identity in the newly devolved nations.

Activity: Census categories

Look at these census categories that were presented to people in the 2001 census.
One set of categories is from the Scottish census and the other is from the census in England and Wales.
What do you notice? Which box would you tick in each?
What issues arise?

Scottish Census Categories: 2001	England and Wales Census Categories: 2001
What is your ethnic group?	**What is your ethnic group?**
Choose ONE section from A to E, then tick the appropriate box to indicate your cultural background.	Choose ONE section from A to E, then tick the appropriate box to indicate your cultural background.
A White	**A White**
Scottish	British
Other British	Irish
Irish	Any other White background,

Any other White background, please write in. . . . .

please write in. . . . .

B Mixed

Any Mixed background, please write in. . . . . .

B Mixed

White and Black Caribbean
White and Black African
White and Asian
Any other Mixed background, please write in. . . . .

C Asian, Asian Scottish, or Asian British

Indian
Pakistani
Bangladeshi
Chinese
Any other Asian background, please write in. . . . . . .

C Asian or Asian British

Indian
Pakistani
Bangladeshi
Any other Asian background, please write in. . . . .

D Black, Black Scottish, or Black British

Caribbean
African
Any other Black background, please write in. . . . . . .

D Black or Black British

Caribbean
African
Any other Black background, please write in. . . . .

E Other ethnic background

Any other background, please write in. . . . . . .

E Chinese or other ethnic group

Chinese
Any other, please write in. . . . .

What were your experiences of using these categories?
How did you feel about using them?
Were you categorized differently depending on the census?
Does what you have ticked adequately represent you and what you think of as your ethnicity?
Are there missing categories?

Looking at these two census categories reminds us that ethnicity and ethnic groupings vary from place to place. Here we can see that one could describe oneself as Scottish in the Scottish census but not in the census for England and Wales even if you considered this to be your ethnic group or national identity. We can also see that some definitions and ethnic identities that people might have wanted to call on are missing or inadequately represented: the labels and categories that were on offer 'do not deal adequately with people of mixed parentage' (Modood et al., 1997: 14), do not include Gypsy Travellers or Romas and do not distinguish differences in the 'White' category for White Western or Eastern Europeans. A further problem was the use of the label 'Other' which can lead to large returns in this category and tell us little. This is a particular problem in education as Sue identified above. An additional problem in education is that ethnic monitoring has not, until very recently, been carried out systematically. This will be discussed below.

It is interesting to note that the published proposals for the 2011 Census in England and Wales detail a number of shifts in how the ethnic question is to be posed, i.e. that:

- a 'Gypsy or Irish Traveller' tick-box is added under the 'White' heading
- an 'Arab' tick-box is added under the 'Other ethnic group' heading
- the 'British' tick-box . . . be renamed 'Welsh/English/Scottish/Northern Irish/British (in England)', 'Welsh/English/Scottish/Northern Irish/British' (in Wales)
- the 'Chinese' tick-box is moved to the 'Asian/Asian British' heading
- the 'African' tick-box is moved to come before the 'Caribbean' tick-box

(Office for National Statistics, 2009a)

In addition, it is proposed that there will also be questions on language (main language spoken, spoken English proficiency and in Wales, knowledge of Welsh) (Office for National Statistics, 2009b), on migration (Office for National Statistics, 2009c) and on national identity (Office for National Statistics, 2009d). Similar changes are proposed for the Scottish 2011 Census (General Register Office, 2010) and for the 2011 Census in Northern Ireland (Northern Ireland Statistics and Research Agency, 2010).

Activity

Look at both the Office for National Statistics and General Register Office 2011 Census websites to see what the changes to the ethnic question and the questions on national identity, language and migration are.

www.gro-scotland.gov.uk/census/census2011

www.ons.gov.uk/census/2011

Make a note of how attempts have been made to address some of the issues identified above as well as to consider the difficulties and issues that remain.

You may want to try completing the ethnic questions on both Census forms and comparing what emerges with your notes on the Reflection Activity undertaken above.

As the above discussion makes clear, ethnic monitoring does not capture anything that is fixed or objective. At the same time there is a real danger that when we talk about the ethnic groups made visible through ethnic monitoring the boundaries between these groups can be overdrawn, the cultural distinctiveness of each exaggerated (Pilkington, 2003: 23), with the implication that ethnic groups are distinct things rather than fluid, dynamic and overlapping.

State education is of course a public service, and schools, colleges and universities are institutions. That does not mean that the use of ethnic monitoring in education has been straightforward and readily accepted as a 'public good'. Ethnic monitoring has not, until very recently, been carried out systematically (Pilkington, 2003: 126–7) and it has been difficult to have a clear up-to-date picture of who is in school (Richardson and Wood, 2000) and how they are faring. In Scotland, for example, there has been a lack of reliable monitoring until very recently (Arshad et al., 2005: 23–4). One reason has been an unease among teachers about the use to which the data collected will be put (an unease identified by Ruth above) and, in 'mainly White areas', which covers most of Scotland, a feeling until recently that such monitoring is not required (Arshad et al., 2005). In England and Wales data from Local Education Authorities (LEAs) and then schools and colleges, in one form or another, have been collected since 1989 but not in a very systematic way (Foster, 1994: 647). This changed with the introduction of the Pupil Level Annual School Census (PLASC) in 2002 (see Chapter 2 for an explanation of PLASC). Foster has considered the reasons put forward for ethnic monitoring in education and warns of some of the limitation in using ethnic data for examining equal opportunities in education. The five main reasons that are put forward for ethnic monitoring in education according to Foster are:

1. To recognize the needs of students and in deciding upon appropriate educational provision to be able to take account of their culture and religion;
2. To be able to use resources more effectively at LEA level;
3. To gather data on achievement so that the effectiveness of educational provision for different ethnic groups can be monitored;
4. To identify where discrimination might be occurring and to examine practices that put ethnic minorities at a disadvantage;
5. To monitor the effectiveness of measures to reduce underachievement (Foster, 1994: 647–8).

Foster, however, feels that there are dangers in being over-reliant on ethnic monitoring in education. He feels that using ethnic background to identify student need can lead to stereotyping – 'The 'cultural needs' of students in the same ethnic background category may . . . vary widely. Ethnic data tell teachers nothing about this variation. Indeed, it . . . (can encourage) teachers to make stereotypical assumptions about students needs' (Foster, 1994: 649). He reminds us that differences in achievement and educational opportunity for different ethnic groups might have other causes or explanations, some of which may be located outside schools (Foster, 1994: 650–1) and argues that inequalities in outcomes (this is what ethnic monitoring would measure) are not a reliable guide to situations where discrimination is or might be occurring. This is because, he claims, inequalities in outcomes could be the result of a variety of factors and, at the same time, discrimination that was occurring might not be revealed in group outcomes if, for example, a particular group of individuals were drawing on other resources to counter discrimination and its effects (Foster, 1994: 651).

While I do not agree with all of the limitations that Foster outlines (he does tend to present racial discrimination and racialism at a personal, individual level rather than something that occurs at an institutional level), his main conclusion, that we need to look at the processes within schools, and not be over-reliant on statistics and fixed ethnic categories, is a good one and is one of the issues that we look at in Chapter 3.

I conclude this section with an example of the process of ethnic monitoring in a specific educational context, an 'Academy' school in an English city, in order to give some sense of the issues that must be faced by a teacher who needs to, and is required to, gather ethnic data about the pupils in her school.

Example of good practice: Ethnic monitoring in an English secondary school

Hannah is a specialist Ethnic Minority Achievement teacher in a large secondary Academy school in a British city. The school has a large number of minority ethnic pupils, including refugee and asylum-seeking pupils. Part of Hannah's job is to monitor pupils in the school in order to see how they are doing and to check if the school is supporting and developing these pupils' learning. In order to do this monitoring Hannah has to complete an ethnic monitoring form for each pupil. The 2001 Census categories were the initial categories that Hannah selected for use, however, these were inadequate for the detailed monitoring that was required and were awkward and inappropriate for use with the students and families who attended the school. In the light of this, Hannah made the following changes:

1. She reordered the categories so that White was not the first and Chinese the last category on the list. Hannah commented on the fact that having White as always first (because of this category being the ethnic majority) implicitly came to suggest some kind of hierarchy when filling in the forms with students and their families. Hannah reordered the categories so that they were in alphabetical order. It made the process of completing forms with students and families more comfortable as there was no implied sense of White always being first and the 'normal category'.
2. Hannah added to the categories by including 'Somali' in the 'Black British or Black' section; 'Eastern European' and 'Western European' as well as 'Gypsy/Roma'; 'Traveller of Irish Heritage' in the 'White' section; added separate sections headed 'Any other ethnic background' and 'I do not wish an ethnic background to be recorded'.
3. Hannah renamed the 'Mixed' category as 'Dual Heritage and Multi-Heritage'.

In addition Hannah decided that it was important to also collect data about

parents', grandparents' and students' country of birth
religion
all languages spoken within the family and by whom

This example gives us some insights into the decisions and issues that can be involved in ethnic monitoring in a specific context. It also reminds us of some of the issues that we have covered in this chapter.

Chapter Summary

In this chapter we have considered what the terms race, 'race' and ethnicity mean and the history of these terms. We have also looked at ethnic groups and ethnic identity and conceptions of 'race' and racism. We finished by considering the issue of ethnic monitoring and some of the difficulties and tensions that arise around this practice. The chapter has raised the issue, one that we meet again and again in this book, of what it means to categorize and name, and be categorized and named, according to some notion of 'race'/ethnicity. We have considered the dangers of this and the necessity of doing this. In the next chapter we turn our attention towards 'race'/ethnicity and education and begin to look at how 'race'/ethnicity affect educational experiences.

Further reading

I have drawn heavily on the following accounts in this chapter and they are all worth consulting further for their accounts of 'race', racism and ethnicity: Pilkington (2003), *Racial Disadvantage and Ethnic Diversity in Britain*; Fenton (2003), *Ethnicity* and (1999) *Ethnicity: Racism, Class and Culture*; Karner (2007) *Ethnicity and Everyday Life*. In addition, Solomos and Back (2000) in their 'Introduction' in *Theories of Race and Racism: A Reader* offer a good account of the concept of race relations, class, the kinds of meaning that can be given to the term and category of race and how racism can be identified as well as 'new racism'. Bhattacharya et al. (2002) in *Race and Power: Global Racism in the Twenty-First Century* offer a good account of the construction of 'race'. See also Bhavnani et al.'s *Tackling the Roots of Racism: Lessons for Success* (2005), Chapter 1 for a discussion of the origins of the concept of 'race'.

For a further discussion of ethnicity and ethnic group see Modood et al. (1997), *Ethnic Minorities in Britain*.

Richardson and Wood in *Inclusive Schools, Inclusive Society: Race and Identity on the Agenda* (2000) offer a good account of ethnic monitoring in schools and Gaine and Burch in their conference paper 'Self-Identification and Ethnicity: "You Can't Be An English Pakistani"' (2004) offer an excellent account of identity categories that young people choose to use.

For a history of the development of ethnic categories for the census, see Leech (1989), *A Question in Dispute: The Debate about an 'Ethnic' Question in the Census*.

Stuart Hall's work on ethnicity and identity is recommended: see 'New Ethnicities', in Donald and Rattansi (ed.) (1992), *Race, Culture and Difference*.

Scourfield et al. in 'The negotiation of minority ethnic identities in virtually all-white communities: Research with children and their families in the South Wales valleys', in *Children and Society* (2005) Volume 19, looks at how ethnic identity is negotiated by children in a predominantly white area of South Wales. It touches on many of the issues discussed in this chapter, including whiteness, the importance of history and context in considering ethnic identity, the socially constructed and fluid nature of ethnic identity as well as links with social class, gender and religion.

Useful websites

www.statistics.gov.uk/Census2001
Office for National Statistics UK
www.gro-scotland.gov.uk/census/censushm2011
General Register Office, Scotland (for Scottish Census, 2011)
www.nisranew.nisra.gov/uk/census
Northern Ireland Statistics and Research Agency (for NI Census, 2011)

2
'Race', Ethnicity and School Achievement

Introduction

The ethnic group you are perceived to belong to would seem to matter in relation to your chances of achieving well in school. Who you are considered to be (which group you are placed in – and perhaps place yourself in) would seem to matter in relation to how well you do in school. If we want to be more circumspect we could say that considering 'race' and ethnicity seem to be important if we want to be aware of how our education system functions – it would seem that the system serves certain ethnic groups better than others or, if we put it another way, it provides opportunities to do well to some groups rather than others.

In this chapter we will look at why the above statements have been made. First, there will be a consideration of how there came to be a focus on ethnic groups and school achievement, what some of the concerns were with talking about 'achievement' and looking at school achievement in relation to ethnic groups. Then there will be a consideration of what statistical studies revealed about how different ethnic groups were doing in school. This will be followed by a discussion of the limitations of these studies and of the explanations that were put forward regarding why some groups do better than others. It is worth reminding ourselves at this point that there are certain issues and problems with the manner in which people are categorized into particular ethnic groups, who does the categorizing and how these categories are constituted. These issues have been discussed in Chapter 1 and they should be borne in mind in this discussion about achievement.

It is also the case that different terminology has been used by those categorizing people into ethnic groups over the years. African-Caribbean people were, in earlier times, usually referred to as West Indian. In this chapter the terminology for categories of people and pupils that the researchers themselves used will be retained. The naming and categorizing of groups of people, in terms of some notion of nationality, geographical origin, culture or skin colour, are, as discussed in Chapter 1, indicative of social, political and historical concerns of the time periods that produced them. Thus, terms that were used in the 1960s, 1970s and 1980s and so on are no longer used and some have negative connotations attached to them now. In the same manner, the terms 'immigrant' and 'indigenous' have also been retained in this account.

Why a focus on ethnic groups and achievement?

British society after 1945 became more diverse with the settlement of visible minorities from the New Commonwealth, Pakistan, the Caribbean and East Africa. This increasing diversity was reflected in the school population (especially in British cities and towns) from the mid-1950s as people began to raise families and dependents from overseas began to arrive to join the original family member who had migrated to Britain.

There were a number of differing responses to the increasing diversity of British class-rooms. There was a concern about cultural differences and the specific language needs that many groups of children had (if they needed to learn English) as well as discussion about the extent to which the educational system could provide equality of opportunity for these groups of pupils and whether changes needed to be made in order to provide for their educational needs (Little, 1975: 117). Craft and Craft (1983) report that many programmes were quickly put together to cater for these perceived needs of migrant pupils. At the same time, a very common reaction from teachers and schools was to see the arrival of these children as a problem (Little, 1975: 121). One of the ways this 'problem' was articulated was through the expression of concerns about the effects of 'immigrant children' on the education of 'indigenous children' (i.e. White British-born children). That is, there were articulated concerns about 'immigrant children' holding back 'indigenous children'. At the same time, there was also hostility in White British society towards migrants, a hostility frequently articulated around 'colour' (Little, 1975: 117), and a popular majority (White) conception that 'immigrants' took vital resources that were already scarce. These attitudes and hostilities found their way into schools and discussions about education. There were concerns about the 'swamping' of White classrooms. Some White parents did not want their child educated in a classroom with lots of ('coloured') migrant pupils in it and expressed concerns about the presence of immigrant children hindering the English language acquisition of their own children. Tomlinson notes that some White parents complained that their children were being held back by the presence of immigrant children in their classrooms. This view of White indigenous children being disadvantaged by the presence of immigrant children made it into the mainstream of educational discussion when it was included as a measure of disadvantage in the Plowden Report of 1967 (Tomlinson, 2008: 54).

These responses to the increasing diversity (of visible minorities) in English classrooms led to studies being conducted in order to find out how children were achieving in school. (There was a lack of discussion and research in Wales, Scotland and Northern Ireland due to the perception that the low numbers of migrants settling in these countries meant that there was nothing to investigate. This response was also to be found later in rural and shire areas of England: see Gaine, 1987.) Concerns about how ethnic minority groups were faring in the English educational system led to studies that measured their performance and achievement (Craft and Craft, 1983). Concerns about whether British-born (indigenous) children were being disadvantaged by the arrival of immigrant children in their classrooms were also investigated.

At the same time, parents, particularly the parents of West Indian children, became increasingly concerned about the education of their children. Having arrived in Britain with high expectations of education and the opportunities it would offer, it was becoming clear to many parents that the education system was failing their children. Many were being placed in lower sets and in some cases designated as Educationally Sub-Normal (ESN) and sent to special schools where they were unable to achieve in the same way as mainstream pupils (Tomlinson, 2008: 36; Coard, 1971). Parents themselves began to take action and ask questions around the issue of equal education opportunity and the achievement of minority pupils. These concerns, particularly of the educational and employment levels of Black school leavers, led to the establishment of a number of House of Commons Select Committee Inquiries between 1969 and 1977 (that looked at West Indian pupils) and then to the Rampton and Swann Committees and Reports of 1981 and 1985 respectively (Mabey, 1986). Rather than focus solely on the achievement of West Indian children it was decided that these committees should focus on the needs of all minority ethnic children (Phillips, 1979).

Early studies, thus, considered 'immigrant' versus 'non-immigrant'/indigenous groups. Studies appeared that considered the effects of the presence of 'recent arrivals' on the reading attainment of 'White' children in the same school (Phillips, 1979; Mabey, 1981). Other studies looked at whether schools were able to provide for 'recent arrivals' and their needs and how such 'recent arrivals' were doing in school (Little, 1975). These studies, and those that followed, were obliged by the nature of their inquiry to look at the performance of different ethnic groups in relation to each other.

Ethnic groups and achievement: 1970s and 1980s

The picture that emerged early on was that ethnic minority children were underachieving in school when compared with their White, indigenous peers. Little (1975) in examining how 'recent arrivals' were doing in school found that there were more immigrant children, than would be statistically expected, in the bottom groups of a sample of streamed junior school classes in London and fewer immigrants than expected in the top two groups. He also found that, while London school children were six months behind the national reading age, immigrant children were one year behind. Phillips (1979) found that Afro-Caribbean and Asian pupils in the West Midlands scored below indigenous pupils when tested at the end of junior school for reading ability and vocabulary. A review by Tomlinson of studies of West Indian and Asian pupils' educational performance in the 1960s and 1970s also concluded that the achievement of immigrant children tended to be below that of indigenous children (Tomlinson, 1980).

It was also found that attending a school with a lot of immigrant children on the school roll did not affect the reading scores of indigenous children (Phillips, 1979: 121). Thus concerns, and hostility, from White parents and society appeared to be unfounded. The tenor of findings from studies at this time was that minority groups were underachieving when compared with their White indigenous peers.

By the late 1970s attention had become focused on the Afro-Caribbean child in relation to other ethnic groups and White pupils. In 1979 a Committee of Inquiry into the Education of Children from Ethnic Minority Groups was set up in response to concerns about the educational achievement of Afro-Caribbean pupils (Gillborn and Gipps, 1996). The findings of the Committee were published as the Rampton Report (Department of Education and Science, 1981) and the Swann Report (Department of Education and Science, 1985). Two sample surveys conducted in London on behalf of the Committee showed that at the age of eight Afro-Caribbean achievement was significantly lower than the achievement of the other groups (Mabey, 1981). This finding was confirmed by another survey in 1986 which showed that at school leaving age, Afro-Caribbean children were still achieving at a significantly lower level than their White peers (Mabey, 1986).

Other studies in the 1980s continued to reveal that Afro-Caribbean and other ethnic minority pupils were not performing as well as White children in school. Craft and Craft (1983) analysed the exam results of an entire cohort of 5th and 6th formers in a single Greater London LEA. They found that West Indian children lagged behind White pupils even when the results were controlled for social class. Mabey (1985), in an Inner London Education Authority (ILEA) Literacy Study, found that at the age of eight Turkish, West Indian, Greek and Indian pupils had reading scores lower than English, Scottish, Welsh and Irish (ESWI) pupils. Mortimore et al. (1988), as part of the ILEA's Junior School Project, found that Caribbean, Turkish, Asian and Greek pupils had lower maths and reading scores than White pupils at entry to Junior school and these differences persisted through Junior school. Smith and Tomlinson (1989) found in a study of 18 multi-ethnic comprehensives that Black pupils did not achieve as highly as their White and Asian peers.

Despite these studies and widespread concern in some quarters, there was very little systematic collection of data about exam results and the differing achievement of minority ethnic groups until 1985 when the ILEA began monitoring 5th-year exam results (Kysel, 1988: 83).

The general picture that emerged from these early studies was that in British schools all minority groups, but particularly West Indian pupils, were underachieving in relation to White, indigenous pupils.

Explanations for underachievement arising from early statistical studies

Despite being statistical studies, explanations for the underachievement of these groups of pupils were put forward. The main explanations that were put forward in the studies considered above and in later statistical studies were:

- **Socio-economic factors, including poverty, unemployment of parents, class:**
  - Mabey, 1981, 1986; Craft and Craft, 1983; Drew and Gray, 1990; Haque, 1999; Sammons, 1995; Sammons and Hind, 1997; Strand 1997; Kysel, 1988
- **Length of time in the UK/late arrival for schooling in the UK:**
  - Newham, 1995; Mabey, 1981; Kysel, 1988; Strand, 1997b; House of Commons, 1987
- **Lack of fluency in English:**
  - Strand, 1997b; Camden, 1995; Birmingham City Council, 1994, 1995; ILEA, 1990; Mortimore et al. 1988; Kivi, 1991; Wandsworth, 1994; Tower Hamlets, 1994; Sammons, 1995; Sammons and Hind, 1997; Newham, 1995, Kysel, 1988; House of Commons, 1987
- **The link between reading attainment and exam success:**
  - Mabey, 1986; Phillips, 1979; Sammons, 1995
- **Parents' education and English fluency:**
  - Haque, 1999; House of Commons, 1987
- **Home background:**
  - Mabey, 1986; Sammons and Hind, 1997; Haque, 1999
- **Low teacher expectations of ethnic minority pupils:**
  - House of Commons, 1987; Kysel, 1988
- **Racism:**
  - Kivi, 1991; House of Commons, 1987
- **Lack of relevance of the curriculum to pupil need:**
  - Kysel, 1988; Kivi, 1991
- **Teacher's ignorance of linguistic and cultural issues ethnic minority pupils faced (poor training):**
  - Kivi, 1991
- **Absences from school:**
  - House of Commons, 1987

However, a clear picture did not really emerge from the studies regarding the reasons why pupils underachieved. Explanations were either put forward without any real basis in empirical research or predictors were put forward regarding who was likely to underachieve or the relationship between different variables that may affect achievement was explored. In some cases different studies come to different conclusions. For example, while the House of Commons Home Affairs Committee (1987), Sammons (1995), Camden (1996), Swann (1985), Sammons and Hind (1997) and Amin (1997) all believed that a lack of fluency in English was significant, Strand (1997b) found in his study that all the English as a Second Language pupils who had started school alongside their monolingual peers had all caught up with the monolingual pupils by the end of Key Stage 1 and that language was not an issue.

The limitations of early statistical studies and reviews

Although the studies considered above presented a clear case for the underachievement of certain ethnic minority groups, it has to be acknowledged that the studies were not without their problems and limitations, and this was noted by many of their authors. These limitations could be summarized as follows:

- **Poor sampling:**
  Many of the samples for the early studies were drawn from inner London and there was an absence of evidence from large, cross-sectional, nationally representative surveys (Tomlinson, 1990; Gillborn and Gipps, 1996; Pathak, 2000; Demack et al., 2000). Tanna makes this criticism claiming that such research relied on imperfect samples, nearly all from inner London, where the population was generally of a poorer socio-economic status and where school standards were lower. As a result of this, statistics and findings could not be generalized to other parts of the UK, especially to non-metropolitan areas, with any confidence (Tanna, 1990: 352). Even where large, national samples could be used, such samples contained relatively few ethnic minorities from a non-manual background which made generalization difficult (Gillborn and Gipps, 1996: 18). Troyna has pointed out the dangers of this tendency to generalize from small samples in particular geographical locations to other, very different, locations (Troyna, 1991b).
- **A failure to consider socio-economic factors and class:**
  There was an absence of a consideration of social class or socio-economic status in many studies and an overdependence on 'free school meals' as a way of measuring social class (Harris, 2001; Richardson and Wood, 2000: 13; Demack et al., 2000: 119).
- **A failure to consider gender:**
  Mirza, in 1992, drew attention to the fact that gender was not considered by many of the statistical studies of ethnic groups and achievement with the result that the high achievement of Black girls was made invisible (Mirza, 1992). There were significant differences recorded in the achievement of White girls versus White boys, yet the effects of gender were not usually considered in statistical studies of ethnic groups and attainment.
- **Inconsistent data collection and analysis:**
  Gillborn and Gipps pointed out that their trying to build up a picture of ethnic minority performance for their review of ethnic minority achievement in 1996 was hampered not only by a lack of

consideration of class but also by the inconsistent ways in which LEAs collected and analysed data (Gillborn and Gipps, 1996). There was also a difference in the number of years LEAs had been collecting data on ethnicity and achievement and this affected the number of years results could be traced back for (Gillborn and Gipps, 1996: 19).

- **The categorization and homogenization of ethnic groups:**
  The categories used varied from survey to survey and made comparing survey results almost impossible and restricted understanding of ethnic minority achievement in the above studies. Gillborn and Gipps describe how the use of 'Asian', as we have already noted, ignored significant differences in the cultural, political and economic profiles of Indian, East African Indian, Pakistani and Bangladeshi pupils (Gillborn and Gipps, 1996: 18). They also critiqued the use of 'Black' in many studies as this was a term that was not used by many ethnic minorities to describe themselves, it was a term that made South Asians invisible and which obscured the significant differences, experiences and achievements between those of an African ethnic background and those of a Caribbean ethnic background (Gillborn and Gipps, 1996: 26–7). These criticisms were echoed by Richardson and Woods (2000) and Amin et al. (1997: 5). Demie also rightly claimed that it was necessary to remember that ethnic groups were not homogeneous (Demie, 2001: 103), and likewise, Mirza pointed out how statistical studies failed to consider differences within groups (Mirza, 1992: 12). Another weakness was the large numbers of pupils who appeared as 'Other' in the survey results.

Other criticisms that have been made of this early statistical work include the manner in which studies frequently used data collected well in advance of the publication date of the studies (Strand, 1999; Gillborn and Gipps, 1996), the fact that few studies were sensitive or longitudinal enough to consider how performance and achievement varied throughout school careers (Sammons, 1995) and the fact that many studies did not include in their measures pupil mobility (Goldstein, 2000). Tanna pointed out that statistical surveys were very limited: the data analysed still left too much unexplained (Tanna, 1990).

Two other patterns emerged from these studies: one was that both Asian and West Indian pupils tended to stay on in education and gain their CSE and 'O' Level qualifications later than White pupils (Murray and Dawson, 1983 cited in Tomlinson, 1986: x). As the studies above considered qualifications at school leaving age this could not be adequately captured. The other trend that emerged from a comparison of the data collected for the Rampton and Swann reports was that West Indian performance improved between 1979 and 1982, while Asian performance remained static (Tomlinson, 1986). These trends begin to hint at some of the complexities of considering educational achievement in relation to ethnic groups. However, before we continue to consider later studies and statistics about ethnic minority achievement that do begin to consider a more complex picture, it is necessary to consider some other important issues, namely: What do we mean by achievement? What are some of the problems in using the terms achievement and underachievement? How can achievement be measured?

The concept of 'achievement'

There are certain issues regarding how we talk about achievement.

What do we mean by achievement and how do we measure it? Meanings can be varied and how we measure it can be very different. The implications of how we define achievement and measure it can be problematic.

Reflection activity

Write down your definition of school achievement.
  Try and limit yourself to just a few words or a sentence or two.

Find a newspaper or web-based article that refers to school achievement in some way.
  Is what is meant by achievement stated clearly or is it implied?
  What definition of achievement is being used in the article?
  Is it the same as yours?
  What are the similarities and/or the differences?

What do we mean by 'achievement'?

The above discussion (and much government policy) tends to assume that achievement is not a contested term and that the achievement of ethnic minority children can be simply measured. There is also a sense that 'achievement' has always been established as a term or problem. This is not the case and the studies and reviews that appeared in the 1980s, 1990s and in the first decade of the twenty-first century can be said to be part of establishing, or constituting, the problem of achievement (or underachievement) in education.

One way of understanding achievement was, and sometimes still is, to consider a pupil's ability and then to measure how well they do in school in relation to their perceived ability or potential. However, this approach requires a measure of 'ability' as well as attainment: an approach fraught with theoretical and practical difficulties regarding 'ability' and what is being measured (and some would argue that 'ability' is a purely constructed concept). How is one to measure a pupil's potential for example? The Swann Committee, among others, concluded that 'there is no really reliable indicator of a child's academic potential' (DES, 1985 cited in Tomlinson, 1986: 3). Smith is a contemporary researcher who approaches the study of achievement in this way. Her interest is in being able to predict underachievement (see Smith, 2005: 115). She comments on the ways in which other researchers have attempted to measure potential through intelligence or standardized tests, or through teacher nominations, and to measure achievement through comparing performance in tests of mental ability with that in tests of academic performance (Smith, 2005: 106). She notes the problems that can occur because of test bias (a bias towards middle class, White males as well as the linguistic biases that can be found in standardized tests) and because ability can only be measured through performance and not separately from it (Smith, 2005: 110).

Generally, however, underachievement has been taken to refer to the 'differences in the average attainments of different groups', average attainments being measured by pupil performance in exams and tests (Gillborn and Gipps, 1996: 10). (Smith refers to this as 'lower achievement', reserving the term 'underachievement' to describe the comparison between potential and performance described above, Smith, 2003: 10.) Thus achievement and under-achievement are used as ways to talk about the performance of groups in comparison with, or relative to, each other rather than the achievement of individual pupils. Achievement and underachievement, understood in this way, appeared as terms in educational circles during the 1970s and 1980s (Gillborn and Gipps, 1996: 10). In this way it was, and still is, thought possible to make judgements about the effectiveness of the education system in providing equality of opportunity. If equality of opportunity exists then different groups of pupils will have similar patterns of exam and test success, assuming that what is referred to as ability and intelligence are randomly distributed across all groups of pupils. As we saw above, early statistical studies using this method of comparison revealed that different groups of pupils did not have similar patterns of exam success and concerns about those groups of pupils who were thus identified as underachieving came to the fore.

Reflection activity

Is this the way in which you conceptualized achievement?
Is this the way that the newspaper or web-based article defined achievement?
What could some of the problems be with conceptualizing achievement in this way?

However, this method of comparing the mean attainment of one group of ethnically defined pupils with another has been criticized and hotly debated (Gillborn and Gipps, 1996: 11). This has mainly come about as a result of the manner in which West Indian underachieve-ment was reported after Swann. Rather than the presentation of this group of pupils, or any minority ethnic group, as underachieving being read as a comment (or indictment) of the failings of the education system, it came to act as a 'given', and in some instances a self-perpetuating explanation, in the education system. In other words it became expected and accepted that West Indian pupils, or minority ethnic groups, underachieve. This in turn created and perpetuated stereotypes of deficient learners and low teacher expectations of such groups of learners. Thus the idea of considering achievement as a way of looking at educational equality came to have a more negative aspect.

Troyna was concerned that by presenting Black underachievement as a national problem and as a 'given' rather than as 'a problematic that requires sensitive and systematic interrogation' (Troyna, 1984: 164), schools and teachers could feel themselves absolved of the problem as it was a 'problem beyond their control' (Amin et al., 1997: 5). Troyna also discussed how the use of the term 'underachievement' could come to signify a widespread failure among Black pupils, 'as if all black students are somehow destined to fail' (1984 cited in Amin et al., 1997: 5) and thus lead to a lowering of teacher expectations about this group and the creation of negative stereotypes about the educational potential of this pupil group (Gillborn and Gipps, 1996: 11). This also shifted the responsibility for underachievement away from the educational system on to the pupils and their families (Amin et al., 1997: 5). Troyna (1984: 158) also claimed that such inter-group comparisons could not be considered a legitimate method of assessing the academic performance of Black pupils because researchers and statisticians were not comparing like with like. Black pupils, Troyna claimed, had a different relationship to society and education because of the existence of racism both inside and outside school. This racism meant that Black students' attainment in exams could not be compared with White pupils (Troyna, 1984: 158). Wright (1987: 125) made a similar claim.

Another criticism of the terms 'achievement' and 'underachievement', and the way they were used, was that they reduced the worth and success of pupils to their exam results. Jeffcoate (1984) claimed that achievement should mean more than succeeding in exams. While acknowledging the danger of reducing the worth of pupils to their exam results, a counter argument to this would be that first, exam success is extremely important for young people in order for them to be able to continue into further or higher education or to find appropriate employment, and secondly, that there was already a tendency for certain minority ethnic pupil groups to be viewed as 'good at sports' or art or practical activities within schools, thereby limiting the opportunities and resources made available by teachers for academic success (and fuelling racial stereotypes at the same time).

Tomlinson felt that it was important to consider who decides what counts as achievement and what kinds of measures of achievement are used (Tomlinson, 1986: 2–3). One of Tomlinson's concerns was that measuring the relative achievement of ethnic groups, and talking of the underachievement of particular groups, obscured 'within group' differences and thus hid the success of many pupils. Some West Indian pupils did well in school but the use of mean group averages, wide group categorizations and the comparison of relative group performance hid this and thus promulgated the view that all West Indian pupils were underachieving in school (Tomlinson, 1986: 4).

Others were concerned that considering 'underachievement' in terms of minority ethnic pupil groups could lead to the creation of a hierarchy of minority ethnic groups based on assumptions about inherent ability (Gillborn and Mirza, 2000: 7), and like Troyna saw the way in which talk about underachievement resulted in reasons for it being located in pupils and their families and not in the education system. They also expressed concerns about ethnic minority learners' efforts to succeed being undermined as their educational experiences were always being viewed through the lens of underachievement (Gillborn and Mirza, 2000: 7).

Thus, achievement and underachievement are contested terms. The terms originally came into being as a way of talking about equality of opportunity for ethnic minority groups in education. As we have seen, some have claimed that their use can have damaging effects on pupils either by perpetuating negative stereotypes and low expectations (e.g. Troyna, 1984) or through judging pupil worth and success only by exam and test marks (e.g. Jeffcoate, 1984). The term can also be used without consideration for the different, contested, meanings of what achievement is and who it is for (Walters, 2001).

Reflection activity

Can you think of any other terms that could be used instead of achievement and underachievement?
 What might be the advantages or disadvantages of using these different terms?
 After considering some alternatives, which terms do you prefer to use?

In response to these concerns some researchers have chosen to use the term 'disadvantaged' rather than 'underachieving' in their work (Drew, 1995; Gillborn, 1997; Wright, 1987 cited in Amin et al., 1997: 5). However, describing pupils as 'disadvantaged' is itself problematic. It can sound patronizing and would not appear to address the issue it was intended to address as it can suggest that it is somehow the home backgrounds or cognitive capabilities of Black pupils that are at fault and not problems within the education system. Many will hear 'disadvantaged' as 'disadvantaged by poor home background, parents and culture', a situation both Troyna and Wright were at pains to avoid in their critique of the term 'underachievement'. Wright's other suggestion of using the term 'educational inequality' (1987: 126) seems a better one.

Gillborn and Gipps in their report for OFSTED on the achievement of minority ethnic pupils use the term 'relative achievement' to discuss the achievement of pupils in different ethnic groups in order to flag up the difficulties of the term 'achievement' (Gillborn and Gipps, 1996: 11).

However, an alternative argument can be made for retaining the term in its original meaning. It can be argued that the terms achievement and underachievement should be retained when it is clear that they are being used in relation to the curriculum and curriculum work in schools. The terms 'achievement' and 'underachievement' can be a useful way of talking about what is happening to children and their learning within the education system. They are not a way of speaking of the worth or potential or ability of a pupil or pupil group, but a way of speaking about where a pupil or pupil group have reached at a particular moment in time in relation to the curriculum and the expected stage posts along the way which they and their teachers are obliged to follow.

Schools and teachers have often avoided considering minority ethnic pupils in terms of achievement as the term somehow challenged their assimilationist expectation that all that was required of them, and the education system, was to help minority ethnic children settle in and be happy in school – Wallace and Conteh have referred to this kind of attitude and response, in relation to English as Additional Language learners, as a 'culture of care' rather than a focus on teaching and learning needs (Afitska et al., 2010: 35) (see also Walters, 2003). To ignore the needs of minority ethnic pupils in this way, to consider achievement as the extent to which a child is happy or well settled in class, or a success on the football pitch, is to ignore the right of all children to have access to other important resources, including the curriculum and examination success, in society. Key Stage test results and exam results, as a marker of achievement, are required by children if they are to have access to the resources of mainstream culture.

Therefore, while acknowledging the dangers of both the manner in which 'underachieve-ment' becomes a deficit explanation of poor performance *and* the way in which current policy and political discourses utilize the concept of 'achievement' in their fixation on standards, the terms 'achievement' and 'underachievement' can be positive, politically use-ful terms that challenge complacency and assimilationist expectations within schools.

In the discussion above we can see that achievement and underachievement are not neu-tral terms especially when used in connection with groups of minority ethnic pupils. Some claim that they can be damaging either by perpetuating stereotypes and low expectations of minority ethnic pupils groups or reducing the worth and success of students to exam results. Others defend the use of the terms and see their use as important ways of exploring equality of opportunity for pupils in school.

How has evidence and information about achievement been collected? How has achievement been measured?

As indicated above, evidence and information about the relative achievement of ethnic minority groups has often been measured by using the exam results of pupils at the end of compulsory schooling, e.g. through an examination of GCSE – General Certificate of Education –results. (GCSEs being the exams that pupils take at the end of Key Stage 4 when they are sixteen. Key Stages are part of the National Curriculum introduced into England, Wales and Northern Ireland in 1988 and occur at the ages of 7, 11, 14 and 16.) In England this is usually done by looking at how many pupils in each ethnic group have gained five or more GCSEs at levels A–C, this being considered a necessary number and grade of GCSE exams that will allow a pupil to continue to the next stage of education.

Richardson and Woods (2000) indicate the other measures that have been used (2000: 8): One is to look at what percentage of pupils in each ethnic group have gained one GCSE (at any level), this giving a picture of how many pupils in each ethnic group have not gained any qualifications at all or. Another method is to assign points to each grade of GCSE, working out the average point score for each pupil/pupil group and comparing ethnic groups in this way. In addition to using GCSE results, Key Stage test results have also been used to compare different ethnic groups of pupils, for example, by looking at how many children in each ethnic group have gained Level 4 at the age of eleven (Richardson and Woods, 2000: 8).

In Scotland, where there are no GCSE examinations or Key Stage levels, each Standard Grade exam grade awarded a pupil attracts tariff points and these are then used to compare the achievement of different groups at the end of compulsory schooling. In Wales, a Core Subject Indicator (CSI) is used. This score represents the percentage of pupils gaining the expected level, or above, in English (or Welsh), Maths and Science in combination. In Northern Ireland, data is gathered via the Summary of Annual Examination results.

In the early studies discussed above, other kinds of test results were compared: for example, IQ tests, non-verbal reasoning tests and reading tests. These kinds of tests, of course, are standardized (i.e. they are prepared for and pre-tested to make sure that they reveal what they say they reveal) on large ethnic *majority* groups of pupils (and if the tests are devised in the US they will be standardized on and for American majority pupils). Gillborn and Youdell point out that a cognitive ability test used in British secondary schools is standardized in two LEAs that do not represent the general secondary school population in England and that the test has not been standardized since 1984 (see Gillborn and Youdell, 2000: 60–2). When IQ tests were developed and standardized minority ethnic children were not included in the standardization (Kamin, 1974 cited in Gillborn and Youdell, 2000: 59). Due to this, these kinds of tests can be criticized for having linguistic and cultural biases that work against minority ethnic and linguistic minority pupils. Just as we saw above, it is very difficult, perhaps impossible, to measure ability because any test for ability can only measure performance, and culture and language are present in any test that is used. According to Tomlinson (1986: 4), Hegarty and Lucas (1979) concluded that it was probably impossible to create a 'culture fair' test.

Another way of comparing the achievement of ethnic groups has been to use the data gathered by LEAs or data from Youth Cohort Studies (YCS), Ethnic Minority Achievement Grant (EMAG) returns, the PLASC and more recently the Longitudinal Study of Young People in England (LSYPE).

LEA data and YCS data (and research findings from a school effectiveness study) were the only data available to researchers like Gillborn and Gipps when they were conducting their review of minority ethnic pupils' relative achievement in the mid-1990s. Some (usually urban, with large minority populations), but not all LEAs, gathered data about the numbers of minority ethnic pupils in their schools (using very broad, and differing, categories of ethnic groups) and monitored the progress of these pupils by exploring their attainment at various Key Stages. YCS data come from a large, nationally representative survey of a sample of 16- to 19-year-old young people that is conducted every 2 years. It allows access to information about exam performance according to ethnicity (although again the categories used are rather broad), gender and social class.

EMAG replaced Section 11 funding in 1999. (Section 11 was funding from the Home Office that had been provided to LEAs and had often been used to support the English language acquisition of bilingual pupils in schools.) The intention behind the change in funding was to place more of a focus on supporting ethnic minority achievement in schools rather than simply language acquisition. (Section 11 funding and EMAG are discussed in more detail in Chapter 5). As LEAs had to bid for the funding, they were placed in a position where they had to monitor ethnic achievement more systematically and thoroughly at both school and LEA level than they had to in the past (Pilkington, 2003: 166). This meant that EMAG data became another data source for measuring the relative attainments of different ethnic groups. PLASC data also became available in 2002. PLASC was, and is, a census of all children attending state schools in England and records each child's ethnicity (using the categories utilized in the 2001 Census), gender, take up of Free School Meals as an indicator of class, and test and exam results. (This is known as the Annual School Census, ASC, in secondary schools.) PLASC data then allows researchers to track and compare the achievement of ethnic groups of pupils as well as individuals without relying on samples. As Gillborn notes, PLASC data made it possible for the first time to explore the attainments of smaller groups of minority ethnic pupils such as Chinese pupils (Gillborn, 2008: 147).

More recently, LSYPE data (Strand, 2007b; 2008, Department for Education, 2010), funded by the government, has been used to explore ethnic achievement among English pupils and school leavers. This is a longitudinal study that collected data from a national sample of more than 15,000 young people aged 13 to 18 years (the 2008 study considered these students' GCSE results) in order to provide a picture of pupil progress as well as achievement at a particular point in time and in order to explore a wider and richer range of variables (particularly variables associated with social class and poverty, home ownership, neighbourhood characteristics, family composition, aspirations, academic self-concept and educational risk) than those covered by YCS studies and PLASC and EMAG data. In order to be able to collect the required data in enough depth to explore the variables, Strand had to work with a sample rather than with a total population and so the ethnic categories become rather broad again.

The different ways in which data about achievement and underachievement have been collected have been outlined above. There are, however, significant issues and debates related to how these data are analysed and compared in order to measure and talk about ethnic minority achievement. Before considering these debates we will look at the picture that has been presented, through the use of statistical studies and reviews, of ethnic minority groups and achievement over the past 20 years. It seems important to consider the picture that was created, through the various writings and reports in this period, and in this way see something of how the problem of achievement became constituted and the way in which it was presented before considering how this picture was critiqued and disputed.

Ethnic groups and achievement: 1990–2010

After Rampton and Swann the picture produced of ethnic minority attainment became increasingly complex as studies began to consider the effects of socio-economic status and gender upon achievement statistics. Work in the 1990s by the London Boroughs of Brent (1994) and Lambeth (1994), Sammons (1994), Tizard et al. (1988), Plewis (1991), Drew and Gray (1990) and the ILEA (1990) amply demonstrated this. For example, Drew and Gray, drawing their data from the Youth Cohort Study, confirmed the findings of previous researchers that there were differences in exam achievements associated with ethnic background. When exam performance was considered White pupils were gaining more 'O' Level exam passes than Asians and Afro-Caribbean pupils and more A–C/CSE grade 1 exam passes (although the gap between Whites and Asians was very small) (Drew and Gray, 1990: 111–2). However, when gender and socio-economic group were introduced into the picture they found that there was a relatively high performance of Asian pupils (especially males) from intermediate and manual backgrounds in comparison with White pupils and Afro-Caribbean pupils (Drew and Gray, 1990: 113). Mirza has drawn attention to how studies during this period often failed to consider gender when analysing and presenting statistics regarding the underachievement of particular ethnic minority groups and the particular invisibility of the high achievement of Black girls in English schools (Mirza, 1992).

Socio-economic status was also, at this time, considered as a factor in the differing performance of Asian pupils in different studies. In one study Asian pupils were underachieving when compared with Afro-Caribbean pupils and White pupils (Phillips, 1979); in other studies they were doing better than Afro-Caribbean pupils but worse than White pupils (Little, 1975; Thomas and Mortimore, 1994). Other studies found that Asian pupils were doing as well as, or better than, White pupils (Rampton: Department of Education and Science, 1981; Brent, 1994; Kysel, 1988; Sammons, 1995). Gillborn and Gipps (1996: 23) suggest that this inconsistent picture may have come about because the research that found Asian pupils to be doing better than White pupils was conducted in London where the socio-economic status of White pupils was much lower than the status of White pupils outside London and that this may have reduced the attainment of White pupils. (Whereas the studies that found Asian pupils underperforming when compared to their White peers were conducted outside London where the generally higher socio-economic status of White pupils may have been reflected in higher achievement.)

Another level of complexity emerged as studies (e.g. Brent, 1994; Birmingham City Council, 1994; Camden, 1995; Southwark, 1994) also began to consider increases in the overall levels of GCSE achievement for each ethnic group **and** the progress that children made during their schooling, taking on board the notion that pupils have different starting points in their school career (i.e. they start school with differing levels of school-valued knowledge and skills). Gillborn and Gipps rightly point out that 'progress' is not the same as 'achievement' (Gillborn and Gipps, 1996: 36). Those that make the greatest progress do not necessarily have the highest achievement: it depends on the relative starting points of each pupil or group of pupils. For example, if one ethnic minority group had attained, on average, 35 per cent in a test at the end of a year of school while White pupils had, on average, attained 65 per cent and then at the end of the next year of school the ethnic minority group had scored 55 per cent (i.e. increasing their average score by 20 per cent) and the White pupils had scored 70 per cent, the ethnic minority group would have made more progress (20 per cent compared with the White group's 5 per cent) but the White group would still, on average, have achieved more highly (70 per cent compared to 55 per cent) (see Gillborn and Gipps, 1996: 37–44). At the same time, through considering the relative achievement of different ethnic groups from year to year reviewers and researchers began to talk about the achievement gaps between groups and whether these were widening or shrinking. To take our example, in Year One the gap between the ethnic minority group and the White group was 30 percentage points and at the end of Year 2 it was 15 percentage points. It could be said that the achievement gap between Bangladeshi and White pupils was narrowing. It is in this way that researchers and policy makers, as well as talking about the relative, average achievement of ethnic groups, have become immured in debates about attainment 'gaps' between ethnic groups and whether these are growing or narrowing and most importantly, how achievement and 'gaps' should be measured. This debate will be discussed below.

Another way in which studies became more sophisticated was through beginning to disaggregate, where possible, some of the ethnic categories used, e.g. the ethnic category of 'Asian' and 'White'. Until this time the 'Asian' grouping included within it Indian, Bangladeshi, Pakistani and East African Asians, pupils from different continents, with different socio-economic backgrounds and profiles, languages, religions and histories of migration. When data were collected and compared for each of these groups separately it became clear that Indians were generally doing well in the British education system and Pakistanis and Bangladeshis very poorly. Disaggregating large 'ethnic groups', which were not really ethnic groups at all, was thus shown to be important in producing a clearer picture of ethnic groups' achievement in British education. However, the need for large numbers to gain secure results in statistical work often meant that Bangladeshi, Pakistani, East African Indian and Indian children continued to be considered under the aggregate heading of Asian in statistical analyses. In addition to this, the White category became disaggregated in some studies into White British, Gypsy/Roma, Irish Heritage, and so on (e.g. Department for Education and Science data cited in Archer and Francis, 2007) and more recently statistics have been collected for 'Mixed Heritage' pupils (e.g. Strand 2007b and 2008).

Many statistical studies of ethnicity and achievement, and reviews of such studies, have been undertaken since the 1990s. What is discussed next are some of these studies and reviews in order to provide a picture of ethnic achievement during this time. The studies or reviews are either key ones that have been often quoted or provide data for particular periods so that what follows covers the years 1996 (Gillborn and Gipps), 2000 (Gillborn and Mirza), 2003 (Bhattacharya et al.), 2004 (Archer and Francis), 2007 and 2008 (Strand). Not only are these studies and reviews important in providing information about ethnicity and achievement but they are also, as indicated earlier, important in constructing a particular discourse about ethnicity and achievement in that they present 'ethnicity and achievement' in a particular way, painting a particular picture of ethnic groups and school achievement.

Ethnicity and achievement 1996 to 2010

In the mid-1990s the Office for Standards in Education (OFSTED) commissioned a review from Gillborn and Gipps into the educational experiences and achievements of ethnic minority pupils as a decade had passed since the Swann Report and it was felt that the issue of 'race' and educational equality had slid from prominent view. The purpose of the review was to 'take stock' of any changes in the educational achievements of ethnic minority pupils (Gillborn and Gipps, 1996: 7). The researchers looked at research that had been conducted in the previous 10 years, as well as data that were available to them from Local Authorities, in order to consider the differences in levels of achievement between different ethnic minority groups. Gillborn and Gipps faced considerable difficulty in this task as the data available were often old, were from samples that it was not possible to generalize from, used crude categories of ethnic groups, were regionally or locally based rather than national (and frequently urban based) and which often did not consider social class and gender. There was also the problem that because of the small number of ethnic minority pupils in the samples from middle-class backgrounds, or from certain minority ethnic groups (e.g. Chinese pupils) generalizing about social class and ethnicity, or the attainment of particular ethnic groups was difficult. They did, however, attempt to comment on the effects of social class and gender and to comment on results when ethnic groupings were disaggregated where this was possible. This is a summary of Gillborn and Gipps' (1996) findings.

Research summary: Gillborn and Gipps' 1996 review

Primary school:
- There was a reasonably consistent pattern of Bangladeshi and Pakistani pupils' lower than average attainment when compared to other ethnic groups.
- African-Caribbean pupils appeared on average to achieve less well than White pupils.

However, the research available did not provide a consistently clear picture. Two studies discussed by Gillborn and Gipps included a consideration of gender but the findings were too limited to deduce any patterns.

End of compulsory schooling (GCSE exams/Key Stage 4):
The research and data available on GCSE performance were not up to date and representative enough to provide an accurate picture of achievement according to ethnic group. Their review of LEA data and research revealed:

- Indian pupils on average appeared to achieve more highly than Bangladeshi and Pakistani pupils and to achieve more highly than White pupils in some urban areas.
- Pakistani pupils achieved less well than Whites in many areas.
- Bangladeshi pupils achieved less well than other groups (although in one London borough they were the highest achieving when compared with Caribbean and English/Scottish/Welsh groups).
- African-Caribbean pupils in many LEAs had significantly lower average achievements than other groups. There was an increasing gap between the achievement of African-Caribbean pupils and other groups in some areas and the achievement of African-Caribbean young men was of particular concern.
- Pupils from a higher social class achieved the highest averages regardless of ethnic origin or gender.
- Girls tended to do better than boys from the same social class.
- Average GCSE performance had improved across the board but not all pupils had shared equally in the improvement. The gap between the highest achieving group and the lowest achieving group had increased in many Local Authorities (see Gillborn and Gipps, 1996: 1–5).

Thus their review of the available data and research findings indicated that despite increases in attainment for all pupils at GCSE level, there were significant differences in attainment between certain ethnic groups even when social class was taken into account although, as indicated above, they were quick to point out the limitations of the data that they were able to use (Gillborn and Gipps, 1996: 19; Gillborn and Mirza, 2000: 8). In particular, they found that African-Caribbean young people, especially boys, had not shared equally in increased attainment, in fact, in some places this group of pupils' performance had worsened. African-Caribbean boys and girls achieved, on average, below the level achieved by other groups while Asian pupils, both boys and girls, achieved as well as or better than White pupils of the same class or gender (Gillborn and Gipps, 1996: 18).

In addition to examining achievement at different stages of schooling, Gillborn and Gipps also considered the progress made between the different key stages by different ethnic groups (Gillborn and Gipps, 1996: 36–42). What Gillborn and Gipps found in relation to *progress* was:

- Some evidence suggested that the gap between ethnic minority pupils and White pupils widened between Key Stage 1 and Key Stage 2. The attainment of ethnic minority pupils was frequently behind that of White pupils at the end of Key Stage 2.
- Between Key Stage 2 and 4 more progress was made by Asian pupils compared to White pupils but the difference in progress between African, African-Caribbean pupils and White pupils was not so consistent and was smaller.

Minority ethnic groups made better progress than White pupils between Key Stages 2 and 4 but (except in some parts of London) they finished school with a lower average attainment than White pupils at Key Stage 4 (from Gillborn and Gipps, 1996: 41).

Thus, they were able to make the important point that while ethnic groups were making good or better progress than White pupils they still underachieved in relation to White pupils at the end of schooling.

Gillborn produced another OFSTED review in 2000, this time with Heidi Mirza as co-author (Gillborn and Mirza, 2000). This review of research explored the relative significance of 'race'/ethnicity alongside class and gender and how different ethnic groups were faring in relation to the rising levels of attainment identified at the end of compulsory schooling. In order to do this, and in the continuing absence of any consistently collected national data, they used data supplied by Local Authorities as part of their EMAG submissions in 1998 (see above for an explanation of EMAG) and data from the YCS from 1988, 1995 and 1997 (Gillborn and Mirza, 2000: 5). This represented the most comprehensive data that had ever been available, although Gillborn and Mirza warned, as do others, that the data did have their limitations (some of the data were given only in percentages and some of the data, as noted by Gillborn and Gipps, were based on very small groups (Gillborn and Mirza, 2000: 8).The report identified the same trends that had been identified by Gillborn and Gipps.

Research summary: Gillborn and Mirza's 2000 review

The EMAG data that Gillborn and Mirza analysed (which did not include data on gender or class) showed that there was considerable variation in attainment – for each of the main ethnic groups studied there was at least one LEA where that group was the highest attaining relative to other groups. This 'suggest(ed)' that even for the groups with the most serious inequalities of attainment nationally, there (were) places where that trend (was) being bucked' (Gillborn and Mirza, 2000: 9). In commenting on these findings, Gillborn and Mirza saw grounds for optimism in that they showed that every ethnic group was capable of high academic achievement somewhere and flagged up the importance of considering locality and context when considering achievement (Gillborn and Mirza, 2000: 11). However, the Youth Cohort Study data also showed that there continued to be a 'significant and persistent problem' of inequality of attainment for many minority ethnic groups (Gillborn and Mirza, 2000: 11). While pupils in all the main ethnic group were more likely to gain five higher grade GCSE in 1997 than they were in 1988, the patterns that Gillborn and Gipps had identified (1996, see above) were still evident: Pakistani, Bangladeshi and African-Caribbean (Gillborn and Mirza include people of Black African and/or Black Caribbean heritage in the category 'African-Caribbean') pupils were less likely than White and Indian pupils to gain five higher grade GCSEs nationally. This 'suggests (again) that pupils of different ethnic origins do not experience equal educational opportunities' (Gillborn and Mirza, 2000: 12). In addition, they found the following which, with regard to *progress* and *achievement gaps*, add to the picture presented by Gillborn and Gipps (1996):

- Indian pupils had the greatest improvements in attainment, enough to close the gap between themselves and White pupils.
- Bangladeshi pupils' rate of improvement matched that of White pupils' and so the gap between their relative attainment remained the same although both groups were improving.
- Black and Pakistani pupils were not improving at the same rate as their White peers and so the gap between Black and Pakistani pupils and White pupils was growing.

Gillborn and Mirza commented, 'African-Caribbean and Pakistani pupils have drawn least benefit from the rising levels of attainment: the gap between them and their White peers is bigger now than a decade ago'.

- There was a decline in the relative attainment of African-Caribbean pupils when compared to White pupils at all the Key Stages of schooling (i.e. at age 7, 11, 14 and 16). Black pupils started school 20 points ahead of the average and finished 21 points behind the average. This pattern was confirmed in London-based research in 1999. (see Gillborn and Mirza, 2000: 12–17).

Gillborn and Mirza also used the YCS data in order to consider *class* and *ethnicity* in relation to attainment after making provisos about how difficult class was to define and capture. The following summarizes their review of findings:

- Pupils from middle-class backgrounds had significantly higher attainment than pupils from working-class backgrounds within each ethnic group examined mirroring 'the strong association between class and educational achievement'. Among African-Caribbean pupils this difference was much less pronounced.
- Even when social class was controlled for there were still significant inequalities in attainment between minority ethnic groups.
- Black pupils were less likely to gain 5 higher grade GCSE passes than pupils of the same social class in any of the other groups. There was a decline in the attainment of working-class Black pupils between 1988 and 1997. Thus inequalities of attainment existed for Black pupils regardless of class.
- Indian and Pakistani/Bangladeshi and White pupils from working-class backgrounds were as successful as Black pupils from middle-class backgrounds. (see Gillborn and Mirza, 2000: 19–20)

Their key findings were that 'ethnic inequalities persist even when class differences (were) taken into account', that the usual difference in attainment between working-class and middle-class pupils was replicated in each ethnic group and that 'social class factors do not override the influence of ethnic inequality' (Gillborn and Mirza, 2000: 21). In fact, in the case of Black pupils, the expected social-class differences were mitigated by 'race' (Gillborn and Mirza, 2000: 21).

Gillborn and Mirza also use the YCS data in order to consider *gender* and *ethnicity* in relation to attainment. The following summarizes their findings:

- The gender gap was considerably smaller than differences of attainment associated with class and 'race'.
- There is a difference in attainment according to gender within each of the ethnic groups studied, with girls outperforming boys. However, significant inequalities of attainment exist between groups regardless of gender e.g. there is a considerable gap in attainment between Pakistani, Bangladeshi, African-Caribbean girls and White and Indian girls.
- Bangladeshi/Pakistani and African-Caribbean girls are less likely to gain 5 higher grade GCSEs than White and Indian boys. (see Gillborn and Mirza, 2000: 23–4)

They conclude that 'when controlling for ethnic origin and gender, the data reveal similar patterns to when it was subjected to controls by social class' (see above) 'race' and ethnicity remain key defining factors in both cases' (Gillborn and Mirza, 2000: 24). What this means is that the difference in attainment between different ethnic groups cannot be completely explained by claiming that their low attainment is because they are predominantly working class or male (two factors that are found to be correlated with poorer academic performance). It means that ethnicity is key in some way. 'Neither (social class nor gender differences) can account for persistent underlying ethnic inequalities: comparing like with like, African-Caribbean, Pakistani and Bangladeshi pupils do not enjoy equal opportunities' (Gillborn and Mirza, 2000: 27).

Gillborn and Mirza's review thus provided an insight into the interactions of class and gender with ethnic group attainments, making clear that class and gender could not account for all of the differential attainment of ethnically defined groups.

In 2003 Bhattacharyya, Ison and Blair summarized and reviewed government statistics from 2001 relating to ethnic group participation and attainment in education and training in England (Battacharyya et al., 2003). This was an update on an earlier review by Pathak (2000). They were able to disaggregate the Black group of pupils to Black Caribbean, Black African and Black Other and the Asian group to Indian, Pakistani and Bangladeshi and include Chinese, Mixed Heritage, Gypsy/Roma and children of Travellers of Irish Heritage as these categories were now being included in data gathering either via PLASC, ASC or the National Census. (Although Bhattacharyya et al. included the categories of Gypsy/Roma, Travellers of Irish Heritage and refugee and asylum-seeking pupils in their discussion they do not present or analyse achievement data for these groups of pupils.) They also included refugee and asylum-seeking pupils although the data about these two groups of pupils were only available via a report for the Department for Works and Pensions (Bloch, 2002) and thus very limited.

Research summary: Bhattacharyya, Ison and Blair's 2003 review

Many of their findings revealed a similar pattern to those outlined above. In addition, Bhattacharyya et al. found that in relation to *achievement* and *progress*:

- Black Caribbean and Black African children made relatively more progress than White children in pre-school education.
- Indian and Chinese children were more likely to achieve the expected attainment levels at each Key Stage than other ethnic groups and make good progress.
- Black Caribbean pupils made the least progress in school.
- Black Other and White made less progress between Key Stage 3 and 4 than Black African, Pakistani and Bangladeshi pupils.
- While GCSE attainment rates continued to rise in general, they fell for Black pupils and remained the same for Indian pupils in 2002.
- The difference in attainment between genders was most marked among Black Caribbean, Black Other and Black African boys and girls where there was a 14–15 per cent discrepancy in the attainment of five or more GCSEs. (see Bhattacharyya et al., 2003: 3; 9–11)

Battacharyya et al. were thus able to include and place Chinese pupils' achievement alongside that of Indian pupils, emphasize how Black Caribbean pupils started school well and made good progress in pre-school education but then made the least progress during the rest of schooling. Generally they were able to add to the picture the kinds of differential progress made by ethnic minority groups between Key Stage 3 and 4 (i.e. during secondary school education) as well as confirming that GCSE attainment rates continued to fall for Black Caribbean pupils. They also showed how gaps in achievement increased during the time pupils spent in school and that differences in gender were more marked among Black pupils, thus building on Gillborn and Mirza's work.

In 2007 Archer and Francis reviewed the research literature and statistics available for 2004. They revealed a picture of ethnic achievement that had similar patterns to that of Gillborn and Gipps, 1996; Gillborn and Mirza, 2000 and Bhattacharya et al., 2003 above. They were able to include in their analysis Chinese, Gypsy/Roma and Travellers of Irish Heritage pupil groups.

Research summary: Archer and Francis (2007)

The picture of *achievement* that emerged was:

- Chinese and Indian pupils did best at all Key Stages.
- Bangladeshi, Pakistani, Black and Traveller pupils underperformed and Gypsy/Roma pupils significantly underperformed at Key Stage 4.
- In the early years of schooling Black pupils (especially Black Caribbean pupils) generally did slightly better than Pakistani and Bangladeshi pupils. However, by the end of schooling Pakistani and Bangladeshi pupils did slightly better than Black pupils.
- The achievement gap between different ethnic groups widened rather than narrowed as pupils moved through school and the Key Stages with Black pupil's attainment reducing through the Key Stages.
- There was a substantial gender gap between Black Caribbean girls and boys in achievement at Key Stage 4. Girls did much better than boys. However, Black girls did not out perform White boys.
- Irish Heritage travellers caught up with and almost matched African-Caribbean attainment. Archer and Francis saw this as evidence of how African-Caribbean attainment slipped down over the years of schooling.
- 5 higher grade GCSEs were gained by 50 per cent middle-class White pupils but only by 20 per cent working-class White pupils.
- Social class was a more important and accurate predictor of achievement for White British pupils than for other ethnic groups: the gap between working-class and middle-class attainment was smaller in ethnic minority groups and in some cases was reversed. For example, working-class Bangladeshi, Black Caribbean and other Black girls did as well or did better than middle-class boys in some minority ethnic groups.
- More girls than boys gained 5 high-grade GCSEs in all ethnic groups except the Gypsy/Roma group.
- Middle-class boys usually outperformed working-class girls from the same ethnic group.
- Gender was less important that social class when considering educational achievement. (see Archer and Francis, 2007: 2–17)

They were thus able to confirm that Black Caribbean pupils did well at the beginning of school and to place Irish Heritage Travellers' attainment in relation to other groups. They were able to show, in addition, that social class was a more important predictor of attainment for White British pupils than for ethnic minority groups. They also showed that Gypsy/Roma girls bucked the trend and did not achieve more highly than Gypsy/Roma boys but confirmed that gender was less important than class in its relationship with attainment. Archer and Francis conclude their analysis by commenting that 'social class, gender and ethnicity inflect together to impact on the achievement of different pupils' (Archer and Francis, 2007: 13) and pointed out that 'ethnicity impacts on . . . gender and social class, in some cases making (gender and social class) less salient predictors of educational achievement' (Archer and Francis, 2007: 13).

More recent studies, by Strand (2007b, 2008), for the Department for Children, Schools and Families (DCSF) and Department for Education (DfE), and by the DfE (2010) were able to use national test data from the National Pupil Database (test results for Key Stage 3 and 4), the Youth Cohort Study (YCS, for the 2010 study) and data from the LSYPE, a study that gathered data about pupil and parental educational aspirations and family circumstances from interviews with young people and their parents as well as the school and neighbourhood contexts of young people's educational experiences. In this way Strand and the DfE were able to explore the relationships between ethnicity, class, gender and other important variables with a large and representative national sample (unlike the studies that we have considered above which were limited to a restricted range of variables and some rather crude measures such as Free School Meals as an indication of socio-economic status). However, due to the nature of the data sets, neither Strand nor the DfE include Chinese, Gypsy/Roma, Irish Travellers or White East Europeans (a growing group of pupils in UK schools in the mid-2000s) as separate categories in their analysis.

Research summary: Strand (2007)

Strand's first report (2007b) using LSYPE and Key Stage 3 data found that:

- There were large gaps in educational attainment between ethnic groups at the age of 14 (the end of Key Stage 3) with Black Caribbean, Black African, Pakistani and Bangladeshi pupils on average the equivalent of a year of progress behind their White British peers.
- When social class, maternal education, family poverty, home ownership and family composition were controlled for this substantially reduced the attainment gaps between White British pupils and minority ethnic pupils with the exception of Black Caribbean pupils (i.e. while social class, maternal education and the other variables considered could account for the low attainment of other ethnic groups relative to White British pupils these factors could not account for the much lower attainment of Black Caribbean pupils).
- When a further set of variables concerning attitudes, aspirations, educational risk and school and neighbourhood characteristics were considered, the low attainment of Black Caribbean pupils still could not be accounted for.
- Black Caribbean pupils were underrepresented in the higher tiers of entry to Key Stage 3 tests (the tests require teachers to decide in advance of the test whether students will be able to achieve at the higher levels or not – the actual test that a pupil sits depends on whether they are likely to achieve at the higher or lower end of the scale. A pupil entered for a lower tier test cannot gain the top marks and be awarded a high level in the text) even when prior attainment and all the other variables related to pupil, family, school and neighbourhood were taken into account.
- A lot of the difference in attainment between ethnic groups at Key Stage 3 (i.e. aged 14) could be accounted for by pupils attainment at Key Stage 2 (i.e. the gaps that existed between different groups at age 14 had been present at the age of 11) and that in this respect there was a need for a focus on what was happening in primary schools. However, between Key Stage 2 and 3 Black Caribbean and Bangladeshi boys made less progress relative to White British pupils, so the gap here increased. (see Strand, 2007b: 5–7)

Strand's second report (2008) considered data from Key Stage 4 (GCSE results) and the LSYPE in order to explore whether ethnic minority groups made stronger *educational progress* between Key Stage 3 and 4, to look at progress between Key Stage 2 and 4 in order to be able to look at the association between ethnicity, educational attainment and progress over the whole secondary school phase.

Research summary: Strand (2008)

The key findings were:

- Black Caribbean pupils had on average a significantly lower attainment than White British, Pakistani, Bangladeshi, Black African pupils while Indian pupils were significantly ahead of all of these groups. Of particular concern regarding low achievement were: White British boys and girls and Black Caribbean boys from disadvantages backgrounds and Black Caribbean pupils, particularly boys, from middle-class backgrounds.
- Social class accounted for the gap in attainment more than ethnicity and gender accounted for the gap the least out of these three variables.
- White British attainment 'was differentiated to a greater extent' (i.e. more differentiated) than any of the other ethnic groups with middle-class White British pupils being one of the highest achieving groups and White British pupils, both boys and girls, from disadvantaged backgrounds being the lowest achieving. Factors such as low social class, low maternal education, relative poverty and living in a deprived neighbourhood had a negative impact on all ethnic groups in relation to attainment 'but seem to be associated with disproportionately low attainment among White British pupils'.
- In relation to progress during their secondary school careers, Indian pupils on average made more progress than White British pupils (and so were substantially ahead at Key Stage 4), while Black African and Bangladeshi pupils who were behind White British pupils at the beginning of secondary school (Key Stage 2) caught up with them by Key Stage 4. Pakistani pupils, who had been substantially behind White British pupils at Key Stage 2, had almost caught up with them by Key Stage 4. Mixed-heritage pupils remained on par with White British pupils from Key Stage 2 to 4. Black Caribbean pupils, as noted above, were substantially behind White British pupils at Key Stage 2 and although they made the same progress as White British pupils they thus remained substantially behind White British pupils at Key Stage 4.
- Progress, like attainment, was affected by gender and socio-economic status of the home so that it was White British pupils from disadvantaged backgrounds, Black Caribbean boys and Bangladeshi boys from disadvantaged backgrounds that made the least progress. (from Strand, 2008: 2–4)

The most substantial findings that emerge from the above are that controlling for socio-economic status could not account for the low attainment of Black Caribbean pupils and the under-representation of this group of pupils in higher tier entry for certain key exams. Strand was also able to contribute to an understanding of pupil progress in relation to ethnicity. He was able to demonstrate that Indians, Black Africans, Bangladeshis and Pakistanis made more progress in secondary school than White British pupils, while Black Caribbean made the same progress as White British pupils.

Strand thus leads us to an outline of relative achievement that is different to the one presented by Gillborn and Gipps (1996) that we started with. This is the outline of the relative achievement of the main ethnic groups at age 16 as presented by Gillborn and Gipps and as presented by Strand.

Gillborn and Gipps (1996):

High	Indian
	White
	Pakistani; Mixed Heritage
Low	Bangladeshi; Pakistani; African-Caribbean

Strand (2008):

Indian; (Chinese: Gillborn and Mirza 2000; Archer and Francis, 2004)

White British; Bangladeshi;

Black Caribbean

Reflection activity

In the light of what has been said and discussed above about the dangers of discussing ethnic groups in relation to achievement:

What problems and dangers are there in presenting the relative achievement in this way?

How could you critique the presentation above?

Compare your notes and thoughts with those presented later in this chapter.

In presenting the above this text has colluded in some of the very negative aspects of the way in which 'ethnicity and achievement' has been constituted and come to be presented. This presentation will be critiqued below. However, for now, we can see that in spite of the limitations identified by the researchers and reviewers (and discussed below), a picture emerges of achievement and underachievement, with regard to the main ethnic groups, that clearly suggests that ethnicity has a part to play in one's chances of doing well in school. Put very simplistically, the picture that emerges suggests that if you are categorized as belonging to the ethnic group of Indian or Chinese pupils you are likely to do well in school, make good progress and achieve highly in relation to White pupils and other ethnic groups of pupils at the end of schooling. If you are categorized as belonging to the ethnic group of Bangladeshi, Pakistani or Mixed Heritage pupils you are likely to now achieve alongside your White peers at the end of schooling, although there are some variations within this according to your gender and class (and this has changed over the 12 years – if you are considered to be part of the Bangladeshi or Pakistani ethnic group you have been 'catching up' with your White British peers in recent years but still tend not to do as well as this group in primary school), while if you are categorized as belonging to the ethnic group of Black Caribbean pupils you are likely to underachieve in relation to all the other ethnic groups even when your social class and gender are taken into account. All of the ethnic groups of pupils are seen to be improving their achievement in school with more and more pupils in each of the ethnic groups gaining the important GCSE A–C grades; however, there are still big differences between the numbers in each ethnic group that do achieve these valued examination results. Even though gender and your social class can explain some of this difference, these two factors cannot explain all of it and so we are left with the finding that the ethnic group that you are perceived to belong to does somehow make a difference to how well you do in school tests and exams and thus to your opportunity to gain qualifications that are valued and needed after school has ended. In addition, your perceived ethnicity would also seem to affect your chances of being excluded from school, you being considered to have Special Educational Needs (SEN) or being referred to a special unit for your education and what type of examinations you take when you take them.

In Scotland, tariff scores for pupils at the end of compulsory schooling (Standard Grade 4) in 2009 showed that the highest achieving pupils were Chinese (222), Indian (195) and Mixed (195), while the lowest achieving were Black Caribbean pupils (111). This is the same pattern as that found by Strand and many other studies in England although Mixed Heritage pupils are achieving relatively more highly in Scotland than in England. Interestingly, in Scotland, Bangladeshi pupils are among the high achieving groups (with a tariff score of 194) while Pakistani (177), White (175), Asian Other (174), White Other (172) and Black Other (172) groups are all clustered around the national average (175) (Scottish Government, 2010a). Girls also outperform boys in all groups (Scottish Government, 2010a). It has to be noted that these statistics are based on very small numbers of pupils – there are fewer than one thousand pupils in most ethnic groups analysed and only 92 Bangladeshi and 23 Black Caribbean pupils (Scottish Government, 2010a). The statistics also show that the effects of poor economic status on achievement were not as great for minority ethnic groups as for White pupils (Weedon et al., forthcoming).

In Wales, at the end of compulsory schooling Chinese pupils also achieved highly while Black pupils had the lowest relative achievement. Using the CSI data which combined averages for 2007, 2008 and 2009, 68.2 per cent of Chinese pupils achieved CSI (i.e. they achieved the expected level or above in the three core subjects) while White (44.1 per cent), Asian (43.5 per cent) and Mixed (42.2 per cent) all achieved close to the national average of 44.1 per cent. Black pupils only achieved a CSI of 30.9 per cent (Welsh Assembly Government, 2010). Again this is a very similar pattern to that found in the English studies.

In Northern Ireland, performance data according to ethnicity are collected but the analysis only compares all minority ethnic pupils as one group with White pupils (Irish Travellers are included in the minority ethnic group). This rather limited analysis, bearing in mind the very small numbers involved (there were only 330 minority ethnic pupils taking GCSEs and 'A' Levels in 2009), reveals that 71.2 per cent of minority ethnic pupils gained 5 GCSEs

A*–C (or equivalent qualifications) compared to 70.1 per cent of White pupils (Department of Education, 2010). The pattern of relative achievement could thus be similar to England, Scotland and Wales but with the aggregation of all minority ethnic pupils it is not possible to see if this is the case.

Exclusions from school

In the above section we have considered the different attainments of ethnic groups in the educational system through some key statistical studies and reviews that were carried out. Another issue that needs to be considered in relation to ethnicity and schooling is that of school exclusions. If a pupil is excluded from school on a fixed-term exclusion then they lose access to important educational resources that impact on their ability to achieve in school for the time they are excluded. If a pupil is permanently excluded then they lose the opportunity to study for and take school tests and exams. In addition, commentators have reported on an increase in 'unofficial exclusions' (e.g. Osler et al., 2000 cited in Gillborn, 2008: 61; Wright et al., 2000: 1–2). All forms of exclusion can have negative consequences for achievement and subsequent access to employment and/or further education. A DfE study found that 'Of those who were permanently excluded from school by Year 11 only 3 per cent had attained Level 3 (qualifications) by age 18 showing that those permanently excluded by age 16 rarely go on to attain Level 3 by age 18' (DfE, 2010: 11).

Research has clearly documented that certain ethnic groups are excluded from school more than others.

> . . . statistics reveal that some groups of children and young people are at a considerably greater risk of exclusion than others. The research evidence indicates that those who are at disproportionate risk of exclusion are African-Caribbean boys of both primary and secondary school age (e.g. Hayden, 1997; Parsons 1996; Wright 1992; Gillborn and Gipps 1996).
>
> (Wright et al., 2000: 7)

In Scotland, the most excluded group of pupils are Black Caribbean and Other Travellers while the least excluded are Indian, Chinese and Asian Other (Scottish Government, 2010b).

Wright et al. are quick to point out that this situation is not a new one and that the over-representation of African-Caribbean pupils in school exclusions was identified in the 1970s and 1980s by Coard (1971), Tattum (1982) and the Commission for Racial Equality (1985) (Wright et al., 2000: 7). In the mid-1980s OFSTED data suggested that nationally Black Caribbean pupils were excluded from school at six times the rate for White pupils (Gillborn, 2008: 61). Battacharyya et al. in 2003 found that Black Caribbean pupils were approximately three times more likely to be permanently excluded compared to their White peers (Bhattacharyya et al., 2003: 3) and in 2005 Parsons et al. found that Black Caribbean, Mixed White and Black Caribbean pupils were 2 to 2.5 times more likely to be permanently excluded from school than White British pupils (Parsons et al., 2005 cited in Strand, 2007b: 93–4). Gillborn presents government figures for 2004–5 that show that while 0.13 per cent of White pupils were excluded from school the percentage for Black Caribbean pupils was 0.39 per cent and for Mixed Heritage White/Black Caribbean pupils 0.41 per cent (Gillborn, 2008: 62). While Black Caribbean pupils are over-represented in exclusion figures, Asian pupils are under-represented and are therefore less likely to be excluded than their White and Black peers (Gillborn, 2008: 63). Gillborn, referencing the work of Richardson (2005), rightly comments that 'Exclusions have become one of the most controversial areas of inequality so far as race and education are concerned. The over-exclusion of Black students frequently emerges as one of the most important issues in the eyes of Black teachers, parents and students' (Gillborn, 2008: 63).

Special educational needs and referral units

It is also worth being aware that there are differences in the numbers of pupils who get referred to special units or who become considered as pupils who have SEN. While being considered to have SEN can gain a pupil additional resources and teacher-time, it can also restrict access to other resources, take pupils out of mainstream education while they work with a specialist, or in many cases a teaching assistant (often on work that is different to that being covered in the mainstream class), result in lower teacher expectations and prevent entry to higher-tiered exams. Being placed in a referral unit can also have many of the same effects. Bhattacharyya et al. found that Gypsy/Roma, the children of Travellers of Irish Heritage, Black Caribbean, Pakistani and Bangladeshi pupils were more likely to be recorded as having SEN than their White peers while Black Caribbean and Black Other pupils were over-represented in pupil referral units (2003: 3). They also found that there was a large variation in the proportions of ethnic minority pupils considered to have SEN across LEAs and schools suggesting that there was a lack of consistency in who was considered to have SEN (Bhattacharyya et al., 2003: 17). Lindsay et al. found that Black Caribbean, Mixed White and Black Caribbean pupils were more likely to be statemented and that they were one and a half times more likely to be labelled as having behavioural, emotional or social difficulties than other pupils, even when the data were controlled for free school meals (FSM), gender, age and neighbourhood deprivation (Lindsay et al., 2006 cited in Strand, 2007b: 94). Tomlinson (2008: 36) writes about the over-placement of West Indian pupils in ESN schools in the 1960s and the prevalent claim that West Indian pupils had lower IQs and were intellectually inferior to White children (see also Coard, 1971).

Achievement after compulsory education

Another aspect that needs to be borne in mind when considering ethnicity and achievement is that of the different routes taken by learners through schooling and education. Research has shown that ethnicity has a part to play in the differing journeys of learners as they make their way from school, into further and higher education.

When conducting their 1996 OFSTED review on the achievements of ethnic minority learners, Gillborn and Gipps found the following with regard to post-compulsory education:

Research summary: Gillborn and Gipps' review – ethnicity and post-compulsory education (1996)

- Within each ethnic group, the higher the social-class background of the learner, the higher the rate of participation in post-compulsory education.
- Participation in first three years of post-compulsory education was higher for all major ethnic minority groups compared to White young people regardless of gender and social class. The participation of Asian young people was especially high even after three years.
- Young women tended to stay on in education more than young men, although more Asian young men stayed on than Asian young women.
- At the age of 18, Asian young people were the most highly qualified group (including White young people) due to a tendency to follow traditional academic courses.
- African-Caribbean young people were more likely to follow vocational courses.
- Relatively more ethnic minority people applied to Higher Education institutions than White people.
- At 'old' (higher status) universities Whites were more likely to be accepted and Black Caribbean and African applicants least likely.
- Chinese young people were more likely to be admitted to university than other groups while Pakistani and Black Caribbean young people were less likely. (see Gillborn and Gipps, 1996: 5–6)

Bhattacharyya et al. also found that:

Research summary: Bhattacharyya, Ison and Blair's review – ethnicity and post-compulsory education (2003)

- Black and Asian people are more likely to stay on in full-time education at age 16 than White young people. Black Africans of working age are the most likely to be currently studying for a qualification.
- Minority ethnic learners were more likely than White learners to enter Higher Education with vocational qualifications, rather than academic qualifications.
- Minority ethnic students were less likely to gain a First-Class or Upper Second-Class degree at the end of their undergraduate study. (from Bhattacharyya et al., 2003: 4)

In Scotland, the same pattern emerges: Indian, Chinese, Asian Other, Black, Mixed Heritage and Black Other pupils are all more likely to go into Higher Education than White UK pupils (Scottish Government, 2009) and in Northern Ireland minority ethnic pupils (50 per cent) are more likely to go into Higher Education than White pupils (42.8 per cent) (Department of Education, 2010).

What clearly emerges from this is that ethnic minority groups of learners stay on in post-compulsory education to a far greater degree than White young people. Drew found that, 'once attainment was taken into account, ethnic origin was the single most important factor in determining the chances of staying on' (Drew, 1995: 180 cited in Pilkington, 2003: 130). In this way these groups of learners improve their qualifications over time, gaining their GCSEs, for example, at a later date than their White peers. The above statistical surveys that consider GCSE achievement at the end of Key Stage 4 do not capture this achievement.

In a recently published study, using YCS and LSYPE data, many of the above findings were confirmed. In this study the DfE looked at the same pupil cohort that Strand had presented in his 2007 and 2008 study (Strand, 2007b; 2008) – young people who had now reached the age of 18 and therefore 2 years after the end of compulsory education. The 2010 study considered the young people's main activity at the age of 18, how many of them had gone on to gain five or more A*–C GCSEs or their equivalent (Level 2 qualifications) or two 'A' levels or their equivalent (Level 3 qualifications) and their participation in Further Education (FE), Higher Education (HE), work or whether they were not in education or employment (NEET).

Research summary: Department for Education – post-compulsory education and main activity at 18 (2010)

Some of the key findings in relation to ethnic groups were as follows:

White young people (41 per cent) were least likely to be in full time education while Black African young people (85 per cent) were most likely (DfE, 2010: 5).

By the age of 18 Black African and Black Caribbean young people were more likely to have stayed on in education and to have acquired Level 2 qualifications with the result that at 18 the percentage of young people without Level 2 qualifications was: White (23 per cent); Black African (14 per cent); Black Caribbean (20 per cent); Pakistani (23 per cent); Bangladeshi (23 per cent). It would seem that Black Caribbean and Black African young people take longer to reach this particular level of attainment yet more young people from these two groups do gain this level of attainment by the age of 18 than the other groups listed (see DfE, 2010: 11).

Regarding Level 3 qualifications: at 18 the patterns of achievement were similar to those outlined in the studies considered above at 16. Indian (68 per cent) and Other Asian (70 per cent) young people are more likely to have Level 3 qualifications than other groups, while Black Caribbean (37 per cent) the least (see DfE, 2010: 11). Pakistani (33 per cent), Black African (39 per cent) and Black Caribbean

(36 per cent) young people were more likely to be in FE than White (12 per cent), Indian (19 per cent) or Other Asian (23 per cent) pupils. As the DfE points out, these two groups of young people were more likely to gain their Level 3 qualifications later than the other groups (DfE, 2010: 18).

Those groups with the highest level of participation in HE were Indian (56 per cent) and Other Asian (56 per cent) and those with the lowest were Black Caribbean (24 per cent) (although this group had a high number of HE place offers which had been accepted so it looks likely that this group will increase their participation in the next year). Again, this seems to add evidence to the picture that certain ethnic groups, for example Black Caribbeans, 'take longer to reach higher levels of attainment than others' (DfE, 2010: 26). White young people were the least likely to apply and be accepted for HE while those that did were more likely to attend an elite university (see DfE, 2010: 31).

Other findings showed that Pakistani (10 per cent) and White (9 per cent) young people were more likely to be NEET for more than 12 months and Indian (2 per cent) and Black African (2 per cent) the least (see DfE, 2010: 35).

These findings regarding post-compulsory education and the pathways that young people follow then complicate the picture of educational achievement a little more and direct our attention to the fact that it takes some ethnic groups, on average, longer to attain important qualifications and to question why this might be.

Limitations of statistical studies

As we have identified, some clear patterns do emerge from the studies and reviews that we have considered and how they raise serious concerns about how the educational system has failed and is failing certain ethnic groups of learners. However, as with all research, we have to be aware of the limitations of statistical research and what such studies cannot show. These will now be discussed.

We have discussed above some of the limitations of the early statistical studies of ethnic groups and achievement and have noted that more recently such studies have been able to address some of those limitations by using nationally collected, more representative data. In the case of Strand and the DfE studies it was possible to consider socio-economic status, gender, family background, community and school context and so on and in other studies it was possible to consider gender and disadvantage as well as disaggregate ethnic categories to allow a much fuller and wider picture to emerge. This is not to say that these studies are without their limitations though. Some of the limitations of these more recent studies are now discussed.

Differences in group sizes

Even where large, national samples could be used there were usually very large differences in the sizes of the group that were being considered and compared – Archer and Francis point out that when percentages are being used there is a danger that we forget that the White British group is made up of over 400,000 pupils while the Chinese group is made up of only just over 2,000 pupils (Archer and Francis, 2007: 2). As Gillborn and Mirza point out a big change between one year's results and the next within an ethnic group might reflect a change in attainment among a relatively small number of pupils (Gillborn and Mirza, 2000: 13). For example, a change in attainment of only 200 pupils in the Chinese group would equal 10 per cent in any data given in percentages whereas a change in attainment of 200 pupils in the White British group would equal 0.05 per cent. Gillborn and Mirza found that the majority of LEAs did not stipulate the raw numbers behind the percentages that they provided in their EMAG data (Gillborn and Mirza, 2000: 8).

Broad categories that hide difference

The small numbers of pupils in some ethnic groups, such as Chinese or Gypsy/Roma pupils, mean that once statisticians begin to control for variables such as social class, the group numbers become too small for such an analysis to be sustained and valid. This means that groups of pupils have to be combined together to allow for such analysis to take place. In this way some of the studies considered above have combined groups of pupils or left them out of their analysis all together. Gillborn and Mirza were not able to consider Chinese or Traveller children for these kinds of reasons. Archer and Francis point out that the use of the broad categories such as 'White' or 'Asian' is 'relatively useless' as the groups included within the categories have such widely differing attainments, e.g. Indian and Bangladeshi pupils who can be included together under the heading 'Asian' (Archer and Francis, 2007: 2). Even Strand's LSYPE studies (2007b and 2008), despite their ability to explore a wide range of variables and provide 'rich contextualised data' (Strand, 2007b: 18) and to ask respondents to self-identify their ethnic group, combined Black Other, Gypsy/Roma, Chinese and Irish Travellers into other ethnic groupings thereby losing these as categories in the analysis (see Strand, 2007b: 22–3). Paradoxically, one of Strand's recommendations in his findings is that the broad category of 'White British' should be abandoned as it disguises the 'high degree of polarisation around socio-economic factors' (Strand, 2008: 4) within this group and that using the category 'Black' should also be avoided due to the significant differences in the attainment of Black African, Black Caribbean and Other Black groups (Strand, 2008: 104).

Data not available for certain ethnic groups

Some of the studies discussed above were unable to comment on some aspects of attainment as data were not provided for some ethnic groups. Bhattacharyya et al. make no comment on the particular attainment of Gypsy/Roma; Irish Travellers; asylum seekers and refugees for these reasons. They also comment that there were no national data available at the time of their study on fixed term exclusions according to ethnicity (Bhattacharyya et al., 2003: 19). Gillborn and Mirza (2000: 8) comment on the missing data that can hamper reviews such as theirs. In their case, many LEAs were compiling ethnically based data on a large scale for the first time and this meant that data were often gathered and reported on hurriedly with sections of forms sometimes left blank. They also found that nearly a third of LEAs were not recording attainment at Key Stage 2 and 4 by ethnicity (Gillborn and Mirza, 2000: 8). In all of the studies we have considered statistics only related to pupils attending state schools and not those in independent schools. Many of the statistical studies that were available to reviewers were figures from England only and so many statistical studies and reviews did not report on ethnicity and achievement in Scotland, Wales and N. Ireland

Different categorizations used for ethnic groups

A difficulty that Gillborn and Mirza faced when trying to analyse EMAG data was that different LEAs used different ethnic categories to group together pupils (Gillborn and Mirza, 2000: 8). Bhattacharyya et al. (2003) also found that categorizations varied across studies making comparisons very difficult and hampering the creation of a bigger picture.

Difficulties in considering social class and socio-economic status

Despite an awareness of the need to consider social class and socio-economic status in relation to attainment data, Gillborn and Mirza (2000), Bhattacharyya et al. (2003) and Archer and Francis (2007) all comment on the difficulty of finding a variable that could accurately represent social class and socio-economic status as well as the difficulty of defining social class and socio-economic status in the twenty-first century. As Gillborn and Mirza comment, there is no single definition or way of measuring social-class background that has universal support, in different studies occupations can be categorized in different (and therefore inconsistent) ways and the range of other factors that can be considered in relation to socio-economic status is disputed (Gillborn and Mirza, 2000: 18). Archer and Francis comment on the extra difficulty of finding a good indicator of social class when considering ethnic minority groups in the UK as their different trajectories and experiences 'often defy traditional British categories of social class' (Archer and Francis, 2007: 10). All of the studies that we have considered above, with the exception of Strand, use FSM as an indicator of social class and socio-economic status, although all agree that this is a poor indicator and only really represents family income. In addition, some data that is gathered, for example EMAG data, does not include any information about social class or socio-economic status, thus preventing an analysis of the role of social class with ethnicity on attainment.

What is being compared with what?

In all of the studies discussed above the researchers or reviewers have compared the educational achievement of ethnic minority groups with the achievements of either White pupils or White British pupils. As Strand points out, we should be clear as readers about which group is being used as the reference group or base group for comparisons as this affects what is said and how the analysis is grounded (Strand, 2008: 19). We can also ask ourselves what the implications are of using the White or White British group as the reference group – if there is underachievement in the White or White British group when compared to Chinese or Indian pupils then is a comparison with White or White British pupils the best way of exploring whether the education system fails to adequately support, or actively discriminates against, other ethnic minority groups of learners? Does using White or White British as the reference group reinforce a notion of Whiteness as the norm to be assimilated to?

Homogenization of ethnic groups

As we have seen in our discussion above, it becomes very easy to slip into talking about 'African-Caribbean', 'Bangladeshi' or 'Chinese' pupils and how well they achieve in school. Even when we include gender and social class and talk about working-class Bangladeshi boys or middle-class African-Caribbean girls we are still in danger of thinking of all working-class Bangladeshi boys and all middle-class African-Caribbean girls as being the same as each other. It is important to remember that the statistical studies we have considered are using mean averages for each of the categories of ethnic group studied. That means that we have only been looking at the average for each group at given points in time and not at the range of pupils within a category. It is extremely important to remember that these studies are only looking at what goes on **between** ethnically defined groups of pupils – they do not tell us anything about what goes on **within** the groups that we have been considering except to tell us something about the differences between girls and boys and middle-class and working-class pupils. We need to resist the easy slip, when reading these studies, into thinking of all Bangladeshi working-class boys, or all middle-class African-Caribbean girls, as being the same.

Creating hierarchies

Despite warnings from the writers or the reports and reviews, and in spite of what has been said about the homogenization of ethnic groups above, there is still a very big tendency to start to organize ethnic groups of pupils into hierarchies with those who do well at school at the top and those that underachieve at the bottom. This was done at the end of the account of the reviews and statistical studies of ethnicity and achievement. In this way this text colluded in presenting homogenized groups, in presenting group experience as individual experience and in ranking pupils in a way that is stereotypical and can lead to low expectations of those pupils who are seen as the 'underachieving' groups. The table and the account have been left in as it clearly indicates how the way ethnicity and achievement are discussed can lead to this kind of thinking and how easy it is to slip into this way of picturing ethnicity and achievement when we have been reading and discussing the statistical reviews and studies. Connolly makes a good argument for expanding and changing the ways in which we represent the statistical data that are collected in such studies through using different graphical representations of statistical data (for example: box graphs presented on their side and the use of box plots) in order to visually remind ourselves of the overlap that there is between different ethnic groups (Connolly, 2006a).

Writers in the 1980s and 1990s, such as Troyna, Tomlinson and Wright, made clear their disquiet. They were particularly concerned with the **finding** about West Indian/African-Caribbean (and other minority group) pupils' underachievement in the school system becoming a given, an explanation, in practitioners', policy makers' and the public's mind, as well as in the minds of pupils themselves, thus creating a situation in which teachers and other commentators had low expectations of this group and resorted to stereotypical and racist views about their academic abilities. In this century, and after the 'achievement discourse' has become more firmly entrenched, disquiets are rightly still expressed. Mirza (2006) has commented on the fact that we are now familiar with the bar chart that shows each ethnic group lined up in order of their achievement in school with Chinese and Indian pupils at the head of the line, followed by White and then Bangladeshi, Pakistani, African and finally African-Caribbean pupils,

> Here we use the measure of getting five examination subjects at GCSE to rank ethnic groups in order of ability. It is seen as a good thing, with Indian and Chinese (the so called 'model minorities') at the top and Africans and Caribbeans (the so called 'failing' minorities) at the bottom. But what does this tell us? Some are gifted, others are not? Are Asians docile and hardworking (like the coolies of the past)? Do Blacks have a chip on their shoulder and rebel (like uppity slaves of the past)? What do you think? What do we think? What do teachers think? (Mirza, 2006: 151)

Reflection activity

What are your responses to Mirza's questions?
  What kinds of things do you notice in how Mirza writes about achievement?

This is a very interesting extract as Mirza here substitutes the word 'ability' for achievement or performance, reflecting the manner in which people generally, and easily, slide from 'achievement' to 'ability' in their thinking (making a slip from seeing the statistical findings as **findings** about achievement to seeing them as **an explanation** of achievement). She then makes excellent links in her questions between current (majority White) discourses about minority ethnic groups of pupils and British colonial history: questions that take us back to issues we considered in Chapter 1. She questions whether we use past stereotypes and understandings, essentialized understandings, about former colonial subjects as contemporary ways of understanding thus challenging us to think of how our past is present in our present as British subjects. She links this explicitly with our thinking asking if we do allow our thinking to take this form and then links this with teachers' and their thinking. The thinking of teachers is one of the key issues discussed in Chapter 3.

While discussing the homogenization of ethnic groups and the danger of creating hierarchies of ethnic groups we should consider one explanation for differences in 'group performance' that has been put forward by some commentators on education and was put forward very powerfully in the US in 1994. It seems important to do this here in order to demonstrate the easy slippage between achievement and ability as identified by Mirza above as well as the manner in which simplistic, stereotypical and dangerous beliefs can emerge from working with the idea of homogenized, hierarchical groups. In addition it is important to reflect on the manner in which ideas about a linkage between some notion of race and intelligence are still dangerously utilized in contemporary discourses (see Chapter 1). In their book *The Bell Curve*, Hernstein and Murray (1994) argued that hereditary genetic intelligence was the reason why White Americans achieved more highly than African-Americans and used a bell curve to argue that African-Americans scored on average lower than Whites in IQ tests (see Mirza, 1998: 113). The argument is then that differences in intelligence are the cause of differences in achievement. This argument has also been made recently in the UK by Dr Frank Ellis, a senior lecturer at Leeds University, who claimed that Black people are genetically less intelligent than Whites (see Gillborn, 2008: 174). This explanation relies on an acceptance that there is such a thing as hereditary intelligence and that intelligence is something that is fixed and measurable, both assumptions that have been rigorously challenged in the literature (see Chapter 3 of this book and Chitty, 2007; Mirza, 1998; Gillborn, 2008; Gardner, 1995). It is also the case that tests can only tell us what someone can do at a moment in time, not what their potential is. IQ tests are also culturally biased (see Mirza, 1998: 114). It is also easily challenged when we remember that first, as we have seen in Chapter 1, the so-called racial groups are not biologically or genetically distinct groups of people; secondly, that pupils' achievement (and IQ scores) can and do shift, change and improve (Pilkington, 2003: 137). It is also clear that many non-White pupils achieve more highly than White pupils. We can also remember that exactly the same explanation was once put forward regarding the difference between men and women, boys and girls, middle-class and working-class people (see Chitty, 2007).

Measuring relative achievement and debates about 'The Gap'

As well as the placement of ethnic groups in relation to each other in a hierarchy coming under attack, the way that the 'gaps' between ethnic group achievement have been measured and described have also been subject to heated debate. In the studies and reviews we have considered, many of the writers have commented, for example, that there is a gap in achievement between Group X and Group Y. In many cases, the measure of achievement being used is the percentage of pupils in each ethnic group who gain five or more GCSEs at levels A–C, what we, after Connolly (2006a: 238), will call the 'GCSE benchmark'. Thus we have statements such as '55% of Group X achieved the GCSE benchmark compared to 40% of Group Y'. Therefore the difference in achievement between these two groups is said to be 15 percentage points. This is the way differences in achievement in the studies that we have considered above have been measured and presented. One problem that emerges is that away from the reports and reviews people begin to speak of percentages rather than percentage points and so the difference between Group X and Group Y becomes discussed as 15 per cent, rather than 15 percentage points. This is mathematically incorrect. A bigger issue emerges though when commentators seek to use percentage point differences over time in order to talk about whether ethnic groups are improving in their achievement and if so by how much and whether achievement gaps between ethnic groups are widening or narrowing.

Let us take improvements in achievement first. To continue with Group X and Group Y, if we say that it was in 2006 that 55 per cent of Group X and 30 per cent of Group Y achieved the GCSE benchmark and that in 2008 60 per cent of Group X and 50 per cent of Group Y achieved the benchmark we have a situation in which it can be said that:

a) Group X improved their achievement between 2006 and 2008 by 5 percentage points. This means that in every 100 pupils in Group X, five more gained the GCSE benchmark in 2008 than 2006.

b) Group Y improved their achievement between 2006 and 2008 by 20 percentage points. This means that in every 100 pupils in Group Y, 20 more gained the GCSE benchmark in 2008 than 2006.

In much commentary these improvements are represented as percentage improvements (i.e. as 5 per cent for Group X and 20 per cent for Group Y). However, Gorard (1999) argues that this is not actually the case as the rate of improvement should be measured as a proportion. To illustrate this, if we take Group X, their improvement was from 55 per cent to 60 per cent in the 2 years. This is an improvement of 5 in the whole group (which is represented as 100); therefore, the proportional improvement is an improvement of 20 per cent (as 5 is 20 per cent of 100). For Group Y the improvement would be 5 per cent. It immediately becomes clear that using percentage points or proportional change as a way of talking about achievement improvements over time for an ethnic group gives completely different, and opposing, results. Group X can be described as improving their attainment by 5 per cent points (using the percentage points method of calculation) or by 20 per cent (using the proportional change method). Group Y can be described as improving their attainment by 20 per cent points (percentage point method) or by 5 per cent (using the proportional method)! These differences have serious implications for the picture that is presented of inequalities in education (The 'gap' debate discussed here has taken place in a wider context than research and statistics about ethnicity and achievement and has included talk about the 'gap' between boys' and girls' achievement as well as the performance of different schools and types of school, employment figures and so on – see Gorard, 1999). As indicated, the key studies have used the percentage point method. When discussing poorly achieving groups the picture that is presented of improvement over time becomes a small one. Let us take another example. If 40 per cent of Black Caribbean pupils achieved the GCSE benchmark in 2006 and 45 per cent gained the benchmark in 2008 then the improvement in achievement would only be 5 per cent points, or in some accounts, 5 per cent, whereas, if the proportional method had been used it would be an improvement of 20 per cent. An improvement of only 5 per cent seems small, indicative of persistent inequalities in the educational system and to indicate that resources must be directed to ameliorate this problem, whereas an improvement of 20 per cent suggests that things for this group are getting better and that there is little need to do anything.

If we now consider the way in which these two ways of measuring improvement and attainment affect the way we perceive the gaps between ethnic group achievement over time we can see more clearly how different ways of calculating lead to radically different pictures. To take our previous example, if 40 per cent of Black Caribbean pupils achieved the GCSE benchmark in 2006 and 45 per cent gained the benchmark in 2008 and 57 per cent of White pupils achieved the GCSE benchmark in 2006 and 65 per cent in 2008 then the percentage point improvements would be Black Caribbean: 5 per cent and White: 8 per cent thus Black Caribbean pupils would be perceived as behind White pupils in their achievement and making less progress than their White peers, i.e. the gap between them and their White peers would be a widening one. If, however, the change was calculated proportionally the improvement would be Black Caribbean: 20 per cent and White: 12.5 per cent, thus Black Caribbean pupils would be perceived as improving at a greater rate than their White peers and the gap between these two groups could be seen as a narrowing one. In this way we can see why Gorard argues that the percentage/percentage point method produces an incorrect picture about inequalities in education. Gorard referred to the percentage method of calculation as the 'politicians' error', referring to the manner in which percentage calculations dominated political and policy discourse in the late 1990s producing what he saw as an erroneous picture (Gorard, 1999: 235–7). His method of calculation produces a picture in which inequalities are actually falling rather than increasing. As Gillborn comments, 'Gorard's proportionate method produces an entirely different set of results to those more cited' (Gillborn, 2008: 47) and gives scope to those who wish to challenge the idea that there are 'race' inequalities in the educational system.

In this manner the debate becomes one with important political consequences. One method of measurement shows increasing inequalities and makes the case for political and policy action (as well as suggesting the role that the education system plays in perpetuating racial inequalities). The other shows decreasing inequalities and makes the case for political and policy inaction (as well as denying that the educational system is complicit in some way in reproducing educational inequalities).

there is no obvious need to do anything specific to ameliorate these gaps. Things are already getting better, and although progress towards the reduction of inequalities may be slow there is no guarantee that any alternative intervention would be any more effective. (Gorard, 1999: 243)

Hammersley argues that both methods are valid, useful and complementary if it is recognized that they are measuring and showing different things. According to Hammersley, one method seeks to compare the situation as it is with how it should be while the other seeks to measure how much improvement there has been (Hammersley, 2001: 293–4 cited in Gillborn, 2008: 48). While accepting that this is the case, Gillborn is aware of the political consequences of the debate: 'it fails to resolve the contradictory conclusions about what the findings mean in terms of race inequality in education, i.e. whether inequalities/gaps in achievement are worsening or narrowing' (Gillborn, 2008: 48). Gillborn also argues that greater progress is not the same as closing the gap. Just because one group is improving in terms of the proportion of its members who attain the GCSE benchmark it is not the same thing as the gap between this group and a higher achieving one becoming smaller. Even if the gap is getting smaller it has to be by a large enough proportion to allow a poorly attaining group to catch up with a highly attaining one.

When the starting point is significantly lower than other groups, a relatively small change in performance will look impressive according to the proportionate model. But a greater proportionate change would have to be sustained year-on-year to make a dent in the actual inequality of achievement (what most people would reasonably view as the 'gap') (Gillborn, 2008: 49)

Connolly has argued that both methods, the percentage point and the proportional, are flawed (Connolly, 2006b: 76–7). He demonstrates how the proportional method lacks perspective and can lead to contradictory results (see Connolly, 2006b: 77–9) and argues for the use of Phi as an indicator of effect. Phi, a statistical method, measures the size of effect, for example, the size of the effect of gender or ethnicity on educational outcomes. He agrees that Gorard is correct to warn about the dangers of using percentage points to talk about change (2006b: 80) but instead of the proportional method, Connolly makes a strong case for the use of Phi.

Thus, as we can see, there is no consensus about the most reliable and valid way to calculate comparative statistics about achievement. A limitation of the work that we have considered is that the 'gap' figures and claims can be challenged and different interpretations made. What we do have to inform us though are statistics about how many pupils, who make up a particular ethnic group, achieve against specific thresholds such as the GCSE benchmark. We can see, in any of the years that figures are available for, the number in every hundred pupils in that group who gain the GCSE benchmark. The differences between groups are significant. Whether gaps are widening or narrowing is a different matter and depends on how you chose to measure and interpret the data. Gillborn's point that proportional improvement does not automatically mean that gaps are narrowing is a correct one. Connolly's point that statistical studies have long worked with the issues of measuring effect and that more appropriate statistical techniques can be taken from this discipline also seems a correct one. In spite of the critiques of percentage point usage, the data that have been presented above still show that there are racial inequalities in the education system when we compare ethnic group performance in relation to the GCSE benchmark.

A final word on the strengths and weaknesses of statistical studies

The statistical studies referred to above established ethnic minority performance in school as an issue and were influential in establishing 'the problem of underachievement'. The studies' strengths lay in their ability to demonstrate differing achievement according to ethnicity and in the manner in which patterns and relationships between variables could be explored. However, such studies were not able, by their very nature, to consider the processes of learning and achieving for ethnic minority pupils. Most of the studies focused on achievement or performance as measured by test results, usually at the end of schooling and thus at one point in time and could not reveal anything about the processes of schooling and the school careers of pupils. This was noted by many of the researchers themselves (Kysel, 1988; Tanna, 1990; Kivi, 1991; Amin et al., 1997; Drew and Gray, 1990; Demie, 2001; Gillborn and Gipps, 1996: 81). In addition, in statistical studies and reviews, data on ethnic minority pupils were often aggregated in ways that lost sight of significant historical, cultural, political and social issues resulting in only 'a partial, and possibly misleading, picture' (Gillborn, 1995: 43).

In the 1980s and 1990s qualitative research studies began to appear which were able to focus on the processes within classrooms and on the experiences of ethnic minority pupils in English schools. This work is to be discussed in Chapter 3.

Chapter summary

In this chapter we have considered how a focus on the educational achievement of ethnic groups came about and what early statistical studies in the 1970s and 1980s revealed as well as what some of the limitations of these studies were. We then considered the concept of 'achievement' and the different meanings that can be attributed to the term, how achievement has been measured and some of the dangers of talking about the achievement of ethnic groups. We then considered what a range of reviews and statistical studies revealed about the relative achievement of different ethnic groups between 1990 and 2010 and noted that despite the limitations of these reviews and statistical studies it certainly seems the case that ethnicity has a part to play in one's chances of doing well in school. Those categorized as Indian or Chinese pupils were revealed as likely to do well in school and achieve highly in relation to White pupils at the end of compulsory education while those categorized as Black Caribbean pupils were revealed as likely to underachieve in relation to all other ethnic groups even when their social class and gender were taken into account. We also considered the higher rates of exclusion from school of African-Caribbean boys and the effects of this on achievement, how certain ethnic groups of pupils are likely to be over-represented in SEN figures and the implications of this and how some ethnic groups of pupils take longer to acquire educational qualifications but do get there two years after the end of compulsory education. We briefly identified ethnic differences in what happens to young people after they have finished compulsory education. The chapter ends with a consideration of the limitations of statistical studies and reviews with a particular focus on the big debate about how one should measure and talk about relative achievement as well as a discussion about how racial stereotypes and hierarchies can be perpetuated through acts of writing and presentation such as this text.

Further reading

Tomlinson provides a list of all research conducted on the attainment of West Indian and Asian pupils between 1960 and 1983 in *Ethnic Minority Achievement and Equality of Opportunity* (1986: 25–6) and directs readers to her reviews of this literature in *Ethnic Minorities in British Schools: a Review of the Literature 1960–82* (Tomlinson, 1983).

Other critiques of the concept of ability can be found in Gillborn and Youdell's *Rationing Education: Policy, Practice, Reform and Equity* (2000) and Gillborn's *Racism and Education: Coincidence or Conspiracy?* (2008: 112–14).

For more information about achievement patterns in Wales, see Welsh Assembly Government, *The Achievement of Ethnic Minority Pupils in Wales* (2003); as well as *Schools in Wales: General Statistics 2009* (2009a); *Schools in Wales: Examination Performance 2008* (2009b); *National Curriculum Assessments of 7, 11, and 14 Year Olds, 2009* (2009c); and *GCSE/GNVQ and GCE 'A', 'AS' and AVCE Results, 2009* (2009d), all of which are available at www.wales.gov.uk/topics/statistics.

For more information about achievement patterns in Scotland see Scottish Government (2010a) *SQA Attainment and School Leaver Qualifications in Scotland: 2008–2009*; Arshad et al. (2005) *Minority Ethnic Pupils' Experiences of School in Scotland*; and Weedon et al. (forthcoming) *Muslim Pupils' Educational Experiences in England and Scotland: Policy and Practice in Scotland*.

For an exploration of achievement gaps at Key Stage 4 in England with a particular focus on pupils eligible for FSM in comparison with those who are not and gaps relating to underachieving minority ethnic groups, see Department for Children Schools and Families' Research Brief 217 available at www.education.gov.uk/research/data/uploadfiles/DCSF-RB217.pdf

For an exploration of the impact of Excellence in the Cities policy on minority ethnic achievement, see *Minority Ethnic Pupils and Excellence in Cities: Final report* (2005) by Kendall, Rutt and Schagen.

Texts to consult for further discussion of the 'achievement debate' and definitions of 'achievement' and 'underachievement' include: Mirza (1992), *Young, Female and Black* (Chapter 2) and (1997), 'Black women in education', in *Black British Feminism: A Reader*; Troyna (1984), 'Fact or artefact? The "educational underachievement" of Black pupils', in the *British Journal of Sociology of Education* 5 (2) and (1987), *Racial Inequality in Education*; Reay and Mirza (1997), 'Uncovering genealogies of the margins: Black supplementary schooling', in the *British Journal of Sociology of Education* 18 (4); Gillborn and Gipps (1996), *Recent Research on the Achievements of Ethnic Minority Pupils*; Gillborn and Mirza (2000), *Educational Inequality: Mapping Race, Class and Gender*; Smith (2003), 'Failing boys and moral panics: Perspectives on the underachievement debate', in the *British Journal of Education Studies*, 51 (3) and (2005), *Analysing Underachievement in Schools* and Richardson and Wood (2000), *Inclusive Schools, Inclusive Society: Race and Identity on the Agenda*.

Useful websites

www.wales.gov.uk/topics/statistics

Welsh Assembly Government publications, statistics and reports

www.education.gov.uk/research

Government (England) publications, statistics and reports

www.scotland.gov.uk

Scottish Government publications, statistics and reports

www.statistics.gov.uk

National Statistics Office

www.education.gov.uk/rsgateway

Department for Education (England) website

3

'Race', Ethnicity and School Experience

Reflection activity

The limitations of statistical work have been outlined in Chapter 2.

What approaches and methods could be adopted by a researcher who wanted to find out about minority ethnic pupils' experiences of school?

Why might this be a good approach?

What might be some of the limitations or problems with this approach?

Introduction

The statistical studies referred to in the previous chapter established ethnic minority performance in school as an issue and were influential in establishing 'the problem of ethnic minority underachievement'. The studies' strengths lay in their ability to demonstrate differing achievement according to ethnicity and in the manner in which patterns and relationships between variables could be explored. However, such studies were not able, by their very nature, to consider the processes of learning and achieving for ethnic minority pupils. Most of the studies focused on achievement or performance as measured by test results, usually at the end of schooling and thus at one point in time, and could not reveal anything about the *processes* of schooling and the school careers of pupils. This was noted by many of the researchers themselves (Kysel, 1988; Tanna, 1990; Kivi, 1991; Amin et al., 1997; Drew and Gray, 1990; Demie, 2001; Gillborn and Gipps, 1996: 81).

In the 1980s and 1990s qualitative research studies began to appear which were able to focus on the processes within classrooms and on the experiences of ethnic minority pupils in English schools. Gillborn situates this work in relation to the statistical work of the 1970s, 1980s and 1990s, claiming that in such work data on ethnic minority pupils were 'often aggregated in ways that lost sight of significant historical, cultural, political and social differences' resulting in only 'a partial, and possibly misleading, picture' (Gillborn, 1995: 43). Concerns were also expressed about the ease of stereotyping as a result of survey work (Connolly and Troyna, 1998). Statistical work could also be critiqued for its tendency to see particular ethnic groups as failing and locating the failure within deficiencies in the groups themselves rather than considering the structural processes, specifically of racism, which existed within society and within schools, as the reason for ethnic minority underachievement (Gillborn, 1995; Mirza, 1992; Mac an Ghaill, 1992; Connolly, 1995). Troyna, at the end of a review of the problems of statistical work, claimed that there had been a failure to

> develop a suitable analytic framework which captures . . . the complex processes through which pupils are allocated to credentialing courses of different statuses

and insisted that

> we need to dive beneath the surface and consider the relationship between ethnicity . . . and who goes where and who (gets) what. (Troyna, 1991b: 363)

Qualitative research has appeared from the late 1980s that attempts to look at 'these complex processes', not just of how pupils get allocated to courses of different statuses but of ethnic minority pupil experiences in school in general, and 'who goes where and gets what'. Most of the early studies show that different groups of pupils receive differing amounts or kinds of attention from their teachers or that setting and banding arrangements in schools are key in creating disadvantage.

In this chapter we will look first at some of the key qualitative studies and what they have revealed about ethnicity and school experience. We will then consider some of the explanations and insights put forward by this work and what these have revealed about the role of 'race' and ethnicity in education. In Chapter 4 we will then consider a major critique aimed at this work.

Qualitative studies

As hinted at above, qualitative research is able to focus on the particular social processes and practices that are lost in survey research. Qualitative research in this respect is research which is based on the researcher or researchers spending a period of time in the site or sites of the research, interviewing the people who are going about their daily lives or practices in those sites and/or listening to what people say as they go about their work and their lives as well as observing (either as a participant observer or a stand-apart observer) what is happening in the classroom, other spaces of the school(s) and sometimes outside the school(s). Qualitative research data are built up from these interviews, conversations and observations as well as sometimes from an examination of written documents that are produced or used in the research site. Data are analysed by looking for patterns and themes that emerge in the collected data. This often involves using the terms, meanings and concepts of the research participants in order to organize the data. The focus in qualitative research is always on processes and how people make meaning of their actions and daily practices in the research site. It is sometimes referred to as an 'interactionist' approach in that it can focus on the interactions that take place in particular settings and contexts between the people in those settings and contexts.

It is thus clear that only qualitative approaches to classroom research can focus on the different relationships that children from the same ethnic background develop with their teachers and their peers and show what is shared and not shared. Through qualitative work, understandings of ethnicity in classrooms can be developed which do not rely on or reproduce, 'insidious stereotypes' (Keith, 1993). In addition, qualitative strategies allow researchers to explore schools, neighbourhoods and classrooms in order to consider the concepts, language, actions and events, and the meanings given to these by participants (and the meanings given to the participants by these). There are also philosophical reasons why a qualitative research strategy can be more appropriate for a study of 'race', ethnicity and school experience than a quantitative strategy. Survey research is located within a traditional scientific paradigm, which assumes that there is a single, constant, objective reality that can be observed and measured. The researcher's role is to look for what is there and report on it. Some, though not necessarily all, qualitative research strategies recognize that the world is a 'function of . . . interaction' and that phenomena are interpreted and not measured and are ever changing and not fixed. A qualitative research study allows for a focus on process and on meaning; how people make sense of their lives, what they experience, how they interpret these experiences and how they structure their social worlds (Merriam, 1988).

At the same time qualitative research also allows for a consideration of how people's social worlds make meaning of them (the participants in that world). Qualitative approaches also give an opportunity for capturing something of the 'messiness' and complexity of classroom and individual life, for allowing the inclusion of things that do not neatly tie up or fit into a 'box'. Qualitative research is thus able to give expression to the multiple, changing, fluid 'realities' of participants' lives as well as to the contradictory ways people understand their world and their actions within it. Qualitative research also allows for multiple viewpoints to be captured and included in analysis.

In the light of these arguments for the strength and need for qualitative studies of ethnicity and school experience let us look at some of the key studies and what they revealed. The main focus will be on studies that examined the experiences of minority ethnic pupils but some mention is made of important studies that focused on the experiences of minority ethnic parents and minority ethnic teachers.

Throughout the chapter I will use the terminology to describe different ethnic groups that the authors of each of the studies used. This 'naming' has of course changed over time.

The experiences of minority ethnic pupils

The 'Afro-Caribbean pupil' dominated qualitative studies during the 1980s and was the focus, with the 'Asian pupil', of most of the studies conducted in the 1990s.

Green: *Multi-Ethnic Teaching and Pupils' Self-Concepts* (1985)

In the 1980s Green considered the social relationships between West Indian, Asian and European children and their teachers. He measured the interaction of a White teacher with a mixed pupil group of West Indian, Asian and European children. His analysis showed that Asian and European pupils were lumped together by the teachers to form a group with which West Indian children were contrasted. European boys were the group most favoured by teachers and West Indian boys were the least favoured group; West Indian boys received less individual attention than other children from their teachers, less praise and more orders. (Green assessed and recorded classroom interactions using Flanders' systematic observation schedule. The study was thus not a qualitative study in the true sense of the term but it is included here as it is a study of what was happening *in* six specific classrooms. It is also frequently referred to by later qualitative studies.)

Wright: *Race Relations in the Primary School* (1992); 'Black students – white teachers' (1987); 'School processes: An ethnographic study' (1986)

Wright (1992) in her study of four inner city primary schools also found that there were subtle differences in the way White teachers treated different groups of pupils. As in Green's study, Afro-Caribbean children were considered by their teachers to be the most disruptive group of pupils and they were the most criticized and controlled group in the school. They were also more likely than any of the other groups to feature in the school's sanction system. As to Asian pupils, Wright found that

> the Asian children (particularly the younger children) were perceived as a problem to teachers because of their limited cognitive skills, poor English language and poor social skills and their inability to socialise within the classroom. However, there was also an assumption that Asian children were well-disciplined and hard working. (Wright, 1992: 57)

She also found that Asian children were the group most likely to experience frequent racial harassment from White peers and to experience the most overt racism in the school (Wright, 1992: 58, 78). This was exacerbated by a 'child culture' within the school in which White children marked themselves off from certain ethnic groups and constructed a status hierarchy from which Asian children were excluded and the fact that the schools had an ambivalent response to this state of affairs.

An earlier study (1986; 1987) of two multiracial comprehensives, which considered fourth- and fifth-year Afro-Caribbean pupils, showed how antagonistic relationships between teachers and Afro-Caribbean pupils influenced teachers' professional judgements of Afro-Caribbean pupils' ability and how this seemed to have led to such students being placed in low sets in school, thus restricting such pupils' educational opportunities.

> Evidence suggests that in their assessment of Afro-Caribbean students the teachers allowed themselves to be influenced more by behavioural criteria than cognitive ones. . . . This in turn led to a situation where Afro-Caribbean students, more so than any other student groups, were likely to be placed in ability bands and examination sets well below their actual academic ability. (Wright, 1987: 123)

Wright found that Afro-Caribbean pupils had the highest average reading scores of all pupil groups, yet they completed school with fewer qualifications.

Mac an Ghaill: *Young, Gifted and Black: Student Teacher Relations in the Schooling of Black Youth* (1988)

Mac an Ghaill presented four case studies, based on ethnographic research, that looked at the experiences of Afro-Caribbean and Asian pupils in a sixth form college and an inner city comprehensive school as well as teachers' and pupils' views of each other and the survival strategies that each adopted. Mac an Ghaill's analysis focused on the creation of student subcultures, and thus student resistances, within these settings and demonstrated how it was the students' experiences of racism that led to the development of these (usually anti-school) subcultures and resistances. Mac an Ghaill saw teachers as of central significance in the difficulties that the students' encountered. Mac an Ghaill's study was of particular significance because he considered class, race and gender together and included a focus on student resistance. His study showed that there were gender differences in pupil resistance: while African Caribbean boys tended to resist institutional incorporation and created male, anti-school subcultures, girls developed 'strategies of institutional survival' which Mac an Ghaill termed 'resistance with accommodation' (Youdell, 2003: 4). He was insistent that racism was an issue to be considered in education.

Mirza: *Young, Female and Black* (1992)

Mirza's study of Black girls in two comprehensive schools in South London also considered the interactions between teachers and pupils and whether pupils performed as well or as badly as their teachers expected. She rejected the explanation that teachers' low expectations of the Black girls in their classrooms (which existed) affected achievement. To the contrary, the teachers appeared to be unsuccessful in eroding Black female self-esteem or passing on their negative expectations (Mirza, 1992: 54). Mirza, left with the question 'How exactly does teacher-pupil interaction function to disadvantage the black child?', suggested that 'the process of discrimination operated by means of the teachers' access to physical and material resources, restrictions to which would result in the curtailment of opportunities' and that ' . . . teachers (were) in a position to enforce their prejudices by restricting access to information and educational resources' (Mirza, 1992: 56). Mirza also suggested that the girls' recognition of the negative assessments that their teachers held of them meant that the girls did not ask teachers for help and support as a means of challenging such assessments, (Mirza, 1992: 83)

Gillborn: *Race, Ethnicity and Education: Teaching and Learning in Multi-Ethnic Schools* (1990)

Another study which looked at relationships between teachers and pupils and pupils and pupils was Gillborn's detailed account of life in a large inner city comprehensive over a period of 2 years (Gillborn, 1990). His interviews and classroom observations revealed, like Wright and Green's work, a complex situation where Afro-Caribbean and Asian pupils experienced school in different ways. While ethnicity influenced choice of friends and teacher expectations, teacher stereotypes of Asian culture (a perception of Asian pupils as hardworking, well-disciplined and from stable home backgrounds which valued education) did not operate against Asian pupils in the way that teachers' stereotypes of Afro-Caribbean pupils worked against them. Asian pupils, Gillborn claimed, had a similar relationship with teachers as White pupils whereas Afro-Caribbean pupils experienced negative teacher expectations which transcended judgements about ability. Like Wright, Gillborn concluded that teacher judgements were the 'prime obstacle' to academic success for Afro-Caribbean pupils (Gillborn, 1990: 100).

Troyna: 'Underachievers or underrated? The experiences of pupils of South Asian origin in secondary schools' (1991b)

This was not a qualitative study but what the figures showed seem relevant to the qualitative studies being discussed.

While both Gillborn and Wright found that Afro-Caribbean pupils were assigned to low ability sets, despite their ability, through 'teacher judgements', Troyna found that Asian pupils in his research school were less likely to be placed in high sets for English even though they were assessed as 'good' by their junior school teachers (Troyna, 1991b). While 91 per cent of White pupils who were assessed as 'good' by their junior school teachers were placed in a high English set, only 82 per cent of Asian pupils were and while 67 per cent of White pupils who were assessed as 'weak' managed to gain a place in a middle English set only 20 per cent of Asian pupils managed this. A similar picture emerged for Maths and Social Science. He also found that children were not moved up into higher sets even if they did well in their exams at the end of their third year (now Year 9 when pupils are aged between 13 and 14). Thus the allocation of pupils to sets on entry to school at age 11 had implications for their access to end of compulsory schooling, GCSE exam entry (and level of entry) as well as the resources available to them during their secondary school years. Troyna concluded that 'the ethnicity of the pupils played a mediating part in structuring their opportunities for placement in the higher ability sets' (Troyna, 1991b: 371) and that referring to Asian pupils as 'underachievers' was less appropriate and precise than referring to them as underrated. (The article in which Troyna reported these findings was heavily critiqued regarding the validity of the claims made, as were many of the studies, and their conclusions, discussed above. These critiques are discussed in depth in Chapter 4).

Reflection activity

Looking back at the pieces of research discussed above (by Green, Wright, Mac an Ghaill, Mirza, Gillborn and Troyna), what kinds of explanations are emerging regarding the differing experiences and performances of minority ethnic pupil groups?

What is your reaction to these emerging explanations?

The above studies had begun to make a case for considering 'racism' and, to use Troyna's phrase, 'who goes where and gets what' (the amount and type of teacher attention, teacher stereotypes, racism and placement in bottom sets etc.) as being key in considering and explaining the educational performance of different ethnic minority groups.

However, Foster's case study of Milltown High, an inner city, multi-ethnic comprehensive school, in 1990, came to different conclusions (Foster, 1990a).

Foster: *Policy and Practice in Multicultural and Anti-Racist Education* (1990a)

Foster's study was specifically concerned with how current anti-racist policies affected classroom practices and how schools should provide for ethnic minority pupils. However, he also looked at racism, school differentiation and equal opportunities in the school. His particular account of pupil achievement restricted itself to Afro-Caribbean pupils. He found that Afro-Caribbean pupils did as well as their White peers in the school and suggested that Afro-Caribbean underachievement was a result of the fact that Afro-Caribbean pupils attended schools that were 'low achieving schools' in which all pupils did badly; that is Afro-Caribbean pupils were caught in a 'loop of disadvantage' and teacher racism was not a cause of their underachievement. In fact Foster claimed not to be able to find many examples of racist attitudes among the teachers in his study. He also claimed that he could not find any empirical support for the ideas and explanations that had been advanced by other researchers, and those involved in anti-racism work, namely that teachers had negative views and low expectations of Afro-Caribbean pupils, that the curriculum neglected and denigrated Afro-Caribbeans (leading to low self-esteem, poor motivation and hostility to teachers) or that teachers lacked the cultural competence to deal confidently and adequately with minority students. He did find that there might be some support for the explanation that evaluations and assessments were culturally biased but this was not something the teachers in the school could be held responsible for. He did find that older Afro-Caribbean pupils were 'more likely to be allocated to lower status groups in the school's system of differentiation' (Foster, 1990a: 81) but that this was because of their poor behaviour, not teacher racism. He argued that Afro-Caribbean pupils 'tended to be regarded less favourably' by teachers as they did not conform closely to their teachers' conceptions of the 'ideal' pupil.

Pilkington, in reviewing the heated debate that ensued concerning whether 'racism' was an issue within schools, pointed out that the key difference between Foster's findings and those reviewed above was that Foster saw teachers as responding appropriately to the behaviour of Afro-Caribbean pupils and playing no real part in generating their behaviour, whereas other researchers had seen teachers as implicated in causing the behaviour that excluded Afro-Caribbean pupils from top exam sets and upper streams in schools (Pilkington, 1999: 413).

> Where Foster and his critics fundamentally disagree is over their explanation of 'bad behaviour'. For Foster, primacy is given to extra school factors. 'There may be a general tendency for Afro-Caribbean students on average to be less well behaved in schools' (Foster, 1991: 168) because of their adoption of a distinctive subculture consequent on a recognition on their part of poor post-school prospects and rejection of racisms in the wider society. For the others, primacy is given to school processes, with some Afro-Caribbean pupils pictured as turning towards a distinctive subculture in order to resist their differential treatment in schools. (Pilkington, 1999: 414)

Two researchers, Paul Connolly (1998) and Tony Sewell (1997) did produce qualitative studies that considered school processes and distinctive subcultures operating both within and outside school:

Connolly: *Racism, Gender Identities and Young Children* (1998)

Connolly responded to Foster's explanation that Afro-Caribbean boys behaved badly, and so got placed in lower sets, by claiming that it was necessary to consider where this behaviour came from. His year-long ethnographic study of an inner city, multi-ethnic primary school looked at exactly this (Connolly, 1998).

Connolly looked at the very complex and subtle ways that children drew on discourses of 'race' in the development of their gender identities, even at the age of five and six and how they reworked their knowledge of 'race', gender and sexuality to make sense of their experiences. He was at pains to explore the ways in which knowledges, perceptions and expectations from both inside and outside schools created particular teacher–child, peer-group relations and identities in the classroom. To this end he explored the ways in which broader discourses on 'race' and the inner city had come to influence the nature of the relationships between the people living on the estate that surrounded the school, how these discourses came to be taken up and reworked by teachers within the school and how these teacher discourses came to influence the ethos of the school, its organizations, social relationships and disciplinary modes (Connolly, 1998: 63–4). He then went on to show how Afro-Caribbean and South Asian boys and girls in the school developed identities through the contexts provided for them by these discourses.

In relation to Afro-Caribbean boys he found that student–teacher relations and peer group relations in the school formed what he termed 'a continuous feed-back loop'. That is, Afro-Caribbean boys were over-represented among those who were publicly disciplined by teachers and they thus developed 'a bad reputation'. This was often perceived by White boys as 'bad' and 'quintessentially masculine'; a reputation that the White boys perceived as a threat to their own masculinity. As a result of this, Connolly claimed, White boys were more likely to publicly challenge Afro-Caribbean boys in order to reassert their own masculinity and this led to a situation in which Afro-Caribbean boys were more likely to be involved in confrontations which reinforced teachers' views that they were troublesome and badly behaved (Connolly, 1998: 89).

In relation to South Asian boys, Connolly found that teacher discourses in the school (praising South Asian boys for hard work, for being quiet, describing them as 'little' and needing to be looked after) positioned them as 'effeminate' and a representation of what boys 'are not'. They became 'the focus through which other boys were able to develop and reassert their own masculine status' (Connolly, 1998: 126). As a result South Asian boys tended to be excluded from social activities in school and to suffer verbal and physical assaults.

South Asian girls in the school were represented by teacher discourses as 'quintessentially feminine' and were seen by teachers as 'model pupils' (Connolly, 1998: 186–7). This had the effect of making South Asian girls invisible to teachers. However, South Asian girls were not invisible to other pupils in the school and as with South Asian boys, the girls were used by other pupils as a means of asserting their own gender identities by treating South Asian girls as a 'sexual Other' (Connolly, 1998: 167).

Sewell: *Black Masculinities and Schooling: How Black Boys Survive Modern Schooling* (1997)

Sewell, like Connolly, also looked at why African-Caribbean boys might behave the way they did in schools (Sewell, 1997). He revealed through his study how the African-Caribbean boys, in the inner city boys' comprehensive school at the centre of his study, were trying to position themselves as pupils in a context that was 'hostile to their gender and race' (Sewell, 1997: 13). In his study school, African-Caribbean boys were over-represented in exclusions from school but had a very good attendance record. Teachers (both Black and White) in the school held middle-class values and ideas about ideal pupils and education and the African-Caribbean boys had great difficulty in positioning themselves in relation to these ideals and values. At the same time, teachers tended to see African-Caribbean boys as a challenge and called on notions, or discourses, of African-Caribbean subculture and challenge (Gillborn, 1990, cited in Sewell, 1997: 63) in order to 'explain' and 'understand' their African-Caribbean pupils and in order to understand any clashes that occurred between teachers and pupils (Sewell, 1997: 63). As Sewell writes, the racism here was not an external set of beliefs called on by teachers but a set of discourses that came to structure the way they thought about the world, their pupils and themselves (Sewell, 1997: 67). All of the African-Caribbean boys in the school, in order to 'make it' (and a number of the boys in the school did value education highly), had to ignore their peer group, ethnicity and anti-school subculture and any sense of solidarity and identification with Black culture. Even when boys did attempt to do this they were often not successful. Sewell became interested in examining how Afro-Caribbean boys coped in a context that was so hostile to their gender and race and examined the different 'response routes' they chose in order to survive in school. He categorized these routes and identities as 'conformists', 'innovators', 'retreatists' and 'rebels'. What was of interest was that he found that the teachers' stereotypes of African-Caribbean pupils (based on a notion of 'challenge') and their 'fears' about the size and supposed physicality of African-Caribbean boys, adopted 'as they attempted to survive the everyday 'stresses' of school life' (Sewell, 1997: 66), were used by the boys themselves as a way of expressing their resistance to the context of schooling and as a way of creating their own identity and reputation within their peer group (Sewell, 1997: 46). In this way, Sewell claims, there were no 'innocent African-Caribbean pupils' versus 'evil racist teachers' operating in the school (Sewell, 1997: 66). However, the boys who adopted a strong rebel position left themselves with no opportunity for learning or for creating for themselves a positive identity (Sewell, 1997: 127) while the teachers at no point saw their part in the production of these rebel identities and behaviours (Sewell, 1997: 127). In the response of these 'rebel' boys, there was a calling on discourses of misogyny, homophobia and hyper-heterosexuality that, while offensive, had to be seen in the context of 'a schooling system that seeks to make African-Caribbean boys intellectually powerless and/or bodily powerful' (Sewell, 1997: 172). These discourses, of course, positioned boys who did achieve some success in school as effeminate and as 'not acting as a Black hyper-heterosexual male' (Sewell, 1997: 111) and therefore subject to the surveillance and judgement of other African-Caribbean boys. Sewell's analysis of his data thus showed how African-Caribbean boys were forced in this school to play to one of two extremes: either a denial of race/sexual identity or an exaggerated phallocentrism (Sewell, 1997: xiv). Thus Sewell challenged the notion that it was simple 'teacher racism' that affected African-Caribbean boys and their performance in school or teachers low expectations of this pupil group (he found no evidence that the teachers thought that the African-Caribbean boys were less able that other boys in the school). What he claimed was that both teacher and pupils were influenced by wider discourse regarding Black males that existed outside the school in the wider society and that these discourses were called on by both teachers and pupils in their efforts to survive their daily experiences of schooling.

In addition, in response to Fosters's work, Sewell argued that there were three occasions in Fosters's depiction of daily life in his research school when racist practices were revealed but these remained unrecognized by Foster (Sewell, 1997: 12).

Other qualitative studies conducted in the 1980s and 1990s that are of interest include:

Haw: *Educating Muslim Girls: Shifting Discourses* (1998)

In this study, Haw adopted a feminist and post-structuralist approach in order to consider how Muslim girls in school are positioned (rather than 'disadvantaged') (Haw, 1998: 29). The study explored the interactions between Muslim and non-Muslim teachers and female Muslim students and whether Muslim girls were more comfortable and empowered studying in a Muslim school rather than in a mainstream school. Haw concluded that the Muslim girls attending the Islamic school were more positive regarding their academic and personal futures and that there were stronger links between parents and the Islamic school.

Bhatti: *Asian Children at Home and at School: An Ethnographic Study* (1999)

This was an interview-led study that examined Asian pupils' experiences of their urban secondary school and set these alongside their teachers' and their parents' views and experiences. Bhatti concluded that race/ethnicity, social class and gender operated together to produce an experience of marginality for the Asian pupils she studied.

Reflection activity

What do the studies by Foster, Connolly, Sewell, Haw and Bhatti add to the notes you made before? What do they add to the explanations that you have already noted regarding the experiences and performances of different minority ethnic pupil groups?

What is your reaction to these explanations?

Are there things that remain unexplained or unexplored?

Findings, explanations and limitations

These qualitative studies then did change the focus of research about ethnic minority achievement from looking at test results and comparing the different attainment rates of different groups to looking at what went on within schools. They did manage to 'dive beneath the surface' of exam results and consider some of the subtle and complex processes to do with 'race', ethnicity and gender that went on within classrooms and schools that affected the educational opportunities of minority ethnic pupils. Some studies were also able to move beyond the dichotomy of 'within school' or 'outside school' explanations to show how both were linked and fed into each other.

Interestingly, what emerges from these studies (with the exception of Troyna's) is an emphasis on behaviour. These descriptions of classroom practices indicate that an important process within schools is the manner in which pupils gain an identity as a pupil and learner through teachers' experiences and expectations of their behaviour, through the type of interactions taking place between teacher and pupil, and how these have consequences for pupils' access to resources and opportunities in school and to placements in exam classes or exam sets.

However, the focus of these studies is generally on the Afro-Caribbean pupil (most frequently on Afro-Caribbean boys) and, except for Troyna and to some extent Wright, none of these studies makes a link between how ethnic minority pupils are perceived, the identities that become theirs and their academic achievement (although Sewell addresses links with exclusion). The explanations put forward concerning poor behaviour leading to placement in low sets (and a restriction on the number and type of exams that can be taken) and thus poor achievement in school can hardly apply in a straightforward way to other, at the time, poorly achieving 'Asian' groups of pupils, for example to Bangladeshi pupils, as in all of these studies, where they are included, Asian pupils are perceived as 'hard working and well behaved' by their teachers. Although able to contribute to the debate about Afro-Caribbean boys' underachievement by describing where

Afro-Caribbean boys' behaviour came from, Connolly's insights about the positioning of South Asian boys and girls in school did not develop into insights into why some South Asian groups of pupils (i.e. Pakistani and Bangladeshi pupils) were underachieving in school at this time. Sewell's account of the ways in which discourse from outside school come to be played out within school and were central to the construction of particular identity positions by both teachers and pupils was only articulated in relation to African-Caribbean boys.

What this research does appear to offer is confirmation that both Afro-Caribbean and Asian children have struggles in school and (with the exception of Foster) that racism of some kind is implicated in this. Green, Wright, Gillborn, Connolly and Sewell all found that teachers had negative expectations or ideas about African-Caribbean pupils, particularly boys, and showed how these worked against this pupil group. Green and Mirza drew attention to how African-Caribbean pupils could receive less individual attention or less access to resources and opportunities in school while Wright, Connolly and Sewell showed how African-Caribbean pupils, particularly boys, could be more frequently chastised and their behaviour negatively sanctioned in school (including the more frequent use of exclusion as a punishment for this pupil group). Wright and Foster both found that African-Caribbean pupils were placed in lower sets than measurements of their ability would warrant. Wright's work suggested that Asian pupils experienced more racism than other children, that they were excluded by 'child culture' and that they were perceived to be a problem to their teachers because of limited cognitive skills, poor English and poor social skills. Troyna's work suggested that Asian children (Pakistani and Bangladeshi pupils in his study) were placed in lower sets than White pupils despite their equal ability. (However, there are serious problems with this publication: his claim that it was the **ethnicity** of the pupils that played 'a mediating part in the structuring of their opportunities for placement in higher ability sets' (Troyna, 1991b: 371) was not adequately supported. See Chapter 4 for a fuller discussion of this).

A criticism that can be made of these studies is that they are focused on pupils and schools in metropolitan, usually inner city, urban areas. It is worth considering what a qualitative study of more isolated learners in a mainly White area, that does consider school achievement and EAL alongside school experiences, might reveal. This was at the core of a research study that considered the learning experiences of Bangladeshi-heritage primary pupils (Walters, 2003). This study sought to (a) explore an aspect of 'Asian' underachievement by considering Bangladeshi-heritage pupils, (b) demonstrate how ethnicity played a mediating part in the structuring of educational opportunities, and (c) explore teacher expectations, assessments and choices and their impact through an unpacking of school processes (which included teacher and pupil accounts of their experiences and actions as well as being based on a year's worth of classroom observation). The findings and issues raised are briefly discussed here.

Non-metropolitan minority ethnic pupils

Walters: 'Bangladeshi Pupils: Experiences, Identity and Achievement' (2003)

The study was focused on the question 'What is it that helps and hinders Bangladeshi pupils as successful learners in the mainstream classroom?' At the time of the research Bangladeshi pupils were, according the statistical analyses we looked at in Chapter 3, underachieving in English schools. The study attempted to answer this question through a portrayal and analysis of six British Bangladeshi pupils' experiences of one year of primary school. The children were all 7-years-old, rising to age 8, during the research year and were in three Year 3 classrooms in a 'mainly White' city in the east of England.

Through six case studies the study demonstrated the complex and subtle processes that positioned these pupils as achieving or underachieving learners, offering them particular identities and resources while denying them others. In doing so, the study confirmed some of the findings of the research we have just considered above but also raised some further issues.

One of the striking things to emerge out of the case study data was that the way in which the case study children took part in classroom life brought them either identities and resources that helped them achieve and learn or identities and a lack of resources that hindered their 'learning'. Their teachers made important assessments of the case study children based on the ways in which the children took part in classroom life and these assessments affected the children's access to resources such as support. When the case study children did not take part in classroom life in the way that was expected, i.e. when they did not present themselves in their teachers' eyes as 'ideal pupils' and could not complete work, when they presented incorrect work or were thought to be not paying attention then their teachers called on explanations and understandings that were based on the children's supposed personality, their ethnicity and their (supposedly deficit) home life (see Walters, 2007). These understandings of the children's home life and ethnicity were often based on stereotypes and misunderstandings. In fact, the research revealed that the children were not able to complete work, or complete work correctly, or 'pay attention' to teacher talk due to struggles they had as EAL pupils; they all had English language learning needs and these were not recognized by their teachers. In this way, the children's learning needs as EAL pupils were not seen by their teachers but what was 'seen' and called on to provide an explanation for their poor performance in the classroom was their personality, ethnicity and a deficit version of home life. One of the case study boy's struggles with reading and writing in English, arising out of his lack of familiarity with English vocabulary, syntax and expectations around what it was to be a good reader in an English primary school classroom, was interpreted as a wilful resistance to the young, female classroom teacher because of his identity as a Muslim boy. As a result this pupil did not receive any support for his EAL or learning needs.

Indicatively, the only support he was offered was a place in a nurture group to help him 'fit in' and mix more with other pupils. When this boy did not complete work, or produced poor work, his teachers did not see that the work was often poor or not completed because of the pupil's language needs. They understood his work to be poor, or not completed, because he was lazy, defiant or lacking in respect for his female teacher. Another of the case study pupils was offered EAL support during the year not because she was identified as having any EAL learning needs but because the class teacher and EAL teacher both judged her to be, as a Muslim girl, too shy, quiet and lacking in confidence, and likely to have a problem with having a man as a teacher, to be able to cope well in class.

It could be seen that the decisions and assumptions made by teachers led to a situation in which the case study children were offered support for their behaviour rather than for their learning or EAL needs as pupils in school. The data revealed how teachers focused through the support provided, not on language development, but on encouraging the children to display appropriate behaviour and fit in with other members of the class (by becoming, for example, more confident, or being able to follow instructions properly).

Thus a key way in which 'race'/ethnicity came to be influential in reproducing educational inequality was in the way that the teachers relied on assumptions about the home life of the children, their Muslim faith and Islamic identity. These assumptions were often wrong (e.g. that the children were forced to fast during Ramadan, that girls' education was not valued by parents) and fed into teachers' explanations for the children's struggles or poor work in school. Many of these assumptions were about gender with the result that ethnicity and gender became intertwined in the teachers' assumptions about the children. The two case studies mentioned above showed how expectations and assumptions about male and female South Asian Muslim pupils' behaviours, and responses to these, can be important determinants of the support that children receive and how children come to be identified. It argues against the assertion that teacher stereotypes of South Asian culture do not operate against Asian pupils in school in the way that teacher stereotypes of African Caribbean pupils do (e.g. Gillborn, 1990).

Another of the key ways in which ethnicity and 'race' came to be influential in reproducing educational inequality was in the way which, whenever the teachers (in all three schools) spoke about the case study children, and their progress, ability or success as learners, the teachers **always** compared the Bangladeshi pupil with the other Bangladeshi pupil in the class, with another minority ethnic pupil in the class or with an older sibling (who had been in the class before). None of the case study children were ever compared with the White English children in the classroom. In this way the case study children are very much located within an ethnic identity and 'Othered' from the White children in the three classrooms. The Bangladeshi pupils' academic performance was not considered alongside that of the White pupils, as if the teachers were operating with two different scales in their heads, one for White pupils and one for Bangladeshi pupils. This indicated that the teachers always saw their Bangladeshi learners as different to and separate from the other learners in the same class and that, in their thinking about their learning and achievement, their Bangladeshi pupils were not to be considered in the same cohort of learners moving through the National Curriculum. Considering the evidence that was presented in Chapter 2, concerning the underachievement of Bangladeshi pupils, this way of thinking seems implicit in low expectations of Bangladeshi pupils.

'Race'/ethnicity also came to play a part in the way that the children's languages were not valued in school. In this way an aspect of the children's identity was placed in a subordinate, lesser role unlike the speakers of French or Italian. The children's other languages, and their bilingualism, were seen as a problem rather than an 'achievement'.

Other researchers (as discussed above) have argued that 'race' impacts on minority ethnic pupils' achievement through teachers' lower expectations, through teachers placing minority ethnic pupils in lower sets and not entering them for exams and through minority ethnic pupils being more controlled, chastised and excluded from school than majority ethnic pupils. The data in this study showed how teachers may come to have lower expectations of pupils through how they interpret the children's interactions with them in the classroom ('she's lazy', 'he doesn't listen', 'he pretends not to understand'). This, of course, is true of all children; however, the Bangladeshi pupils were more vulnerable because their teachers did not recognize that the reasons for such behaviour were often connected to the child's unmet language needs.

EAL, or more specifically minority ethnic pupils' lack of English, is often put forward as an explanation for poor achievement (see for example Chapter 2). However, the high achievement of Chinese and Indian pupils shows that having to learn English while learning the curriculum in English is not a satisfactory, single explanation. EAL, as we have seen in this study, can be linked in complex ways with 'race'/ethnicity, identity and resource provision. Studies, including this one, reveal how other factors are at play (e.g. racism and socio-economic status) in hindering achievement in addition to pupils' lack of English fluency, and lack of support for language development, as well as how teachers' positive view of certain EAL pupils (i.e. Chinese pupils. See Archer and Francis, 2007 below) would appear to be part of the reason why their EAL status does not impede their achievement.

The data, as noted above, also suggest that teachers were in danger of having lower expectations because they only compared Bangladeshi pupils with each other in terms of achievement and not with other children and this study also showed how children could be placed in lower sets so that they could receive support and then find themselves stuck there even though they were working at a more advanced level than the other children in the set.

In terms of minority ethnic pupils being chastised more than White pupils, this study was able to show something of how some of the case study children came to be chastised. The argument put forward is that these children were chastised because their teachers misunderstood their English language ability and thought that the children were being naughty or lazy when in fact the children were trying to take part or were not able to understand. However, the data also suggest that the case study children may have also been enacting some 'resistance' to teacher structures through the way they behaved. (For instance, through holding themselves apart in the classroom or not asking for help. Mirza refers to this as a form of resistance in her study of Black female secondary school students, 1992). Further details can be found in Walters, 2003 and 2004 regarding what the study revealed in relation to Bangladeshi underachievement and how ethnicity played a mediating part in the structuring of educational opportunities for this pupil group and in Walters (2007) regarding the impact of teacher expectations, assessments and choices.

More recent studies

Qualitative research work has continued to inform understandings of ethnicity, 'race' and education in the twenty-first century. Two key studies are discussed here.

Gillborn and Youdell: *Rationing Education: Policy, Practice, Reform and Equity* (2000)

Gillborn and Youdell's study of two secondary schools in London explored the impact of recent policy reforms. They found that the schools studied adopted a range of approaches or strategies in response to these policy reforms, namely:

- setting, selection and pupil grouping according to a fixed and limiting notion of 'ability' (what Gillborn and Youdell termed the 'new IQism');
- the imposition of 'tiering', whereby teachers had to make decisions about whether pupils should be entered for GCSE papers limited to the top end of GCSE grades or the lower range of grades;
- a focus on what Gillborn and Youdell call the 'A–C economy' in schools whereby a school focuses all of its resources and efforts on raising the number of A–C grades their pupils can achieve. Gillborn and Youdell found that this resulted in a 'rationing' of educational resources that privileged those who were considered to be capable of gaining a C grade or higher.

Gillborn and Youdell argued that their data showed that these approaches and strategies exacerbated and extended educational inequalities rather than reduced them, especially for Black pupils and working-class pupils. Their study is an important contribution to explorations of 'sorting' processes that occur in secondary schools. (However, their emphasis on recent 'New Labour' policy as the 'cause' of schools adopting these approaches and strategies is a little overstated. The setting, selection and grouping of pupils, and the use of a fixed, essentialized, notion of ability certainly existed in secondary schools, and even in primary schools, in the 1960s, 1970s and 1980s and tiering existed pre-GCSEs when teachers had to make early decisions about whether pupils should be entered for General Certificate of Education 'O' Levels or Certificate of Secondary Education exams).

Youdell: *Impossible Bodies, Impossible Selves: Exclusions and Student Subjectivities* (2006)

Youdell's work exemplifies a move towards utilizing a post-structuralist framework (calling on the work of Michel Foucault, Pierre Bourdieu and Marilyn Butler) in order to reveal how certain pupils become excluded from educational success and others included. Her analysis focuses on the discourses that pupils and teachers call on (and which are constituted at the same time) in their everyday lives and practices in school and how these, while not fixed and immutable, create pupils as either acceptable or unacceptable (impossible) learners, thereby creating or limiting opportunities for educational success. Her work 'demonstrates that 'who' a student is – in terms of gender, sexuality, social class, ability, disability, race, ethnicity and religion, as well as popular and subcultural belongings – is inextricably linked with the 'sort' of student and learner that s/he gets to be, and the educational inclusions s/he enjoys and/ or the exclusions s/he faces' (Youdell, 2006: 2). Youdell's data exemplify the subtle ways in which these processes play out in ordinary classroom interactions and the resulting ways in which pupils are understood and positioned as acceptable or unacceptable learners ('bad' students and impossible learners) in school. One of her findings was that in many cases the higher a pupil's status was within the student subculture the lower it was within the official school organization, often precluding the pupil from being seen as an acceptable learner. The strength of Youdell's study is not simply in the findings but in her development of a theoretical approach and methodology that allows us to see these processes in action. In an earlier account Youdell explicates how a counter discourse circulates within the student subculture in the research school that ranks Black above Mixed-Race, above Indian, above Pakistani as desirable ethnic identities, yet, as noted above, the success of Black students in this student subculture was inverted within the school's official culture (see Youdell, 2006: 21). She clearly makes the case for understanding the discursive practices of teachers and students as constitutive of the 'selves' that can be recognized and understood in school, how certain 'selves' can become identified as undesirable learners and how pupil subcultural identities as well as their gender, sexuality, race and ethnicity are taken up and deployed in teacher and school discourses as evidence of 'undesirable learner identities' (Youdell, 2003: 3).

Wright, Weekes and McGlaughlin: *'Race', Class and Gender in Exclusion from School* (2000)

Utilizing data from interviews with pupils and staff in five secondary schools as well as with excluded pupils and their parents, this study argued that the over-exclusion of African Caribbean pupils, particularly boys, had to be understood in relation to changing education policy, particularly the marketization of education since the Education Reform Act of 1988. Such policy meant that schools were more likely to use exclusion as a way of dealing with pupils that became seen as 'troublesome' or 'undesirable'. The study took account of ethnicity, class and gender and considered the processes that led up to school exclusion as well as the after-effects. The concept of student resistance was addressed by the researchers who noted the way that this had become racialized.

Shain: *The Schooling and Identity of Asian Girls* (2003)

The main focus of Shain's study was on the strategies utilized by a group of Asian girls in order to deal with their experiences of education and society. She argued that the experiences of the girls were shaped by a multiplicity of factors, including race, ethnicity, class, gender, religion and region. She found that the girls were actively engaged in making choices that were influenced by these factors and most of all by discourses that surrounded descriptions of Asian girls. The girls used conscious strategies of resistance, survival, rebellion or religious prioritization in order to respond to these discourses and deal with their everyday experiences of school.

Archer: *Race, Masculinity and Schooling* (2003)

This study explored secondary school Muslim boys' views and understandings of their schooling experiences and how they conceptualized their identities at school and at home. Archer argued that 'race', religion, class and gender all structured the boys' sense of who they were and their experiences both in and outside school. Her account demonstrated the manner in which the boys' masculinity was relational, shifting, contested and changing and how they did not 'inhabit' simple, clearly bounded 'Muslim' identities but how they performed or challenged a range of identities. In their accounts they shifted between identities as Black, Asian, English, Bangladeshi/Pakistani and British. There was also a reliance on their accounts of Muslim girls as passive, located in the domestic sphere and in need of protection for the enactment of their own identity as non-passive Asian young men. Archer suggests that this was in relation to school and teacher discourses and practices that position young Asian men as effeminate and weak. Racism emerged as a major topic of concern in the boys' accounts of school life. A wide variety of experiences of racism in school were described including physical bullying. The boys did not describe overt racist behaviour from their teachers, but identified tacit subtle forms of teacher racism as well as institutional racism in their schools. This institutional racism took the form of the schools' unwillingness to tackle incidents of racism and the unfair punishment of Asian boys when they physically fought back when racially taunted by their White peers.

Archer and Francis: *Understanding Minority Ethnic Achievement* (2007)

This study, through focusing on British-Chinese pupils in mainstream school settings, considered 'high achievers' in the education system in order to understand how this achievement was accomplished and what it might reveal about underachievement. Interviews with parents, pupils and teachers explored views of education, aspirations and how British-Chinese pupils were understood by their teachers. Archer and Francis found that although teachers held very positive views of this pupil group (as hard working, conscientious, high achieving), they also problematized this by perceiving them as not quite learning in the right way and seeing them as rather passive and repressed by their parents and culture, particularly the girls. While the teachers held stereotypical views of their British-Chinese pupils that could be seen to be positive, these also acted in narrow homogenizing ways. Pupils were seen as the same as each other, as 'naturally clever' (thus misrepresenting and making invisible the work and effort that pupils put into their studies) and, because of their supposed 'quiet', 'shy' demeanour, vulnerable to being seen by their peers as 'weak, effeminate, powerless and victims' (Archer and Francis, 2007: 154). One clear finding was that British-Chinese pupils did experience racism at school (Archer and Francis, 2007: 147) either through these teacher stereotypes and their effects or through comments about their physiognomy, or accent or ability to speak English and therefore their 'right to belong to some notion of Britishness' (Archer and Francis, 2007: 149). In the study Francis and Archer explore how gender meshes with ethnicity in the construction of learner identities, as well as argue that dominant discourses in education about 'ideal learners' position all Black and minority ethnic pupils as 'other' (Archer and Francis, 2007: 66–7). In exploring how Chinese parents and their children achieve 'achievement' and educational success, Archer and Francis show how parents use their own 'valuing of education' and drew on the teachers' discourses of the 'successful Chinese pupil' that was somehow connected to their 'race/ethnicity' by teachers, to fashion a positive construction of Chineseness (Archer and Francis, 2007: 86) that was different to 'White' attitudes to education. In this way they called on a positive stereotype to compensate for a lack of cultural capital. Thus, the discourses of 'Chinese valuing of education' and 'the good Chinese pupil' were drawn on by teachers, parents and pupils in order to 'position British-Chinese pupils as outstandingly diligent and high achieving' (Archer and Francis, 2007: 113). In this manner Archer and Francis's study and findings reflects that of Sewell, and Shain, in that they find that the discourses that surround a particular ethnic group can be and are called on by teachers and pupils and have profound effects on classroom practices, behaviours, the resources provided and on achievement in school although here this has a different outcome than it does for the African-Caribbean boys in Sewell's study.

Minority ethnic parents

The importance of a good relationship between home and school, and the support of parents in their children's learning, has been a regular feature of much recent education policy and discussion (see www.standards.dcsf.gov.uk/parentalinvolvment/pwp). Parents are referred to in this literature as a child's first teachers and an important part of children's continuing learning as they move through school. By the late 1990s the need to involve parents in the education of their children was high on the political agenda (Whalley et al., 2001: 6). At the same time, since the reforms of the Education Reform Act (1988), parents have been positioned as consumers of education and offered the opportunity of 'school choice' for their children (Vincent, 2000: 3). For this reason, some researchers have considered the role and experiences of minority ethnic parents in their children's learning at school and in relation to this 'school choice' agenda.

Bhatti: *Asian Children at Home and at School: An Ethnographic Study* (1999) and Archer and Francis: *Understanding Minority Ethnic Achievement* (2007)

As noted above, both Bhatti (2000) and Archer and Francis (2007) included a focus on the parents of minority ethnic pupils in mainstream schools in their studies of South Asian (Bhatti) and British-Chinese (Archer and Francis) pupils. Both studies examined the relationship between parents and teachers and found that in both cases parents did not have a close relationship with their children's school. While Archer and Francis were able to demonstrate the ways in which Chinese parents, despite their discomfort, were able to make use of their children's teachers' 'positive' stereotypes of 'the good Chinese pupil' and 'the Chinese valuing of education' as a way of perpetuating a particular image of their children and overcoming their lack of cultural capital, this was not a strategy that the South Asian parents were able to utilize in Bhatti's study. In addition to the lack of positive stereotypes of this pupil group held by teachers, these parents experienced a lack of access to knowledge about the British educational system (Bhatti, 2000: 45) and mothers felt self conscious about their lack of English literacy (Bhatti, 2000: 47). The parents reported that they were concerned by the lack of meaningful communication between themselves and school and felt that the school did not tell them about their child's needs and difficulties and did not involve them in their children's education (Bhatti, 2000: 84). They reported feeling a sense of powerlessness and of being stared at in school which reinforced a feeling that they did not belong there (Bhatti, 2000: 90).

Blackledge: *Literacy, Power and Social Justice* (2000)

Blackledge, in his study of Bangladeshi mothers and their relationship with their children's schools, also found that parents reported experiencing difficulties in communicating with their children's teachers despite their wish to find out more about how to help their children develop their English literacy and about their progress in school. He also found that the same parents were very keen to support their children's education and literacy learning but were frustrated in this because the literacy and language of the school was exclusively English. His examination of teachers' accounts of working with parents revealed that teachers' assumptions about Bangladeshi women and homes positioned mothers as lacking the cultural resources required to contribute to their children's learning and therefore barred them from any meaningful partnership work with the school (Blackledge, 2000).

Crozier: *Parents, Children and the School Experience: Asian Families' Perspectives* (2004)

Crozier considered how Bangladeshi parents' traditions, cultures and values corresponded or conflicted with those of their children's schools. She explored the understandings that Pakistani and Bangladeshi-heritage parents had of the English education system and how they saw their role in their children's education. She found that most Bangladeshi parents and many of the Pakistani parents had little knowledge of the English education system and rarely raised concerns about their children or visited their children's schools due to cultural, language and practical constraints. This was particularly so in secondary schools (Crozier, 2004: 7). Pakistani parents did express concerns to the interviewers about teachers' low expectations of their children while all the parents expressed a valuing of education. Many of the Bangladeshi parents felt unable to support their children with their homework (Crozier, 2004: 1). The teachers interviewed believed that Bangladeshi parents were not interested in their children's education (Crozier, 2004: 2). One thing that surprised the researchers was the extent of the racism that the children experienced in their daily school life (Crozier, 2004: 11). They noted that children frequently protected their parents from potential embarrassment and insult by creating barriers to their parents' involvement in school life (Crozier, 2004: 7)

Haque: 'Exploring the Validity and Possible Causes of the Apparently Poor Performance of Bangladeshi Students in British Secondary Schools' (1999) and Centre for Bangladeshi Studies: *Routes and Beyond* (2001)

Haque's study of Bangladeshi pupils' achievement in school found that in their interviews Bangladeshi secondary school pupils reported that they got very little parental help at home with homework and that they relied on their older siblings instead as they knew and understood the British system (Haque, 1999: 101). The pupils claimed that they were expected to help at home with housework (girls) or with looking after their younger brothers and sisters (both boys and girls). Interestingly, a study conducted by the Centre for Bangladeshi Studies which looked at educationally successful young Bangladeshis found that parents had played an important part in the young people's educational success, not necessarily through helping with school work but through allowing their children to get on with their school work at home and not expecting them to help out with household chores (the girls) or take a part-time job to support the family financially (the boys) (Centre for Bangladeshi Studies, 2001: 12). The interviews with the young people also revealed that the support of school friends was also important: being part of a supportive group of friends with similar ambitions to do well in school made a great deal of difference to the young people and their work.

In terms of parents' knowledge about their children's experiences of school, Haque's study found that none of the parents thought that their children suffered from racism at school (Haque, 1999: 122). (Tomlinson and Hutchinson also found this when they interviewed Bangladeshi parents in Tower Hamlets, despite the fact that their children all reported having to deal with racism at school: Tomlinson and Hutchinson, 1991). One clear finding of the Centre for Bangladeshi Studies research was that all the young people interviewed had experienced racism, in the form of name calling and sometimes in the form of physical assault, during their school career (Centre for Bangladeshi Studies, 2001: 37).

Wright, Weekes and McGlaughlin: *'Race', Class and Gender in Exclusion from School* (2000)

Wright et al. (2000) explored the experiences of parents of African-Caribbean pupils who had been permanently excluded from school. Their discussion situates this parent group within the parental rights and 'choice' discourses of post-ERA legislation, pointing out that social divisions like 'race' and class impact on 'school choice' (Wright et al., 2000: 5) and that the concept of 'choice' can become problematic for many parents when their child is not seen as a 'desirable' pupil by a school. This can particularly affect working class and Black children. African-Caribbean boys, as we have noted above, can carry with them a 'reputation' (a teacher expectation) for being 'troublesome', particularly children at the risk of exclusion (Wright et al., 2000: 5–6). Wright et al. found that African-Caribbean parents were aware of these 'constructs of marketability' and how their children could be viewed as 'undesirable' (Wright et al., 2000: 98) and took the choosing of a good school for their children very seriously (Wright et al., 2000: 102). They also found that this parent group was often dissatisfied with the quality of education that their children received (Wright et al., 2000: 106) while maintaining a 'deep and consuming passion for credentials and education' (Wright et al., 2000: 109). Teachers' perceptions of Black parents were that they were either oversensitive or did not have much interest in their children's education. This affected the ways in which teachers related to parents as service users (Wright et al., 2000: 109).

Minority ethnic teachers

So far in this account there has been a tendency to present teachers and school staff as White, monolingual and ethnically different to their minority ethnic pupils. There is a lot of truth in this picture but there are Black and minority ethnic (BME) teachers and staff employed in mainstream schools. It is often the case that these members of staff often remain invisible in research on teachers' lives and professional identities (Osler, 1997: 1).

Osler: *The Education and Careers of Black Teachers: Changing Identities, Changing Lives* (1997)

Osler's study of a small group of BME teachers and senior managers looked at their professional experiences and what encouraged or excluded BME adults from a career in teaching. She was interested in what people's working lives were really like and the opportunities these members of staff felt they had to transform schools, challenge racism and improve pupils' life chances. She also considered the experience of BME students on teacher training courses. She found that the BME members of staff did express a concern for their BME pupils and the need to challenge White teachers' attitudes to this student group. However, she also found that her interviewees also struggled with their BME students' understandings of 'blackness', particularly Black masculinity. A common response of Black pupils to successful Black teachers and senior managers was to accuse them of 'acting white' (Osler, 1997: 111–12). She also found that BME staff felt isolated in schools, faced difficulties in gaining promotion and gained most support from networks with other BME colleagues.

Emerging themes

In the studies that we have considered above from 1980s onwards it is possible to trace some key themes:

There is a declared intention in all of the work of moving away from and challenging 'pathologized' accounts of minority ethnic pupils and families. That is, in all of the research studies that we have considered, ideas about some kind of deficit, related to 'race'/ethnicity, that is located within pupils and/or their families and home backgrounds, have been challenged or dismissed.

There has been a move within these studies away from 'mono-causal' or single case explanations (Mac an Ghaill, 1992: 42). That is, in these studies researchers have rejected the idea that minority ethnic pupils' experiences of school can be understood through looking at the issue of 'race'/ethnicity on its own as a factor in their experience. They have moved beyond this to include a consideration of gender and social class as acting alongside or intermeshed with 'race'/ethnicity in determining minority ethnic pupils', and their families', experiences of education. In some cases, researchers have also considered sexualities alongside 'race'/ethnicity, social class and gender. In the beginning, some researchers 'added' these different kinds of discrimination or oppressions on top of each other and would talk of Black girls as doubly oppressed (by racism and sexism) or of working-class, South Asian girls as triply oppressed (by racisms, sexism and class). However, the focus is now very much on how these factors are intermeshed and a recognition that they cannot be separated out from each other. We have been able to see examples of this in Sewell's and Archer and Francis's work where African-Caribbean boys and British-Chinese boys are constituted as both boys and

African-Caribbean or British-Chinese at the same time and in ways different to African-Caribbean or British-Chinese girls.

This move to a consideration of social class, gender and in some cases sexuality has necessitated a shift and development of theory and theoretical approaches as researchers have attempted to think through how these different variables can be considered together ('intermeshed'). Alongside this, some researchers have been looking for a way to move beyond explanations for social phenomena, in this case the experiences of minority ethnic pupils in school (and in some cases their achievement), that are limited to 'structure' or 'agency' explanations (i.e. it is either the way that pupils and teachers chose to behave in school (agency) or the way society is organized and the expectations that exist around schooling and education (structure) that result in differing experiences and achievement) and have as a result, adopted and developed theoretical approaches that utilize post-structuralism and the theories of Bourdieu among others. In this way they have been able to usefully consider discourses, power and resistance in the construction of particular (fluid and dynamic) learner identities. This has been an important development in research into minority ethnic pupils', teachers' and parents' school experiences. For a good explication of this theoretical work see Archer and Francis (2007, Chapter 2) and Youdell (2006, Chapter 2).

This shift has allowed researchers to begin to see and explore 'power' and the ways in which minority pupils (and sometimes their families) resist racism and sexism in their schooling environments and the 'different coping and survival strategies' that they utilize (Mac an Ghaill, 1992: 43). In this manner, these researchers have been able to demonstrate that different groups of ethnically defined pupils have differing experiences of schooling (Mac an Ghaill, 1992: 43), that different resources and opportunities come their way and that minority ethnic pupils (and sometimes their families) resist or make use of the discourses that surround them inside and outside school. Shain, Sewell, Mac an Ghaill and Wright et al. above have all used theorizations of resistance in their accounts of minority ethnic pupils' lives in school.

Explanations for differing achievement

'The major problem in the schooling of black youth is that of racism'

(Mac an Ghaill, 1992: 56)

Qualitative studies have put forward or revealed particular explanations for the underachievement (or in the case of British-Chinese pupils the high achievement) of certain minority ethnic groups in education. The overriding insight provided by studies is that school practices and processes, and the discourses that produce these practices and processes, position pupils (and teachers and parents) in certain ways, creating and producing particular ('raced', gendered and classed) learner identities that hinder or support achievement.

Walters's research (2003, 2007) showed how teachers, in the management of their class-rooms and lessons, did not see their minority ethnic pupils' language needs as EAL pupils and in order to be able to 'explain' these students' behaviour to themselves (because it did not fit their conceptions of 'ideal pupil'), and take action as teachers, they called on notions regarding the children's ethnicity. The teachers saw 'ethnicity' and not 'English language need' as an explanation for poor achievement with the result that the children's language and learning needs remained unaddressed and the children vulnerable to underachievement as they moved through school. Mirza (1992) claimed that, in a similar manner, teachers' restricted access to resources for Black girls. Archer and Francis's research (2007) also proposed that teachers utilize a concept of 'ideal pupil' and that minority pupils are not allowed to 'fit' this conception but are always compared against it and placed outside of it.

Qualitative research has also explicitly named racism as a primary explanation for the poor achievement of certain minority ethnic groups in education. Some studies have discussed and described teacher racism while others have discussed and described both teacher racism and institutional racism. (For an explanation of individual racism and institutional racism see Chapter 5.)

Wright's work (1992 and 1987) and Gillborn's work (1990) pointed to the fact that the teachers in their studies had lower expectations of Black pupils and Wright (1992) and Green (1985) found that teachers chastised Black pupils more frequently than other pupils and offered them less individual attention and praise. Teachers' lower expectations were the 'prime obstacle' to academic success for African-Caribbean pupils (Gillborn, 1990) and led to minority ethnic students being placed in lower sets (Troyna, 1991b) or placed in lower tiers of exam entry (Gillborn and Youdell, 2000). At the same time Wright (and Troyna and Hatcher, 1992) found evidence of racism from White peers in the classroom and the manner in which clear boundaries between ethnic groups were clearly drawn and marked by primary children. Wright et al. (2000) pointed to the way in which schools' perceptions of African-Caribbean boys as 'undesirable', 'troublesome' learners were factors in their over-exclusion from school.

Other work has drawn attention to the way in which institutional structures, that is the practices, organization and discourses of the education system and schools, prevent certain pupil groups from achieving. A clear account of this is provided by Gillborn (2008) in his analysis (using Critical Race Theory) of race equality in education policy and assessment. His thesis is that education policy 'is not designed to eliminate race inequality but to sustain it at manageable levels' (Gillborn, 2008). Institutional racism and its relationship to education has become a central issue in debates around the reproduction of educational inequalities since the murder of Black teenager Stephen Lawrence and the subsequent Macpherson Report.

Other research that we have considered above (Connolly, 1998; Sewell, 1997; Shain, 2003; Archer and Francis, 2007; Archer, 2003) considered racism in and outside school and how the discourses (and attitudes or stereotypes) created are called on and used by both teachers in their assessment of and engagement with pupils in school and by the pupils themselves as a form of resistance and/or as a means of developing an identity in an attempt to survive everyday life in school. In this manner underachievement is perpetuated for many minority ethnic pupils.

Much of this research, particularly the studies by Youdell (2006) and Archer and Francis (2007), has challenged and developed our ways of conceptualizing learner identities and the relationship between 'race'/ethnicity, gender, sexuality and social class and how these 'factors' can be theorized and held together in an appropriate model for understanding, researching and analysing the social and educational world and the reproduction of social and educational inequalities.

In this chapter we have looked at the wealth of research studies conducted from the 1980s onwards and their findings as well as the developments they offer in theory and methodology when researching minority ethnic pupils' experiences of education. These findings and methodologies were however heavily critiqued and this critique takes us to the heart of key issues in educational and social science research. In Chapter 5 this critique is considered as well as other issues that arise in relation to researching 'race' and ethnicity.

Chapter summary

Through a consideration of a range of qualitative studies conducted since the 1980s, a number of insights have emerged regarding the school experiences of minority ethnic pupils as well as explanations for their differing achievement at the end of compulsory schooling. Early studies revealed how different, ethnically defined, groups of pupils received different kinds and amounts of attention from teachers and how setting arrangements in schools were key in creating disadvantage. A consideration of the interactions between teachers and minority ethnic pupils revealed the complex and subtle processes that positioned pupils as achieving or underachieving, offering particular 'raced', gendered and classed learner identities and affecting access to important school resources. Other studies directed attention to national policy and how this exacerbated racial inequalities in schools particularly for Black and working-class pupils. In many accounts racism, either teacher racism or institutional racism, was explicitly named as a primary explanation for poor achievement. The qualitative work discussed in the chapter also challenged pathologized, deficit accounts of minority pupils and their families and considered the difficulties that many minority ethnic parents face in working with their children's schools in order to support their children as learners. The studies discussed have also been important in developing ways of conceptualizing learner identities and the relationship between 'race'/ethnicity, gender, sexuality and social class and how this relationship can be theorized. They have demonstrated a shift away from mono-causal explanations for educational performance to explanations that present 'race'/ethnicity, gender, sexuality and social class as intermeshed and have at the same time been able to move from a view of power as something that only teachers and school adults hold to include in their accounts examples of pupil (and family) resistance.

Further reading

All of the studies outlined in this chapter are worthy of further reading, particularly: Connolly (1998), *Racism, Gender Identities and Young Children* for his focus on primary school; Sewell (1997), *Black Masculinities and Schooling: How Black Boys Survive Modern Schooling* for his close analysis of identity production and resistance;

Walters (2003), *Bangladeshi Pupils: Experiences, Identity and Achievement*; (2004), '"I don't think she knew I couldn't do it": Bangladeshi pupils and learning to read in the Year 3 classroom', in *Ethnographies of Educational and Cultural Conflicts*, Jeffrey and Walford (eds); and (2007), '"How do you know that he's bright but lazy?" Teachers' assessments of Bangladeshi English as an Additional Language pupils in two Year 3 classroom', in *Oxford Review of Education*, 33 (1) for her focus on achievement, identity, literacy and EAL; Gillborn and Youdell (2000), *Rationing Education: Policy, Practice, Reform and Equity* for their analysis of the effects of policy and assessment on minority ethnic pupil experience and opportunity; Youdell (2003), 'Identity traps or how Black students fail: The interactions between biographical, sub-cultural, and learner identities', in *British Journal of Sociology of Education*, 24 (1) for her analysis of how inequities in the achievement of African-Caribbean pupils have come to be so enduring; Youdell (2006), *Impossible Bodies, Impossible Selves: Exclusions and Student Subjectivities* for her use of post-structuralist theory in analysing and understanding minority ethnic pupil experiences; and Archer and Francis (2007), *Understanding Minority Ethnic* Achievement for their account of high-achieving Chinese pupils.

Also recommended are:

Troyna and Hatcher's (1992) book *Racism in Children's Lives: A Study of Mainly-White Primary Schools* for their account of how concepts of 'race' do play a part in the lives of primary school children;

Scourfield et al.'s (2005) article 'The negotiation of minority ethnic identities in virtually all-white communities: Research with children and their families in the South Wales valleys', in *Children and Society* 19 for data on children's experiences of racism in their daily lives inside and outside school in South Wales;

Hatcher's chapter 'Racism and children's cultures', in Griffiths and Troyna's (1995) book *Anti-Racism, Culture and Social Justice in Education* for his examination of 'race' in the cultures of White children.

Elton-Chalcraft's (2009) book *'Its Not Just About Black and White Miss': Children's Awareness of Race* which looks at young children's attitudes to race and racism in primary schools as well as their perceptions of their own and other cultures. Implications for practice are also considered.

Gaine and George's (1999) book *Gender, Race and Class in Schooling: A New Introduction* for school experience and race.

The Runnymede Trust's (1997) publication *Islamophobia: A Challenge For Us All* for an account of 'Islamophobia' and its consequences in society as well as suggestions for practical action.

Cline et al.'s (2002) research report 'Minority Ethnic Pupils in Mainly White Schools' for its wide coverage of issues relating to the educational experiences of minority ethnic pupils and their parents and teachers in mainly White areas.

Brooker's (2003) article 'Learning how to learn: Parental ethnotheories and young children's preparation for school' for an analysis of parents' differing cultural belief systems and how these prepare children for school in different ways, with implications for school experiences.

Tomlinson's chapter 'Ethnic Minorities: Involved partners or problem parents?', in Munn's (1993) edited book *Parents and Schools, Customers, Managers or Partners?* This chapter makes the case that the history of home–school relationships over the past 30 years, in the context of a society 'still marked by racial and cultural antagonisms', makes it more difficult to develop home–school relationships. It also discusses how teachers are not well informed about the backgrounds, expectations and desires of minority ethnic parents and how they stereotype families as problems.

Crozier's (2004) report *Parents, Children and School Experience: Asian Families' Perspectives* for insights into Asian parents' relationships with their children's schools.

Arshad et al.'s (2005) report *Minority Ethnic Pupils' Experiences of School in Scotland* for an excellent account of minority ethnic pupils' school experiences in Scotland. They include within this account the experiences of minority ethnic pupils with Special Educational Needs.

Connolly and Keenan's (2002) article 'Racist harassment in the white hinterlands: Minority ethnic children and parents' experiences of schooling in Northern Ireland', in *British Journal of Sociology of Education* for an account of pupil experiences of racism in Northern Ireland's schools and responses of schools.

Derrington and Kendall's chapter 'Still at school at 16? Gypsy Traveller students in English secondary schools', in Bhatti et al.'s (2007) edited book *Social Justice and Intercultural Education: An Open Ended Dialogue* for its look at the retention of Gypsy Traveller students in secondary schools and issue of racism, cultural dissonance and cultural alienation. This edited collection also includes a chapter by Bhatti, 'The irresistible attraction of ICT: Experiences of trainee teachers from minority ethnic backgrounds' that considers the experiences of a group of minority ethnic student teachers on a PGCE course.

Haynes et al.'s (2006) article 'The barriers to achievement for White/Black Caribbean pupils in English schools', in *British Journal of Sociology of Education* for the experiences and achievement of mixed-race White/Black Caribbean pupils and a discussion of work on mixed-race identities.

Bourne, Bridges and Searle's (1994) *Outcast England: How Schools Exclude Black Children* for its consideration of reasons for exclusion and accounts of exclusion.

Richards's book *The Way We See It* (2008) for its look at the root causes of African-Caribbean school exclusion as well as identifying some solutions. Maud Blair's book *Why Pick On Me? School Exclusion and Black Youth* (2001) for her consideration of why some schools exclude while others are able to enable success.

Ball et al.'s (2002) article '"Ethnic choosing": Minority ethnic students, social class and higher education choice', in *Race, Ethnicity and Education* for its consideration of the issue of minority ethnic access to higher education. Shiner and Modood's (2002) article 'Help or hindrance? Higher education and the route to ethnic equality' also considers this issue.

Abbas's (2004) 'The Education of British South Asians' for 'race'/ethnicity and subject selection.

Useful websites

www.runnymedetrust.org/publications
The Runnymede Trust

'Race', Ethnicity and Research

Introduction

In Chapter 3 we considered the contribution and findings of qualitative research in relation to 'race', ethnicity and education. Early research demonstrated that African-Caribbean and Asian pupils had struggles in school and that teachers had negative expectations and ideas about African-Caribbean pupils, particularly boys, and showed how these worked against this pupil group. The research directed attention to the manner in which teachers negatively sanctioned African-Caribbean behaviour more often than that of White pupils (including the use of exclusion) in the schools studied and how this pupil group could often be placed in lower sets than an assessment of their learning would warrant, thus contributing to their lower educational achievement at the end of schooling (see Chapter 3). The research then directed attention to within-school processes (and their links with out of school processes) and how these negatively affected minority ethnic pupils as well as to teacher racism (both intentional and unintentional).

Between 1990 and 1995, however, there was a sustained critique made of early qualitative studies. The critique was mounted by Peter Foster (whose study of Milltown High we considered in Chapter 3), Martyn Hammersley and Roger Gomm. The focus of their critique was on methodology, the presentation of data and the validity, reliability and generalizability of the qualitative studies they critiqued. However, the overall theme of the critique was to question the findings that 'teacher racism' and within-school processes were implicated in the underachievement of certain minority ethnic groups. In fact, read together, these papers and chapters reject this explanation and the integrity of the research methodology on which the findings are based. The 'debate' became one about theoretical and philosophical differences in research approach (based around notions of 'objectivity' and 'partisanship') and the role of research and the researcher as well as about whether teacher racism and racism in general existed in schools.

This chapter will consider this debate and its implications and then consider other issues pertaining to 'race', ethnicity and research that need to be considered and addressed by anyone about to conduct research or when reading research accounts. These issues include the 'race'/ethnicity of the researcher and the need to consider the category of 'White' and 'whiteness' within any research methodology.

Objectivity, credibility and research values

The further reading section at the end of this chapter gives an outline of the key papers, books and chapters that constitute this 'debate' or controversy. You may want to consult this when reading through the discussion that follows.

Whose side are we on?

In advance of any critique being made by Foster, in 1990 (of the qualitative research that indicated that 'teacher racism' and/or in school process were implicated in the underachievement of certain minority ethnic groups), Troyna and Carrington published a paper, in 1989, that raised many of the issues to do with research ethics and approach that became contentious during the early 1990s. In their paper Troyna and Carrington were making links between their belief in the importance of anti-racist education and their approach to research and asked the following questions:

> First, how can antiracist researchers reconcile their partisanship with objectivity? Second, what role (if any) should white researchers play in antiracist research? Third, what role should research play in promoting racial equality in educational access, treatment and outcome? Fourth, to what extent ought the research act itself actively challenge commonsense (for example, stereotypical, racist, populist) beliefs and perceptions? Fifth, can antiracist principles be reconciled with the need for external sponsorship and funding? Finally, what steps can be taken to facilitate the development of greater reciprocity and collaboration between the antiracist researcher and those whom she/he researches? (Troyna and Carrington, 1989: 205)

The debate that we are about to look at and the subsequent discussion about 'race'/ethnicity and research are all touched on by the questions that Troyna and Carrington asked in 1989. In many ways their questions could be construed as setting an agenda although few of the commentators that we now consider refer to this paper.

In their paper, Troyna and Carrington argued that a commitment by researchers to anti-racism and to challenging racism in education and society necessitates a considered approach to research methodology as research approaches and methodologies are not neutral. They argue for a research approach that is 'transformative', building their argument on work previously undertaken by feminist researchers, such as Lather, who propose what is often referred to as a 'feminist standpoint' or 'feminist epistemology' approach (Stanley and Wise, 1990, see Youdell, 2006: 62). This approach not only reports forms of inequality but sees the 'research act itself as constituting a deliberate challenge to the status quo . . . the ultimate purpose of research . . . (being) to contribute to a body of empirically-grounded 'emancipatory knowledge' . . . (that) by interrogating commonsense conceptions of the world . . . may serve to 'empower the oppressed' by enabling them to 'come to understand and change their own oppressive realities' (Troyna and Carrington, 1989: 206–7 quoting Lather, 1986). Objectivity, they argue, is maintained through a commitment on their part as researchers, not to Black or White pupils and teachers but to 'the fundamental principles of social justice, equality and participatory democracy' (Troyna and Carrington, 1989: 208). In the rest of the paper, Troyna and Carrington, in answering their questions, consider how previous research, conducted by White researchers, has been problematic, often resulting in the encouragement, reinforcement and reproduction of racial stereotypes (Troyna and Carrington, 1989: 213) and thus potentially of continuing racial inequalities, and the perpetuation of the status quo.

Reflection activity

Consider the following questions and write down your thoughts and responses.
  What is the purpose of research?
  What should the outcome of research and the research process be?
  Do you think that a researcher can be, and should be, neutral as a researcher?
  Can research be a neutral, value-free activity?
  What role should research play in promoting equality and challenging inequality?
  Is the knowledge gained through research activity neutral?

The title of Troyna and Carrington's 1989 paper, 'Whose Side Are We On? Ethical Dilemmas in Research on "Race" and Education' was a nod to an influential paper by Howard Becker published in 1967 entitled 'Whose Side Are We On? In this paper Becker states, 'To have values or not to have values: the question is always with us' (Becker, 1967: 239). Becker makes the claim that it is impossible to be neutral as a researcher: that personal values and political sympathies always inform and infuse research choices and methods. He identifies how sociological accounts of institutional life can favour the official view, the view of 'superordinates', those in charge, like prison governors in prisons, who are seen as knowing best, rather than that of 'subordinates'. Many sociologists researching 'subordinate' experiences and views can find themselves in deep sympathy with and taking the side of 'subordinates' and challenging the 'superordinate' or official view. Becker insists, however, that 'Whatever side we are on, we must use our techniques impartially enough that a belief to which we are especially sympathetic could be proved untrue' (Becker, 1967: 246).

The debate proper begins with Foster's findings from his study of a secondary school's teachers' responses to multicultural and anti-racist educational initiatives(as reported in Chapter 3). Unlike the other qualitative research studies of school processes, Forster claimed that the school's teachers had succeeded in creating a non-racist environment, that racism did not 'influence social relationships' within the school and that 'both Afro-Caribbean and white students enjoyed equitable treatment' (Foster, 1990a: 149 cited in Connolly, 1992: 133). This was remarked upon and debated by other researchers who found that, in their eyes, Forster had ignored aspects of his data that demonstrated unequal treatment of African-Caribbean pupils or had found explanations for his data that ignored or legitimized 'patterns of racialized control and selection', in which teachers were centrally implicated (Gillborn, 1995: 50). (Some of these responses to Foster's findings are discussed in Chapter 3).

In 1990, Foster published an article in which he critiqued two studies (Carrington and Wood, 1983; Wright, 1986) that he claimed placed 'teacher racism' and in-school processes at the heart of explanations for Afro-Caribbean pupils' underachievement (Foster, 1990b). He made the following methodological criticisms of this work:

- there was a lack of adequate evidence provided for the claims that were made.
- observational evidence should have been used rather than a reliance on interview data, references to 'a few' or 'many teachers' were too vague and clearer numbers should have been provided.
- a case was made from only one or two teacher interviews.
- phrases from teacher interviews were taken out of context in order to make a case.
- the questions put to teachers may have influenced their responses.
- pupil accounts of their experiences cannot be held to be reliable.

He also claimed that other explanations were just as plausible for the poor academic achievement of Black pupils. What is striking in his paper and in his subsequent reply to Wright (1991) is his insistence on seeking explanations for poor African-Caribbean school performance outside the school and in seeing some stereotypes of African-Caribbeans as holding some elements of truth (see Foster, 1990b: 338).

Wright did respond to Foster's critique of her work (see Wright, 1990) claiming that Foster had totally misrepresented her work and that it was not possible to include the range of interview data gathered in her study in the space of an academic article. She insisted that her research, and that of others, led her to believe that the factors implicit in the reproduction of racial inequality 'do not simply operate outside schools but inside them as well' (Wright, 1990: 355). This response was subsequently replied to by Foster (1991: 165) who restated much of his original article namely that her study could not be used to support the argument that there were racist teachers and that such racism may result in the underachievement of African-Caribbean students (Foster, 1991: 169).

Another broader methodological argument broke out between Troyna who wrote a paper making the case against the use of the positivist paradigm and quantitative methods for studying 'race' and racism in schools (and noting how influential positivist, quantitative studies had become in informing policy) (Troyna, 1991a) and Hammersley (who incidentally was Foster's supervisor for the Milltown study) (1992a). Troyna claimed that quantitative methods, and their positivist approach towards or understanding of the social world failed to 'capture sensitively the general nature of race relations in education and particularly its dynamic in the social, cultural and institutional worlds of young people' (Troyna, 1991a: 426). He also claimed that statistical studies and the methodologies chosen by researchers such as Smith and Tomlinson (who only interviewed parents about the experiences of racism of their children) were not a good enough method for exploring the overt and implicit racisms that young people experienced in school (Troyna, 1991a: 428) and that studies, such as Milner's, exploring self-identity and self-image, that used researcher-chosen stimuli to elicit responses from children, gave prominence to physical differences and racially defined characteristics, thereby naturalizing/reinforcing 'race' difference (Troyna, 1991a: 431–2). Troyna's overall argument was that he was 'sceptical about the application of quantitative research because I believe it is too crude to capture the subtle and complex nature of racism in education' (Troyna, 1991a: 429) (see also Chapter 3 where this argument is briefly presented as a reason for the development of qualitative studies in the late 1980s). In his response to Troyna's paper, Hammersley attacked the claim that qualitative methods gave a better access to social reality and challenged what he saw as Troyna's failure to 'show similar scepticism towards qualitative research' that he showed towards the weaknesses of quantitative research findings (Hammersley, 1992a: 175).

> Many of the incidents cited as instances of racism are open to plausible alternative interpretations; and in some cases excessive reliance is placed on informants' accounts. Furthermore, relatively small numbers of instances are used as a basis for generalisations about particular teachers and even about whole schools. Finally, these studies have often been treated in the literature as convincing evidence of widespread racism on the part of teachers in British schools. . . . (ignoring) how problematic the generalisability of qualitative findings can be. (Hammersley, 1992a: 176)

This then was a debate about the merits of particular paradigms and their appropriateness for research into issues of 'race' and racial inequality as well as about the validity or 'truth' status of findings produced by different paradigms.

Foster continued to publish papers that critiqued early qualitative work (1992a; 1992b; 1993b). In his 1992a article, 'Equal Treatment and Cultural Difference in Multi-Ethnic Schools', he critiques the work of Mac an Ghaill (1988) and Gillborn (1990) and their findings that Afro-Caribbean students were treated unequally because teachers had particular 'ethnocentric' conceptions of appropriate behaviour in school and that teachers' attachment to monocultural expectations of classroom behaviour led to 'actions which were racist in their consequences' (Gillborn, 1990: 44 cited by Foster, 1992a: 91). The work that he critiques had found that African-Caribbean pupils were more likely to be excluded from school, disciplined in the classroom and represented in special behavioural referral units and was offering 'teacher ethnocentrism' as an explanation for this. Again, Foster criticizes this early qualitative research for not offering evidence that provides 'convincing support' for the claims being made (Foster, 1992a: 92). He claims again that more observation of classroom processes is needed to support the interview data (Foster, 1992a: 92) (although he later critiques the use of observation data when he claims that Gillborn has relied on his observations of teachers rather than what they have to say; Foster, 1992a: 94) and that more interview data, and from more teachers, needs to be provided (Foster, 1992a: 92–3) as well as care taken about generalizing from one school or one classroom to others (Foster, 1992a: 94–5). He also, for the first time, raises the issue (already raised by Troyna and Carrington in the 1989 article) that research findings are based on the particular values of the researcher although this discussion is weak and rather suggests that only some research (qualitative research) is affected in this way (see Foster, 1992a: 95). It is not something that he applies here to his own work. In the rest of the paper, Foster switches to a discussion of some key educational and ethical issues with regard to the schooling of African-Caribbean boys basing his discussion on the findings of qualitative research which is suddenly not to be rejected because of its weakness or lack of credible evidence. This would appear to be because this research (by Furlong) supports his argument that African-Caribbean boys behave differently in the classroom, that their behaviour constitutes an overt challenge to their teachers and that teachers are therefore correct in excluding them or using behaviour as a criteria for set allocation and so on; that these behaviours on the part of teachers are not racist, nor part of the reproduction of inequalities, but are part of how teachers ought to behave (see Foster, 1992a: 97–9).

In relation to his critique about the inadequacy in the amount of evidence provided, it has to be noted that this lack of presented evidence may be because of the conventions of publishing and writing and the fact that journal articles and book chapters limit researchers to about 7–8,000 words in which to present their research methodology and their findings. For statistical studies a lot of data can be presented in a simple table or bar graph; this is not the case for qualitative researchers, particularly ethnographers, who must present the research context and the many layers of data that combine to provide 'findings'. Foster does not explicate what would be enough data or evidence or how many interviews or observations would warrant enough evidence. We seem to have here a concern with how qualitative research should be presented and what constitutes enough evidence rather than the grounds for the rejection of researchers' findings. There is also implicit in Foster and Hammersley's arguments a belief that some research approaches, and therefore researchers and their findings, are neutral and objective while only some are partial and defined by the value position that they take. This is obviously not the case.

Connolly (1992) joins the debate in making exactly this point (i.e. that values affect all research). He starts, just as Troyna and Carrington did, with directing attention to the importance of the theoretical underpinnings of research, the value base of the researcher, and how this affects the research study, its methodology and analysis.

> . . . the use of research methods cannot be seen in isolation, as an autonomous entity working under their own internal logic . . . the researcher's theoretical standpoint . . . will dictate which categories and areas within the field are to be studied and how such data is to be gathered and analysed. . . . Further, the ethical position taken as regards who is to be studied, what for and for what purpose . . . will also determine the research methods to be used. (Connolly, 1992: 135)

He takes Foster's own study of Milltown High and, after demonstrating how Foster's theoretical base is one of 'Weberian political sociology' (a research/theoretical paradigm that has as its goal the influence of political action and social policy – see Connolly, 1992: 135–6), shows how his research is circumscribed by its theoretical underpinnings, as all research is. Such a paradigm 'regards the social structure not in terms of fundamentally antagonistic and contradictory relationships between the powerful and the subordinate, but in terms of a political pluralism, in which numerous class and status groups compete with each other over access to, and control over, society's scarce resources and rewards' (Connolly, 1992: 136), thus centring the focus of any research study on 'race' located within this paradigm on how to 'secure and maintain equal opportunities' (Connolly, 1992: 136). If we think back to Troyna and Carrington's article discussed above we can see that this is in direct contrast to the 'standpoint' research paradigm that they argue for (a paradigm based on a view that does see the social structure in terms of antagonistic and contradictory relationships between the powerful and the subordinate).

Connolly then continues to demonstrate that Foster's study can be critiqued for many methodological weaknesses (which ironically repeat many of the same critiques that Foster has made of others) as well as for its 'unquestioning acceptance . . . that equal opportunities can be based upon 'universalistic values of society' (Connolly, 1992: 138) and that the education system is in someway neutral and not implicated in the reproduction of existing social relations (Connolly, 1992: 138–9). He also discusses how different conceptualizations of 'racism' affect research analysis and findings. In Foster's case the conceptualization used is one of understanding racism as the result of 'cultural ignorance' whereas the conceptualization favoured by Connolly and others (e.g. Troyna) is that of understanding racism in terms of 'relations of power' (Connolly, 1992: 144). Foster's adoption of the 'cultural ignorance' view means that his analysis and presentation of social relations within his research school plays down the pupils' reported experiences of racism, experiences that he generally dismisses. Connolly's key claim is that Foster's study, because of its theoretical approach and methodology, cannot find or see instances and experiences of racism even though they are present in the data he reports (Connolly, 1992: 142). Connolly's argument thus returns us to the claims of Troyna and Carrington (1989), namely that all research is rooted in a particular value base, no research is pure, neutral and objective and that researchers need to reflect upon and consider the effects of their research and research methodologies.

> ## Reflection activity
>
> Where do you stand in this debate?
>   Look back at your original notes – have you changed your mind about anything?
>   How should we judge the evidence presented in research accounts?

Just as the debate was distilling into one about research stance, research paradigms and the nature and presentation of evidence to support claims, Troyna published a paper that presented findings from a study looking at the allocation of pupils to ability groups for teaching (and exam entry) in three secondary schools, to explore whether there was an unfair treatment of ethnic minority pupils in group allocation (Troyna 1991b). The key claim made was that 'the ethnicity of pupils played a mediating part in structuring their opportunities for placement in the higher ability sets' (Troyna, 1991b: 371) and that it was more accurate to speak of the Asian children included in the study being underrated by their teachers, that is that teacher assessments of pupils' ability were tempered by their responses to their pupils' ethnicity, rather than speaking of the underachievement of this pupil group. Troyna wrote that the data and evidence provided in his paper gave 'clear cut evidence' of his claims (Troyna, 1991b: 373). However, the paper is by any standards very weak in that it only uses numerical data about set allocation and test results as its evidence (and uses this data poorly, see below), does not present any of the interview data collected and therefore does not explore teachers' decision making and reasoning about set allocation, imputes explanations to teachers' actions without presenting any evidence and fails to explore many other explanations and factors that may have been part of the decision-making process. In addition to this, Troyna makes claims that are not based in fact or in the research data. For example, that the English language ability/development of the Asian pupils would not have been a factor in their set placements as the pupils had all been attending UK schools for some time and had attended school in Pakistan and Bangladesh (Troyna, 1991b: 368). No evidence is presented that this was the teachers' view and even a cursory experience of work with EAL pupils reveals that English language development for academic work in school can take more than a year to develop. A current estimation is that it takes between 5 and 7 years (see Thomas and Collier, 1997). In this respect the paper, unlike other careful and thoughtful work by Troyna, seems to confirm the very criticisms aimed at early qualitative research reports by Foster and seems a gift to this group of critics (as if they had wished an ethnographer into writing a paper that was an example of everything they wanted to critique about qualitative, ethnographic work).

Roger Gomm (another of Hammersley's PhD students) took the opportunity of responding to Troyna's paper and heavily critiquing its methodology and method of presentation (Gomm, 1993). He claimed that Troyna had misused numerical data by not using appropriate statistical methods for his analysis and by trying to make very small numbers represent significant patterns (Gomm, 1993: 150–4 and 160) and that Troyna had failed to explore alternative explanations for set allocation and to define, and measure, 'ethnic inequality' and 'ability' clearly (Gomm, 1993: 155–8). He also claimed that Troyna had used 'selective data' to support his arguments (Gomm, 1993: 163). The language of the piece was, however, less than restrained: Gomm talks about Troyna's 'unprincipled' use of data, use of 'innuendo and sleight of hand' and 'illegitimate tactics' (Gomm, 1993: 149 and 163).

Troyna continued the debate by labelling Foster, Hammersley and Gomm as 'methodological purists' 'who explicate the allegedly dubious empirical grounds on which claims of racial inequality in education have been mounted' asking if it is possible to have data, when investigating social injustice, that are not amenable to alternative interpretations (although this was not a criticism made by Gomm, he critiqued Troyna for not exploring alternative interpretations). He also asked at what point do data and evidence become valid and plausible for such critics (Troyna, 1993a: 168).

Hammersley responded to Troyna's 1993 paper by developing and challenging Troyna's label of 'methodological purists' to describe the response of himself and Gomm and Foster to early qualitative work (Hammersley, 1993a). In the paper he denies that they require or even presuppose 'absolute proof' and 'evidence that leaves no possible doubt' (Hammersley, 1993a: 339) and states that the problem under discussion is one of what constitutes adequate evidence (Hammersley, 1993a: 340). He refers readers to his proposed solution to this dilemma (to be found in Hammersley, 1991; 1992b), namely that claims and evidence must be judged on the basis of 'plausibility in relation to knowledge we currently take as beyond reasonable doubt, and credibility in relation to judgements about the likelihood of various sorts of error' (Hammersley, 1993a: 340). He claims that this allows for disagreement between members of the 'research community' about what is plausible and credible and that this 'disagreement can be resolved . . . through the search for, and argument back from, what is common ground amongst disputants' (Hammersley, 1993a: 340). This then is taking a stand that is opposite to that taken by standpoint researchers. Hammersley's answer to what constitutes adequate evidence operates on an assumption that those who will decide are the academic community and that community members will behave reasonably.

Reflection activity

What is your response to Hammersley's proposed solution to the problem of what constitutes adequate evidence?

The debate between Foster, Hammersley and Gomm and Troyna and the other qualitative researchers rounds off with a series of publications by Troyna (1995), Hammersley and Gomm (1993), Hammersley (e.g. 1993b), Foster (e.g. 1993b) and Foster et al. (1996). Troyna returned to making a strong case for the idea of 'partisanship research' and its legitimacy, writing of researchers as always situated within and by the research process, never able to take up a position outside of it as well as exploring the contribution of post-positivist and post-structuralist research approaches to our thinking about how knowledge is produced and by whom and to what ends. For Troyna these were key questions and insights and he continued to reject the notion put forward by Hammersley, Gomm and Foster that research was somehow a neutral, value-free activity and that knowledge was rational, objectively gained and neutral.

Hammersley (1993b) continued to situate the debate as a disagreement about the purposes and nature of sociological research. However, unlike the early qualitative researchers, who, through writers such as Troyna and Carrington (1989), had already articulated this insight, he expressed the opinion that while an insistence on absolute proof had to be abandoned in social science research, this was not to be replaced by 'relativism, standpoint theory or instrumentalism' (Hammersley, 1993b: 432) and proposed again his approach to assessing the validity of research findings through judging the findings' plausibility and credibility, forcefully rejecting 'partisanship'. Foster (1993b) reiterated Hammersley's approach to assessing evidence and accused Gillborn and Drew of being simplistic, patronizing, misleading and using insinuation and selective quotation in their article (Foster, 1993b: 551).

As we can see from the above, the debate became starkly defined in relation to two very different understandings about the nature of research, the researcher, knowledge and how the validity of evidence is to be assessed. If we take the view that social science research work was opening itself up at this time to new theoretical insights that challenged notions of objectivity and rational thought, that turned attention to the ways in which knowledge is produced, by whom and to what ends and argued that there was no 'real' objective 'reality', then Hammersley, Foster and Gomm's proposal that research evidence and findings should be assessed by whether they were plausible and credible can be seen as a defensive stand on behalf of what was being challenged and undermined. As articulated by Gillborn (1995: 63) and Connolly (in Connolly and Troyna, 1998), Hammersley's proposal can be seen as essentially conservative and as a move to keep the definition of what is accepted, known and constitutes valid knowledge firmly, at that time, within the confines of White, middle-class male academics. If we take the premise that research evidence and findings should be judged by whether they are plausible in relation to knowledge we currently take as beyond reasonable doubt, we have to ask who the 'we' is in this statement and to wonder what this knowledge that is beyond reasonable doubt might be. We can all think of knowledge that has been claimed by one group or another as beyond reasonable doubt which has been erroneous and in need of being challenged (and has successfully been challenged). One of the key purposes of research is to challenge and add to what we think we already know or premise and to make us see the familiar anew. The importance of social research is to raise questions, suggest ways of understanding, nudge us into challenging our thinking and the commonsense notions we hold in order to help us reflect on ways forward. At the heart of Hammersley's proposal lie issues of power; an implicit claim is being made about who should decide if something is true or not. Within the writings and approach of Troyna, and other 'partisan' researchers there is at least an acknowledgement of power and a call for an explicitness about where power lies and how it infiltrates the research process and responses to research. This explicitness about power is not present in the 'purists" proposals.

Gillborn presents Hammersley, Foster and Gomm's project as 'closed, authoritative and certain' (1995: 52–3) and claims that it would have been more helpful of them to focus on opening up the complex and contingent world of social processes. To rely on members of the research community to decide on plausibility and credibility, and whether something is 'beyond reasonable doubt', is an approach to research that supports and sustains the status quo. He asks, as I have above, 'who has the power to judge what is relevant?' (Gillborn, 1995: 53). Gillborn directs attention to the manner in which Hammersley calls on a notion of a world that has political and non-political elements and how within this world view 'political' equals 'untrustworthy' (Gillborn, 1995: 54). What is striking is Hammersley's calling for/clinging to a notion of spheres of public, social life and research being non-political, or being able to occupy a non-political, rational, objective ground, at a time when such a view of the social world had been successfully challenged within the social sciences.

Gillborn finds that the implications and potential outcomes of Foster, Hammersley and Gomm's project to be:

- A 'privileging of the status quo'
- A 'protection of current educational process and practices'
- A placing of 'the onus of proof for the existence of racism' on those seeking to challenge inequalities
- A limiting of the definition of racism to 'overtly identifiable and intentional acts, therefore denying institutional racism and more subtle, indirect and unintentional forms'
- A denial of the 'inherently uncertain nature of social research and the complex nature of racism'(Connolly, in Connolly and Troyna, 1998: 7).

Pilkington notes that both 'purist' and 'partisan' positions have implications for policy in that 'purists' 'lean to a conservative privileging of current practices while 'partisans' radically challenge current practices (Pilkington, 1999: 416).

Our account has so far favoured the 'partisanship' camp. However, it needs to be said that Foster, Hammersley and Gomm were right to critique and problematize early qualitative work. As well as critique forming an essential part of sociological work and the building of knowledge, the methodological weaknesses of qualitative and ethnographic work needed to be addressed and debated, particularly the tendency for findings from specific schools and classrooms to be generalized and applied to all schools and classrooms and the dangers of 'selective perception' (Pilkington, 1999: 413 and 415). However, one can question whether this important critique should have been used to reject carte blanche any findings that did not concur with Foster's findings in his Milltown study.

Foster's critique of early qualitative work did push for some important things in relation to methodology. Later qualitative work, as we saw in Chapter 3, does go on to explore within-school processes more deeply using observation, interviewing and other methods of capturing meaning-making and decision making within the classroom. This research was able to present a range of evidence regarding the ways in which teachers' responses, school processes, methods of assessment and so on do position ethnically defined pupils in ways that support or hinder their educational achievement. This work moved beyond a simple 'Black'/'White' dichotomy and a simple view of teacher and institutional racism to an awareness of the more subtle and complex processes working both within and outside school (and in tandem) that position pupils and teachers. The work of Connolly and Sewell (see Chapter 4) both considered processes within and outside school and how these were mutually constitutive of pupil and identities and teacher responses within school as well as implicated in achievement. My own research work and that of Youdell and Archer and Francis takes a careful look at how pupils are positioned and known by teachers and the educational implications of these forms of 'knowing' (see Walters, 2003, 2007; Youdell, 2006, Archer and Francis, 2007; and Chapter 4). Interestingly, echoes of the debate initiated by Foster have recently resurfaced in an article by Stevens (2009).

In the article Stevens presents data from his study into how pupils themselves 'perceive differential teacher treatments and how such views relate to pupils' claims of teacher racism and racial discrimination' (Stevens, 2009: 413). Stephens claims that pupils perceive differential teacher treatment of pupils in the classroom as legitimate if the pupils are understood to be ill or as stragglers (i.e. behind the class because they are newly arrived or have some other legitimate reason for being behind) or deviant (i.e. not conforming to expectations about how one should behave in the classroom). It is seen as acceptable for the first two groups of pupils to receive more attention and support from the teacher and for the latter group to receive less by pupils in general. What Stephens explicates from his data is that pupils who are considered 'deviant' by their peers, and thus deserving of less attention and support from their teachers, do not always see themselves as 'deviant' and therefore see themselves as unfairly treated (and 'scapegoated') by their teachers. It is these pupils that describe their teachers as racist and refer to their reduced support from these teachers as 'racial discrimination'.

In some ways the article makes a good contribution to the work of Sewell and Gillborn in the way in which it shows how 'the deviant is considered a legitimate recipient of less favourable teacher treatment than those who conform to their (the teachers') role expectations' (Stevens, 2009: 419). 'Teachers who label pupils as deviant can treat them as suspicious and become wary of everything these pupils say and do. They are therefore kept under surveillance and excluded and isolated from the 'good pupils' because they are perceived as dangerous, contagious and contaminating' (Stevens, 2009: 419). However, Stephens, through the presentation of his data, is also challenging the claim that racism (i.e. responses to pupils' 'race'/ethnicity) is occurring in these contexts. His claim is that pupils' call on notions of racism and racial discrimination is because they feel they are not getting enough positive teacher attention and support in the classroom. The reason for not receiving this support is their behaviour that does not conform to expectations (of teachers and other pupils) about how pupils should behave in these educational settings. This leads us back to something of the argument that Foster made (see above) and this is acknowledged by Stevens in the article (Stevens, 2009: 425). Stevens goes on to question the definitions of 'institutional racism' in the light of his findings and to suggest that pupil claims of teacher racism cannot be accepted at face value (Stevens, 2009: 427).

While there may be some agreement from other researchers that how pupils 'take part' in the classroom is key to the ways in which teachers come to understand and provide for them and for the learner identities that come into being in those settings, they would challenge Steven's removal of 'race'/ethnicity and racism from the equation. For example, in Walters's research (2003; 2007) while teachers were indeed basing their judgements and provision for pupils on how the pupils took part in classroom interactions, 'race'/ethnicity and racism still had a part to play in (a) the explanations that teachers called on in explaining 'deviant' behaviour, (b) the way in which minority ethnic pupils were only compared with other minority ethnic pupils when it came to considerations of achievement and (c) the devaluing of minority ethnic pupils' culture and languages. Other research (e.g. Sewell, see Chapter 3) would of course lead us to consider that 'deviant' behaviour itself arises out of how minority ethnic pupils are positioned within and outside school and that minority ethnic pupils find that there are few alternative positionings open to them in the harsh, antagonistic (towards their 'race'/ethnicity) settings they find themselves in.

Researching 'race'

The above debate has been explored in some detail as it touches on some of the key issues to do with researching 'race'/ethnicity in education and also raises the question of whether research findings can ever be thought of as true and uncontested as well as the role of research, the impact of research and the manner in which research methods and theory impact on the very data and findings that a research study can find and present. The debate itself is also reflected in the wider terrain of sociological and social science work and work on 'race' and ethnicity that is not specifically focused on education.

In her book on researching 'race', Hasmita Ramji outlines how there have been disputes in the social sciences grouped around two key questions: 'What is race?' and 'How can it be measured and/or understood?' (Ramji, 2009: 1). In this we can see the bare bones of the debate we have considered above. Ramji points to how the first question is a question about the theoretical underpinnings of research (the value base and world view of the researcher) and the second is a question about methodology (how the researcher chooses to collect and interpret/analyse and present data). As Troyna and Carrington argued in 1989, the theoretical and methodological are, in all social science research, 'intimately connected' and both inform each other (Ramji, 2009: 1).

Ramji also directs our attention to an issue that we considered in Chapter 1: the danger of using ethnic categories to describe groups of people, categories that then become fixed and essentialized in research. In order to conduct research and talk about the research, researchers need to use language and categories like 'African-Caribbean' or 'Bangladeshi' (imagine Sewell's research account that we considered in Chapter 3 if he couldn't use the term 'African Caribbean'), but in doing so they run the danger of making these categories seem real, seem as if they have always existed and always will and that they are water-tight, bounded-off, discrete categories. In this way they are implicated in reproducing the category, this way of grouping people, as if it was always so and not problematic and part of a way of defining a group of people as different/other, and different/other in ways we know about. As Ramji, following Rattansi (1994), writes, 'There is a tension . . . between a theoretical perception of race as non-essentialist and socially constructed and employing research methods which however unintentionally fix the meaning of race so that it can be studied' (Ramji, 2009: 7). She argues, as is argued here, that this is something that needs to be considered and addressed in our research work and that we need to work with a notion of 'race' as being produced in social contexts and that this is what research work can and should elucidate (Ramji, 2009: 13 and 17). If we consider some of the later research accounts we considered in Chapter 3, we can see how some research accounts did achieve this (Walters, 2003; Youdell, 2006).

Ramji also directs attention to the manner in which there has been a profound debate in the social sciences over what constitutes truth/validity and knowledge just as we saw in the debate between the 'purists' and the 'partisans' above. Postmodern theoretical developments in social science theory have led to insights in the way in which truth and knowledge are linked to the time and place in which they are produced. Such theoretical insights allow us 'to see that the consensual, collusive values paraded as universal. . . . have a historical background; which is understood, known and located through the aegis and frameworks of Western rationalism and historicism' (Ramji, 2009: 21). This takes us back to Hammersley's claim that we should judge research findings by what is generally agreed by the academy and the critiques that were made of this by other researchers into 'race'/ethnicity and education. Our other researchers (the 'partisans') were part of a movement towards seeing truth and knowledge as contested and determined by the context (time and place) in which they are produced while Hammersley et al. were arguing for a more traditional and accepted view in the social sciences that truth and knowledge could be empirically found out about and that knowledge emerged from a rational and objective exploration and discussion rather than from the time, place and discourses present in the society that produced it. Recent theorists and researchers in the social sciences, following a more postmodern approach to research, have argued that a rationalist perspective is of limited use and that all knowledge (and truth) 'should be viewed as partial and situated' (Ramji, 2009: 25). Interestingly, Ramji produces a box of questions that social science researchers should consider when thinking through their research on 'race'/ethnicity that uncannily reproduces many of the question proposed by Troyna and Carrington with which we began this chapter (Ramji, 2009: 27).

Research and power

Of course the issues highlighted above touch on issues of power and how power is implicated in the production of knowledge. A central thesis, following Foucault, is that power and knowledge are 'intimately connected'. As Ramji states, 'Those most powerful will have their version of knowledge accepted as truth' (Ramji, 2009: 34).

One aspect of power relations in research, and their relation to the production of knowledge, that attention has been drawn to is the status of 'whiteness' and how 'whiteness' must be made visible in research accounts and considered as a racial/ethnic category. In much conventional work, 'whiteness' has been invisible and presented as 'non-racial' or outside of ethnic categorizations of people: it is 'non-white' people who are ethnic or who are 'raced' and it is against the norm of 'whiteness' that these subsequent categorizations of people are defined/placed ('race being the defining property and experience of 'Other' groups', Ramji, 2009: 27) and subsequently pathologized and negatively valued (Ramji, 2009: 29). Thus in conducting research, and in reading research accounts, it is necessary to consider the ways in which 'whiteness' manifests itself in the knowledge being conveyed. Ramji argues that researchers themselves, in conducting and then producing their research accounts, can disrupt these easy assumptions that 'whiteness' is the norm and 'Others' are to be judged in relation to this norm, through the use of reflexivity. That is, researchers should challenge their own accounts and make explicit their own positionings, and that of their research subjects/participants, in relation to 'whiteness', as well as deconstruct the categories and concepts utilized through unpacking and examining them (see Ramji, 2009: 29–30).

Reflexivity in social science research refers to the process whereby a researcher reflects on the way in which research is carried out, the values and beliefs that underlie their research and research methodology and the way the knowledge produced shapes the world. It is an awareness that the way you write or talk about the social world is itself potentially part of the problem being addressed in your research (e.g. reproducing racial stereotypes as you categorize and name groups of people and infer common characteristics 'owned' by that group) and thus an awareness that the way you write and talk can be implicated in continuing the reproduction of inequality and disadvantage. Being reflexive in one's research activity and accounts is an attempt to counter, or at least be explicit about, these potentially negative aspects of research work. In this way, some White researchers have responded to the challenge of considering power and their own whiteness by paying attention to their practice and by explicitly locating themselves and their ethnicity (and class and gender) within their research (Edwards, 1990; Haw, 1996; Fine, 1994).

Other aspects of the way in which power and knowledge are implicated in research work become visible if we consider the history and motivations for the commissioning (and funding) of research studies. For example, the history of survey research lies in the desire of newly emergent nation states to collect information (statistics) about their populations in order to be able to monitor, control and manage these populations.

Interviewing

Another of the key ways in which 'race' and ethnicity has occupied social science methodology is with regard to interviewing. This debate has focused on whether the 'race'/ethnicity of the researcher should match that of the interviewee in order to establish a good rapport and thereby gather good data. In essence this debate is concerned with who is best placed to conduct 'race' research.

Reflection activity

If the perceived 'race' or ethnicity of an interviewer is different to that of the interviewee, does this create a barrier to interviewee disclosure?

If a White researcher is interviewing an African-Caribbean person will the perceived difference in life experiences, background and power relationships between them affect what the African-Caribbean person will be willing to say?

Would an African-Caribbean researcher be a better interviewer in this situation?

Make notes of your responses to these questions.

There have been two responses in the research literature to this question. One is to argue for 'race matching' between interviewer and interviewee in order to facilitate the collecting of good research data. In this view 'race difference' is seen as a barrier to maximizing the research potential of the interview in that 'race' and/or issues pertaining to ethnicity will not be openly and honestly talked about, recruitment and participation to the research study may be affected with participants only comfortable and/or interested in talking with someone they perceive as like themselves and the level of understanding and rapport within the interview being negatively affected (Ramji, 2009: 58). The second, and more accepted, response has been to challenge the understandings of 'race' that the concern and first response are premised on. This second response argues that 'race' needs to be 'more fluidly understood. It cannot be given priority or essentialized and hence cannot be "matched for"' (Ramji, 2009: 56). Racial matching in this view is based on a misunderstanding of the nature of 'race' in the interview process in that it makes 'race' the only factor that is important in the relationship between the researcher and researched. That is, it fails to acknowledge that there are many other factors that create difference between interviewer and interviewee, including age, class, language, educational level, power-differentials within the place in which the research is taking place and so on and that by 'race matching' these other differences may be ignored and not accounted for in the research study (Edwards, 1990). It is also argued that not sharing a perceived 'racial' or ethnic identity with an interviewee can have many benefits in a research interview in that the interviewer is often in a genuine position of enquiry and needs to ask the interviewee to elaborate and provide fine detail about an experience that the interviewer has not experienced. A danger in having a perceived commonality between researcher and research participant is that both parties may assume that experiences or insights are already shared and known about and do not need to be articulated or that the interviewer may bring a preconceived understanding about the issue at hand so that they fail to explore in detail that experience or insight during the interview. An 'outsider' may well follow things through, asking for more detail and explication and be in a position to encourage more from the interviewee than an 'insider'. At the same time, rapport can also be lost because the interviewer and interviewee do share a certain insider status. For example, a Bangladeshi woman may be less willing to state what concerns she has about her children's education and the difficulties they are facing in school if she is being interviewed by another Bangladeshi mother who lives in the same community or who is from a different class and educational background to herself whereas she might feel comfortable in discussing these issues with an African-Caribbean man or a White woman.

Data analysis and writing up the research

Above we have considered some of the research issues that need to be considered in relation to theory and the methods used to collect data. It is also necessary to consider the analysis of data and the writing up of research findings when we are thinking about the issues that pertain to research and 'race'/ethnicity.

The analysis of data is a time when the researcher has the opportunity to open up and interrogate their own understandings of 'race'/ethnicity, to consider, in ethnographic or qualitative work that has interview data, how 'race' comes to have meaning for people and comes to be present in their everyday interactions with people and the world. We can think of this as analysing data in order to see how 'race' and ethnicity are constituted in people's everyday and institutional worlds. It is also an opportunity to explore how specific contexts and localities create 'raced' and ethnic identities and actions (and how they affect what constitutes 'race', racism and ethnicity) and thus to challenge notions of research as a simple reflection of a real world (see Ramji, 2009: Chapter 5). Analysis is the 'active occasion' when meaning is produced (Ramji, 2009: 88). We have seen in Chapters 2 and 3, and above, that researchers can be complicit in reproducing insidious stereotypes about minority ethnic people (pathologizing people and giving them a negative value) if care is not taken in how the research study is conceptualized, conducted and data analysed and reported. It has been claimed in the past that White social science researchers have been involved in portraying minority ethnic people and groups as caricatures in their research accounts (Troyna and Carrington, 1989) and as agents in their own racial inequality (Ladner, 1975). It has also been claimed that they have been responsible for reproducing, for a White audience, a sense of minority ethnic people's 'oddness, differentness (and) exceptionality' while leaving Whiteness as an unexamined norm 'the natural, inevitable, ordinary way of being' (Dyer, 1988: 44).

The reporting of research thus leads to a consideration of the language used by writers (see comments above and in Chapter 2 about naming categories of people for example). It also leads us to a consideration of the actual construction of research accounts. The 'turn to language' in more post-structuralist theorizing in social science has meant that as well as attention being paid to how discourses construct or imbue the world in which we live (and constitute us as subjects), attention has been paid to how research accounts (thesis, research reports, journal articles, books) are themselves only pieces of writing and are as such constructions in themselves using conventions and rhetoric in order to convince us that they are the world that they describe as well as hiding how they are implicated in constituting the world they describe.

Chapter summary

In this chapter we have looked in some detail at an important and rather antagonistic debate between educational researchers and debates within the wider social science world in order to consider how theory and methodology are inexorably intertwined in research work. We have considered how theory affects the whole research enterprise and explicated how a difference in theoretical stance can affect research findings as well as considered how we should read and respond to research. This chapter has argued against a theoretical position that sees research as a positivistic, objective and rational enquiry and it has presented some recent discussions that have been rooted in a more post-structural understanding of the social world. This is the direction that research seems to be taking in relation to issues of 'race'/ethnicity and is the direction that would appear to produce interesting, fruitful research insights that help us understand how inequalities are reproduced and become constituted in everyday and institutional worlds.

Further reading

The debate

The following is an outline of the key papers, books and chapters that constitute the 'debate' or controversy:

Troyna and Carrington (1989), '"Whose side are we on?" Ethical dilemmas in research on 'race' and education', in R. Burgess (ed.) *The Ethics of Education Research*

Foster (1990a), *Policy and Practice in Multicultural and Antiracist Education*

Foster (1990b), 'Cases not proven: An evaluation of two studies of teacher racism', *British Educational Research Journal*, 16 (4), 335–49 (critiques Carrington and Wood (1983) 'Body talk', *Multiracial Education* 11 (2), 29–38 and Wright (1986), 'School processes: An ethnographic study', in Egglestone et al. (ed) *Education for Some*)

Wright (1990), 'Comments in reply to the article by P. Foster 'Cases not proven: An evaluation of two studies of teacher racism', *British Educational Research Journal*, 16 (4), 351–5

Foster (1991), 'Case still not proven: A reply to Cecile Wright', *British Educational Research Journal*, 17 (2), 165–70

Troyna (1991a), 'Children, 'race' and racism: The limitations of research and policy', *British Journal of Education Studies*, 39 (4), 425–36

Foster (1992a), 'Equal treatment and cultural difference in multi-ethnic schools: A critique of teacher ethnocentrism theory', *International Studies in the Sociology of Education*, 2 (1), 89–103 (critiques Gillborn (1990), *'Race', Ethnicity and Education: Teaching and Learning in Multi-Ethnic Schools* and Mac an Ghaill (1988), *Young, Gifted and Black: Student Teacher Relations in the Schooling of Black Youth*)

Foster (1992b), 'Teacher attitudes and Afro-Caribbean achievement', *Oxford Review of Education*, 18 (3), 269–81

Hammersley (1992a), 'A response to Barry Troyna's "Children, 'race' and racism: The limits of research and policy"', *British Journal of Education Studies*, 40(2), 174–7

Connolly (1992), 'Playing it by the rules: The politics of research in 'race' and education', *British Educational Research Journal*, 18 (2), 133–48

Blair (1992), 'Review of policy and practice in multicultural antiracist education', *European Journal of Intercultural Studies*, 2, 63–4

Foster (1993a), 'Some problems in establishing equality of treatment in multi-ethnic schools', *British Journal of Sociology*, 44 (3), 519–35 (critiques Green (1985), 'Multi-ethnic teaching and the pupils' self concepts', in *Swann Report*, 46–56)

Hammersley and Gomm (1993). 'A response to Gillborn and Drew on 'Race', class and school effects', *New Community*, 19 (2) January, 348–53 (critiques Gillborn and Drew (1992), 'Race', class and school effects', *New Community*, 18 (4), 551–65 and Smith and Tomlinson (1989), *The School Effect: A Study of Multi-Racial Comprehensives*)

Foster (1993b), '"Methodological purism" or "A defence against hype"? Critical readership in research in "race" and education', *New Community*, 19 (3) April, 547–52 (critiques Gillborn (1990), *'Race', Ethnicity and Education: Teaching and Learning in Multi-Ethnic Schools*)

Hammersley (1993b), 'Research and 'anti-racism': The case of Peter Foster and his critics', *British Journal of Sociology*, 44 (3) Sept, 429–48

Gomm (1993), 'Figuring out ethnic equity: A response to Troyna', *British Educational Research Journal*, 19 (2), 147–63 (critiques Troyna (1991b),'Underachievers or underrated? The experiences of pupils of South Asian origin in secondary schools', *British Educational Research Journal*, 17 (4), 361–76)

Troyna (1993a), 'Underachiever or misunderstood? A reply to Roger Gomm', *British Educational Research Journal*, 19 (2), 167–74

Hammersley (1993a), 'On methodological purism: A response to Barry Troyna', *British Educational Research Journal*, 19 (4), 339–41

Gomm (1995), 'Strong claims, weak evidence: A response to Troyna's 'Ethnicity and the organisation of learning groups', *Educational Research*, 37 (1), 79–86 (critiques Troyna (1992), 'Ethnicity and the organisation of learning groups: A case study', *Educational Research*, 34 (1), 45–55)

Troyna (1995) 'Beyond reasonable doubt? Researching 'race' in educational settings', *Oxford Review of Education*, 21 (4), 395–408

Some chapters/journal articles that refer back to the debate

Hammersley (1995), *The Politics of Social Research*, Sage, Chapter 4

Gillborn (1995), *Racism and Antiracism in Real Schools*, OUP, Chapter 1

Foster, Hammersley, Gomm (1996), *Constructing Educational Inequality*, Falmer

Connolly and Troyna (eds) (1998), *Researching Racism in Education* Preface and Introduction (Connolly); Chapter 2 (Hammersley); Chapter 3 (Gillborn)

Pilkington (1999), 'Racism in schools and ethnic differentials in educational achievement: A brief comment on a recent debate', *British Journal of Sociology of Education*, 20 (3), 411–17

Theory/methodology/analysis

For more on the relationship between theory and methodology see Ramji (2009), *Researching Race: Theory, Methods and Analysis*, Chapter 2. For more on analysis see Chapter 5 of the same book.

5

Taking Action around 'Race' and Ethnicity

Chapter Outline

Introduction

In two previous chapters we have seen how 'race' and ethnicity do play a part in people's educational experiences and outcomes. We have seen that some ethnically defined groups of young people achieve well in school while others achieve poorly and would appear to be disadvantaged by the education system. In this chapter we will consider the actions that have been taken by official 'majority' organizations and institutions (e.g. government, local education authorities and schools) in order to address this disadvantage and the actions taken by minorities themselves through initiatives such as complementary or supplementary schooling and through taking a stand against racism, disadvantage and complacency in official quarters.

Government education policy

Reflection activity

Central government policy on ethnicity and education has never been underpinned by a clearly formulated coherent philosophy. Nor has it generally involved specific policies aimed at ethnic minorities (Pilkington, 2003: 159).

Make a note of any government policies you know of that have been aimed at making educational provision for minority ethnic pupils or addressing educational disadvantage in school.
Do you agree with Pilkington's statement?

The 1960s

During the 1960s, despite the era being considered one of liberal reform in education, the government had very little explicit policy or planning in place regarding provision for 'immigrant' pupils. Responses from government and LEAs were limited to 'bussing', the provision of Section 11 funding and the teaching of English.

'Bussing' was introduced in 11 LEAs in 1965 in response to a government circular, and then an official policy recommendation, that no school or classroom should have more than 30 per cent 'immigrant' pupils and where this was the case these pupils should be dispersed, or 'bussed', to other schools (Tomlinson, 2008: 21). The policy was abandoned 10 years later when it was ruled in court that the practice was discriminatory and therefore illegal (Tomlinson, 2008: 30). There were many criticisms of 'bussing' and two LEAs with large numbers of 'immigrant' pupils refused to take part in this practice (Tomlinson, 2008: 30). Troyna and Williams describe 'bussing' as the 'forced removal of black students' from their local schools (Troyna and Williams, 1986: 18) and note that this occurred without any consultation with Black parents and prevented relationships being established between Black parents and their children's schools. Dispersal policy, they claim, was enacted due to concerns about the effect of the presence of 'immigrant' children on the educational attainment of White pupils and a belief that by being dispersed 'immigrant' pupils would acquire English more quickly (Troyna and Williams, 1986: 19).

Section 11 grants were provided by the Home Office to LEAs to make any special provision that was required due to 'the presence within their area of substantial numbers of immigrants from the Commonwealth whose language and customs differ(ed) from those of the community' (Local Government Act, 1966: S11 cited by Tomlinson, 2008: 31). The money was generally used by LEAs to provide English lessons for pupils and parents. As Tomlinson notes, this was the only money that the government provided during the 1960s,

1970s and 1980s to alleviate 'racial disadvantage' (Tomlinson, 2008: 31). Section 11 funding became EMAG (the Ethnic Minority Achievement Grant) in 1999.

The teaching of English to 'immigrant' pupils was seen as a priority by the government. In addition to Section 11 funding, short courses for teaching English as a Second Language (ESL) were set up and materials were developed for teachers and specialist ESL teachers. As part of an Urban Aid programme from 1968 money was provided in some LEAs for separate language centres for 'immigrant' children in which they could learn English before entering mainstream schools (see Tomlinson, 2008: 32). However, such segregated provision was found to isolate 'immigrant' children both linguistically and socially and to fail to provide for their English language and educational development. The findings of the enquiry by the Commission for Racial Equality in Calderdale in 1986 ended the provision of separate language centres and led to 'immigrant' children being placed directly into mainstream schools (Department for Education and Science, 2006).

The 1970s

During the 1970s there was an increasing pressure on central government to develop policies and to provide funding to support the educational needs of ethnic minority pupils (Tomlinson, 2008: 52). The government made positive responses but in effect few policies were actually developed. The government insisted on considering ethnic minority pupils within the category disadvantaged pupils, believing that the needs of these groups of learners were the same (Tomlinson, 2008: 53–4). At the same time, politicians were wary of discussing and showing any support for providing resources and policies to support ethnic minority children in school as the national political context was such that any explicit action in support of ethnic minorities was likely to be an act of political suicide (Tomlinson, 2008: 67). This was an era of talk of 'swamping' and of 'immigrants' taking and using limited national resources such as housing and welfare benefits and the openly expressed concerns of White parents. As a result, despite a recognition of racial disadvantage in many quarters (e.g. a Race Relations Act was introduced in 1976 that made discrimination unlawful in education, housing, employment, training, public services and advertising and a Green Paper was introduced in 1977 which noted the need for curriculum change in order to acknowledge the presence and needs of ethnic minority children), it was left to LEAs, schools and parents to get on with tackling these issues and making changes (Tomlinson, 2008: 53–4). The government did continue the provision of English language teaching to ethnic minority pupils as it was seen as essential to the assimilationist understandings of the time that ethnic minority pupils learnt English in order to be able to integrate. While there was a recognition in some quarters (e.g. the Bullock Report in 1975 entitled 'A Language for Life') that ethnic minority pupils should not be required to forget about their other languages there was no official provision made for the development and support of children's mother tongue or heritage languages (this was done by parents, see below) (Tomlinson, 2008: 59–60).

The 1980s

The 1980s saw a radical restructuring of education with the centralization of the education system and the introduction of market forces, competition and 'choice' through ten parliamentary acts culminating in the Education Reform Act (ERA) (1988). At the same time there was a move away from seeing ethnic minority learners as subsumed within the category of 'disadvantaged pupils' to a growing recognition that the education system needed to be responsive to the needs of a multi-ethnic society (Tomlinson, 2008: 71) and that racial discrimination needed to be combated (Tomlinson, 2008: 82). The government, by this time Conservative, supported curriculum developments in line with this and provided grants to support in-service teacher training (Tomlinson, 2008: 83). These curriculum developments were to encourage all pupils to develop tolerance of other 'races' and cultures as well as respect for other religions and so applied to 'mainly White' schools as well as those with high numbers of ethnic minority pupils. While 'mainly White schools' continued to see such issues as not applicable to them (see Gaine, 1987 and 1995 for a discussion of this), other teachers and teaching organizations, left with the responsibility for developing good practice, worked hard to establish a recognition that education for a multi-ethnic society needed to take place in all schools (see Tomlinson, 2008: 83). However, there was resistance to changing the curriculum in order to prepare all children for life in a multi-ethnic society from schools in areas of high ethnic minority settlement. This resistance was most famously represented by Ray Honeyford, the headmaster of a Bradford Middle school. He claimed that it was the responsibility of ethnic minorities to settle and integrate and denounced ethnic minority parents as the cause of any problems ethnic minority pupils might face in school. He rejected the claim that racism was the reason for ethnic minority pupils' underachievement in school, insisting instead that underachievement arose from the values of the home and from 'misguided radical teachers whose motives are basically political' (Honeyford, 1984: 31 cited in Troyna and Williams, 1986: 96). Tomlinson details how other LEAs attempted to make curriculum changes and how they were opposed by groups of White parents, heads and teachers (see Tomlinson, 2008: 89–91) and situates this within the denial by those on the Right that non-whites and 'alien cultures' could be included into any version of British heritage or identity (Tomlinson, 2008: 97). This version of Britishness, which focused on an imagined White, homogeneous Britain (often conflated to England), was also coming, in the late 1980s, to dominate education policy reforms (Gillborn, 1995: 1). Notions of 'our culture' and 'our way of life' became prevalent in policy formulation (see Gillborn, 1995: 21) with minority ethnic people positioned as an 'alien threat' having no place within a notion of Britishness or British society.

Two important reports were published during the 1980s: The Rampton Report (Department of Education and Science, 1981) and The Swann Report (Department of Education and Science, 1985). These reports arose out of the establishment of a Committee of Inquiry into the Education of Children from Ethnic Minority Groups in 1977. The

Committee was chaired first by Anthony Rampton who resigned after the interim report was published (in 1981) and then by Lord Swann. The Rampton Report collected evidence and made a number of recommendations regarding the education of West Indian children and was the first government report to openly refer to racism as a factor in West Indian pupils' underachievement in school (Tomlinson, 2008: 98). The Swann Report, entitled 'Education For All', is now considered by many to be the high point in advancing multicultural education (Tomlinson, 2008: 10), although it was critiqued for being premised on the view that racism was simply a product of ignorance and individual prejudice (e.g. Troyna, 1993b: 6–7) as well as for its acceptance of 'cultural reasons' for underachievement. While the report noted the social and economic disadvantage experienced by many ethnic minority groups it also looked to the stability of the family and parental support as explanations for underachievement (Pilkington, 2003: 141). Many commentators were dissatisfied with this lack of attention to class (see Troyna, 1993b: 64). The Swann Report presented a range of evidence about the experiences and achievements of ethnic minority pupils and insisted that education had a role to play in 'laying the foundations for a genuinely pluralistic society' (Tomlinson, 2008: 84). The report acknowledged what it saw as the difficulty of promoting shared values in a nation while accommodating cultural and religious diversity (Tomlinson, 2008: 83). The government responded to the recommendations by creating Education Support Grants (Tomlinson, 2008: 84) but in other respects the report and its recommendations were effectively rejected by the then Minister for Education, Sir Keith Joseph, on the day of its publication (Gillborn, 2008: 74). While there was support for many of the initiatives in schools and LEAs, despite the indifference of government and the hostility of the media to the report's recommendations, this support was cut short by the rise of the New Right and the introduction of the ERA in 1988. Commentators generally see the Swann Report as advocating a cultural pluralist approach (see below for a discussion of cultural pluralism, assimilation, multicultural and anti-racist education), while still retaining many elements of an assimilationist approach, and advocating a form of multicultural education (Pilkington, 2003: 162). Pilkington (2003: 162) describes Swann as containing some elements of anti-racist education while Troyna and Williams (1986: 119) claim that it demonstrated a limited understanding of racism and therefore made naïve policy recommendations.

Teacher training became a focus in the 1980s as it was recognized that teachers were often ignorant or very unsure of how to provide an appropriate education for the increasingly diverse learners in their classrooms and how to prepare their pupils to live in a multiracial society (Tomlinson, 2008: 85). Training was offered to teacher trainers themselves, while teaching unions, such as the National Union of Teachers (NUT), provided guidance on combating racism and on multicultural and anti-racist education to teachers. At the same time both the Council for the Accreditation of Teacher Education and the Council for National Academic Awards were required to make sure that all teacher training courses included training for teaching in a multicultural society (Tomlinson, 2008: 85–6).

The 1990s and the new century

During the 1990s the restructuring of the education system continued as did the shift to talking about history, culture, heritage, religion and nationhood instead of 'race' and racism (Gillborn, 1995: 29). When New Labour was elected in 1997, education policy continued to be based on the principles of consumer demand and market forces. In this period tensions around immigration rose to the surface again: this time in relation to refugees and asylum seekers and White economic migrants from Eastern Europe (Tomlinson, 2008: 100, 123). There was also an increasing majority unease regarding Islam and British Muslims. The term 'islamophobia' was coined to describe this phenomenon (seen to be arising from White majority fears regarding the perceived radicalization of some Muslim groups, particularly young British Muslim men). However, racism against all ethnic minority groups continued to be an issue and a series of studies conducted in White rural counties and shires found that racism was rife in these locations despite a majority view that, to quote Gain again, 'there was no problem here' (Gaine, 1987, 1995; Derbyshire, 1994; Jay, 1992). (Despite this, in the popular consciousness it was White deprivation that was becoming the dominant issue). While there was an insistence politically, that policies should be 'colour-blind' (Tomlinson, 2008: 124), there was evidence that the government's 'choice agenda' was not acting in a 'colour-blind' way and that it was creating inequalities for minority ethnic pupils leading in some instances to increasing segregation and unfair treatment in training and education (Tomlinson, 2008: 107). Tomlinson describes minority ethnic groups as paying 'the ethnic penalty' in education (Tomlinson, 2008: 107). Gillborn claims that while 'race' and racism were rarely, if ever, mentioned in education policy, such policy still had a negative affect on the experiences and possible outcomes for some groups of minority ethnic pupils: in effect, existing inequalities were disguised, sustained and promoted in education policy at this time (Gillborn, 1995: 18). While achievement in school was considered to be rising for all groups of pupils, the gap was widening between the most successful and the least successful groups (see Chapter 2). At the same time, the support that had been provided by the government to meet the needs of minority ethnic pupils and to develop a curriculum for a multi-ethnic society began to disappear (Tomlinson, 2008: 124). Section 11 funding was scaled down and the training of teachers for a multi-ethnic society began to diminish. Tomlinson claims that during this period OFSTED were failing to report on race equality during school inspections (Tomlinson, 2008: 132). In this context of funding cuts and an increasing hostility to curriculum change, the government chose to ignore rising racial tensions in schools (Tomlinson, 2008: 101) and society. Gillborn speaks of the 1990s as a time when there was a return to 'deracialized' education policy and as a time in which 'race' and 'racism' were replaced by 'proxy concepts' such as culture, religion, nationhood, language and 'our way of life', thus creating a policy terrain 'in which race equality is effectively removed from the agenda' (Gillborn, 1995: 29 and 21, 26–7).

It was the murder, by White youths, of a Black 18-year-old student Stephen Lawrence in 1993 that finally forced some political and public focus on the deeply ingrained racism in British society and its public institutions. The Macpherson Report (1999), that arose from the public enquiry that was eventually held into the flawed police handling of the murder investigation (a public enquiry that was initially refused), made an explicit reference to 'institutional racism' when discussing the failings of the police force (see below for a discussion of what was meant by institutional racism). It also made it very clear that it was not just the police force that needed to address these issues but that education also had a very important part to play. The thrust of the report's findings in relation to 'institutional racism' was that publicly accountable institutions such as the police force and the education system could be and were 'institutionally racist' in that, whether wittingly or unwittingly, they were implicated in reproducing racial inequalities through the manner in which they operated. The enquiry and report led in turn to the Race Relations Amendment Act (2000) which made it a statutory duty that all public institutions, including schools, colleges and universities, looked at their practices and took steps, through developing race equality schemes, to address any of their practices and procedures that resulted in racial inequality. In schools this meant monitoring all school procedures and activities for signs of bias (e.g. in assessment procedures and results) and developing a written policy of race equality (Gillborn, 2008: 128). Despite the requirements of the Race Relations Amendment Act, both Tomlinson (2008: 146) and Gillborn (2008: 128) claim that the response in educational institutions regarding the development of policy promoting race equality was very poor.

Reflection activity

If you are a teacher or school governor or if you are attending a university or college:
  What policies and monitoring procedures are in place in your institution?
  Are they followed?
  How effective do you think they are?
  In what way are they effective or ineffective?
  Would you agree with Tomlinson and Gillborn that the response to promoting race equality in your institution has been poor?

The term 'institutional racism' was first used by Carmichael and Hamilton in the US in their book *Black Power* published in 1967. In the book they contrasted 'individual racism' with 'institutional racism' and, alongside others writing at this time, considered how the interrelationships between institutions reinforced racial inequality (Troyna and Williams, 1986: 49–50)

The concept was in use in Britain from 1971 where it was utilized to describe how British institutions 'effectively maintain(ed) inequality between members of different groups . . . even if operated partly by individuals who (were) not themselves racist in their beliefs' (Dummett, 1973: 131 cited in Troyna and Williams, 1986: 51). In 1982, Fenton utilized the term to describe how racism was to be found in the 'regular practices, rules and the enduring features of society' (1982: 59 cited in Troyna and Williams, 1986: 52) and Troyna and Williams included an extensive discussion (and critique) of institutional racism and education in their book *Racism, Education and the State* in 1986 (see pages 52–9).

The term moved into popular discourse with the publication of the Macpherson Report in 1999 at the end of the public inquiry, chaired by the High Court Judge William Macpherson, into the murder of Stephen Lawrence (see above). The concept of 'institutional racism' was used by Macpherson to describe,

> . . . the collective failure of an organisation to provide an appropriate and professional service to people because of their colour, culture or ethnic origin. It can be seen or detected in processes, attitudes, and behaviour which amount to discrimination through unwitting prejudice, ignorance, thoughtlessness and racist stereotyping which disadvantage minority ethnic people. (Macpherson, 1999: para. 6.34 cited in Pilkington, 2003: 85)

What is of interest is that the definition retains the element of non-intentionality, through the use of the term 'unwitting', that appeared in earlier British writing, i.e. the idea that racism need not be intentional to be racism. As Gillborn states, what is important is not intention but outcomes (2008: 123). The definition of whether something was racist lay in the power of the person or group – if they felt that an action was racist in its outcomes then it was racist. This is stated in the Macpherson Report in the following way, 'A racist incident is any incident which is perceived to be racist by the victim or any other person' (Macpherson, 1999: 328–9 cited in Gillborn, 2008: 123). (However, the notion of the interrelationship between institutions and how they operate together to perpetuate racial disadvantage has been replaced in Macpherson by a focus on racism within an institution such as the police force or education).

Reflection activity

Troyna and Williams suggested in 1986 that looking at education through the lens of 'institutional racism' would enable us to see and acknowledge how the ordinary assessment procedures used in schools resulted in large numbers of ethnic minority children being consigned to Special Education units or streamed out of exam entry and directed towards vocational rather than academic subjects (1986: 45).

What would looking at your school, college or university through the lens of 'institutional racism' reveal?

How do you feel about using this concept to consider your institution?

Arising out of the Macpherson Report, and its focus on institutional racism, was the Race Relations (Amendment) Act in 2000 which required public institutions, including education, 'to work towards and monitor race equality treatment and outcomes' (Tomlinson, 2008: 132).

By the end of the century, there was an increasingly articulated commitment by government (now New Labour) to the principles of social and racial justice and to a view of a national identity that recognized diversity and the fact that the UK was made up of a number of minority groups 'whose claims to be part of the society could not be ignored' (Tomlinson, 2008: 132). At the same time the concerns about community and national cohesion and what constituted a British identity continued. The notion of 'citizenship' moved to central stage with its focus on rights and responsibilities. In relation to taking action around supporting the needs and rights of minority ethnic learners, the newly-formed Social Exclusion Unit briefly examined the over-exclusion of Black pupils from school and Section 11 funding was discontinued – a new source of financial support was provided directly to schools through the Ethnic Minority Achievement Grant (and administered by the Department for Education and Employment rather than the Home Office). This change indicated the focus the government wished to place upon ethnicity and 'race' as factors in the underachievement of certain minority groups in education, insisting that schools and LEAs were to consistently collect statistics regarding the educational achievement of all pupils and monitor the achievement of minority ethnic pupils in order to identify any issues that were preventing these pupils from doing well in school. In addition, all LEAs were to use this data in order to set targets for minority ethnic groups and raise achievement in this way. Another action taken by government was to introduce the Pupil Level Annual School Census (PLASC), in 2002. This was the collection of key information about each pupil (for example, their gender, ethnicity and socio-economic status – disadvantage being measured through entitlement to free school meals) together with information about their achievement in national tests on starting school and as they progressed through school. This made it possible for schools, LEAs and national government to know the achievement of each pupil year on year and therefore to be able to explore the patterns of ethnic minority achievement more systematically than before. Another response from government at this time was to offer state funding to Muslim schools so that they could be established in the same way as other faith schools in the state sector.

In addition to these actions, the government also produced a plethora of policy documents relating to ethnicity, 'race' and achievement in school. OFSTED commissioned two reports on ethnic minority achievement in education (Gillborn and Gipps, 1996; Gillborn and Mirza, 2000). They also published:

OFSTED (1999) *Raising the Attainment of Minority Ethnic Pupils: School and LEA Responses*

OFSTED (2001) *Managing Support for the Attainment of Pupils from Ethnic Minority Groups*

OFSTED (2002) *Achievement of Black Caribbean Pupils* (Secondary Schools)

OFSTED (2002) *Support for Minority Ethnic Achievement: Continuing Professional Development*

OFSTED (2002) *Unlocking Potential: Raising Ethnic Minority Attainment at Key Stage 3*

OFSTED (2003) *The Education of Asylum-Seeker Pupils*

OFSTED (2004) *Achievement of Bangladeshi Heritage Pupils*

OFSTED (2004) *Managing the Ethnic Minority Achievement Grant: Good Practice in Primary Schools*

OFSTED (2004) *Managing the Ethnic Minority Achievement Grant: Good Practice in Secondary Schools*

While the Department for Education (and Skills – DfES or Science – DES or Employment – DfEE depending on the date and government) published the following:

DfEE (1998) *Making the Difference: Teaching and Learning Strategies in Successful Multi-Ethnic Schools* (Blair and Bourne)

DfES (2002) *Removing the Barriers: Raising Achievement Levels for Minority Ethnic Pupils*

DfES (2003) *Minority Ethnic Attainment and Participation in Education and Training* (Bhattacharyya et al.)

DfES (2003) *Raising the Achievement of Gypsy Traveller Pupils – A Guide to Good Practice*

DfES (2004) *Understanding the Educational Needs of Mixed Heritage Pupils* (Tikley et al.)

DfES (2004) *Aiming High: Guidance on Supporting the Education of Asylum Seeking and Refugee Children*

DfES (2004) *Aiming High: Supporting the Effective Use of EMAG*

DfES (2004) *Aiming High: Understanding the Educational Needs of Minority Ethnic in Mainly White Schools*

DfES (2005) *Ethnicity and Education: The Evidence on Minority Ethnic Pupils*

DfES (2006) *Special Educational Needs and Ethnicity: Issues of Over- and Under-Representation*

DfES (2006) *Evaluation of Aiming High: African-Caribbean Achievement Project*

In the first decade of the new century, education under the New Labour government came to be increasingly presented as central to improving the competitiveness of the national economy as well as being a key institution for creating a cohesive society with a focus on standards. Work in schools around multiculturalism and anti-racism became subsumed into 'citizenship' with a focus on the rights and responsibilities of citizens within the nation. Some claim that the focus on raising standards supported all learners; however, the majority of academic commentators see that education since 1997 (under New Labour) as continuing or returning to being 'colour blind' and involved in increasing the reproduction of inequalities. This is picked up on below.

Critiques of government action

The above account gives a brief overview of the way in which government has taken action in relation to racial disadvantage in education since the 1960s. Many commentators have argued that considering the seriousness of the issues, and the levels of inequality revealed to be inherent in the educational system for minority ethnic pupils, there has been a lack of engagement by government in tackling racism, discrimination and the underachievement of certain groups in education as well as a lack of a coherent philosophy (Pilkington, 2003: 159). Some of these critiques will now be considered.

Troyna and Williams (1986) are among those who condemned repeated government failure to confront and tackle the issue of racism in education. They argued that successive governments took a 'deracialized' approach to educational policy and thus failed to effectively tackle racism and disadvantage.

Archer and Francis argue that,

> . . . issues of 'race'/ethnicity have been subject to a pernicious turn in policy discourse which removes the means for engaging with inequalities, naturalises differences in achievement between ethnic groups and places the responsibility or blame for achievement differentials with minority ethnic individuals. This discourse effectively denies racism as a potential cause of differences in achievement and hides inequalities within congratulatory public statements. (Archer and Francis, 2007: 1–2)

Gillborn and Mirza (2000: 28–9) argue that target setting by LEAs can lead to increased inequality as the targets set for the percentage of White pupils who will gain A–C grades is often such that even if the African-Caribbean pupils (or other groups such as Pakistani pupils) were to make their target they would still be underachieving in relation to White pupils. In this way Gillborn and Mirza argue that racial inequality is built into the system and into policy. Thus, once again government actions to tackle underachievement are presented as resulting in increased inequality.

At the same time, Gillborn (2008) and Archer and Francis (2007) argue that in government policy documents and briefings to the press, when discussing achievement, the government has played down the inequalities that exist between groups in their attempt to talk up the success that their policies are having in raising achievement and standards overall (Gillborn, 2008: 65–7; Archer and Francis, 2007: 1–2).

Gillborn and Youdell (2000)and Gillborn (2008) have mounted the strongest criticism of government policy in relation to challenging disadvantage and racism.

Example of research: Gillborn and Youdell (2000), *Rationing Education: Policy, Practice, Reform and Equity*

Gillborn and Youdell consider what happens to government education policy when it is put into practice in schools: they are interested in how policy 'plays out' in real school contexts with a particular focus on the impact of this policy on race equality (Gillborn and Youdell, 2000: 33). They discuss the education policy introduced by New Labour since their election success in 1997. Their main argument is that while policy initiatives like 'Excellence in Schools' explicitly discuss race inequalities in education and acknowledge that teachers and schools can themselves increase inequalities through their practices, 'race'/ethnicity remains as an 'add-on' issue in how policy issues are conceived. As a result, they claim, racial inequalities are likely to increase (Gillborn and Youdell, 2000: 28). They pay particular attention to government education policy and how it affects schools' assessment and selection practices. These are carefully described using data from their research schools. They show how government policy which expects to see a rise in the number of pupils gaining five or more A–C grade GCSEs at the end of compulsory schooling (what Gillborn and Youdell term 'the A–C economy') results in schools carefully sorting and selecting pupils based on their ability for particular sets, groups and exams so that they can raise the number of pupils gaining A–C grades. These decisions by teachers are based on their assessments of pupils' ability through using standardized tests and through their own judgement and experience of pupils. Gillborn and Youdell show how these assessments can, and are, in turn, based on an elitist notion of innate, or fixed, ability where intelligence is understood as something that is there or not there in a person, rather than ability as contextual (Gillborn and Youdell refer to this as the 'new IQism'). Such assessments are also based on teachers' own assumptions about racial/ethnic groups (see Chapter 3 of this book) and in this way 'elitist and racist assumptions come to lie at the heart of processes of selection' (Gillborn and Youdell, 2000: 33). The tiering of GCSE exams also has similar results in that teachers have to make decisions about who should be entered for the higher grade papers in GCSE subjects and who should be entered for the lower grade papers. This also has an effect on what schools do. 'Teachers call on what they 'know' about students' abilities but there is the potential for teachers' judgements of 'ability' to be shaped by wider social forces such as gendered, classed and racialised notions of appropriate behaviour, motivation and attitude' (Gillborn and Youdell, 2000: 200). Together with the government policy of publishing league tables to show how well each school is doing in gaining A–C grades for its pupils, these policies (introduced by the government to raise standards and benefit all pupils by ensuring that they are provided with a good education) increase racial inequalities according to Gillborn and Youdell (2000: 33).

All of the above critiques of government action to address racial inequality in education claim that policy has become 'colour blind', i.e. it does not focus specifically on racism and race inequality nor contain specific policies to address these issues. At the same time these commentators argue, the 'colour blind' policies that are introduced that are supposed to benefit all pupils and raise achievement are working to increase racial inequality rather than to eradicate it. However, as Pilkington argues, it is possible to see the policies introduced by New Labour since 1997 in a more positive light (Pilkington, 2003: 166). There has been for the first time a systematic and explicit focus on issues of monitoring and achievement in relation to minority ethnic groups of pupils (e.g. through the introduction of EMAG and changes to the way in which OFSTED inspected for these issues) as well as the setting of targets which has at least required some notion of accountability from schools and LEAs. There have been clear statements and commitments made publicly to racial equality and there has been a raising of expectations about schools and what they deliver. It can be argued that while Gillborn and Youdell can rightly show how racial inequalities are produced and reproduced within schools in the implementation of national education policy, their account makes the mistake of claiming that these processes and practices arise out of the 'colour blind' policy initiatives of the late 1990s. Yet all of the practices and processes that they describe were present in secondary and primary schools in the 1970s and 1980s; they are a persistent feature of any educational landscape that includes any form of national assessment either during or at the end of schooling and which is founded on understanding pupils in terms of their 'natural' ability. While many of the pronouncements of government since the late 1990s may be little more than pronouncements, one of the key things that these pronouncements have allowed for, and a feature that is ignored by the critiques of government policy during this time, is the creation of some 'discursive space' in which practitioners and activists who wish to challenge racial inequalities in school and work towards addressing racial disadvantage in achievement can operate and make the case for something to be done. If there is a policy statement making a commitment to racial equality or a requirement for monitoring and accountability then it is easier for practitioners to manoeuvre in order to make these things happen.

Reflection activity

To what extent do you agree with the statement made above?

A much stronger critique of government policy has been mounted more recently, a critique that would reject much of what has been suggested above.

In *Racism and Education: Coincidence or Conspiracy* (2008), Gillborn argues that instead of acknowledging and trying to eradicate racial disadvantage in education, governments have focused on social control and assimilation, giving in to the fears and feelings of White people regarding social cohesion and protecting their own political careers at the same time (2008: 86). But more than this, Gillborn argues that the English education system is based on 'white supremacy' (Gillborn, 2008: 36) and that racism is 'an ingrained feature of our landscape' (Delgado and Stefancic, 2000: xvi cited in Gillborn, 2008: 27). He does not present government education policy in terms of a lack of effectiveness nor in terms of government indifference to racial inequalities but government as actively creating and supporting a system that perpetuates racial inequalities. He gives as an example the way in which government policy regarding assessment creates and perpetuates racial inequality. He argues, for example, the assessment system in England is rigged so that when Black children succeed, as they used to in 'baseline assessments' at the start of schooling, the assessments are 're-engineered' so that Black children fail, as they did when 'baseline assessments' were changed to 'Foundation Stage Profiles' in 2003 (Gillborn, 2008: 91, 99 108; 117). In considering policies regarding assessment in schools generally, he argues that selection processes within schools have a racist impact, inscribing White domination from the start of schooling (see Chapter 5 of Gillborn, 2008 for a full account). For Gillborn, White people, and government, actively construct and legitimize racist inequalities in education (Gillborn, 2008: 4). Rather than analyse the ways in which the government failed to act to address racial inequalities in education, Gillborn analyses the ways in which the government actively creates and perpetuates racial inequalities in education. In doing this he utilizes concepts from Critical Race Theory (CRT) and discusses government policy in relation to the CRT concepts of 'interest convergence' and 'contradiction closing cases'.

The concept of 'interest convergence' describes how advances in policy to address race inequality only come about when such changes are also in the interest of White people (Gillborn, 2008: 32). 'Contradiction closing cases' are those that appear to be landmark victories for racial equality, for example the Macpherson Report and the subsequent Race Relations Amendment Act in 2000, which presaged huge changes in national and local policy responses to institutional racism. Such cases are referred to as 'contradiction closing cases' because they occur when the contradiction between the espoused values of a society and the real, everyday experiences of people becomes too noticeable.

> . . . these cases come around when there is a contradiction between, on the one hand, the public rhetoric, the national story that we are the land of the free, that we have equal opportunities, that racism is only something that happens occasionally through really nasty far right groups. When that rhetoric is contradicted by the reality something has to change, the contradiction has to be closed. (Gillborn, 2009: 6)

However, such cases, according to this analysis, rarely lead to any real, lasting change. A claim could be made, for example, that proposals in the new Equality Act (2010) support the argument that major reforms and landmark cases rarely lead to any lasting change. It is proposed that the new Act makes no requirement that schools or Local Authorities need draw up equality policies (a cornerstone of the Race Relations Amendment Act 2000) but need only publish 'equality objectives' and that these 'objectives' need not be in accordance with national priorities if there is evidence that there is no local- or school-level need (Richardson, 2010: 10).

A return to 'disadvantage'

In the last few years, in policy discussions and proposals, there has been an increasing emphasis on class, poverty and disadvantage rather than on 'race'/ethnicity, in discussions of achievement, relative achievement and achievement gaps. This is reminiscent in many ways of the focus on 'disadvantage' noted in the 1970s by Tomlinson (2008 see above).

What has emerged is a new focus on White working class disadvantage and poverty as inequalities that are to be tackled rather than those associated with 'race'/ethnicity. This can be seen in the way that, according to Rutter, policy makers and commentators 'have increasingly articulated the view that white, working-class communities have been neglected by government' (Rutter, 2010: 5) and in the way that both the new Equality Bill and the Communities and Local Governments' new race equality strategies place an emphasis on narrowing socio-economic disadvantage and directing attention to class and income as factors in determining opportunity (Rutter, 2010: 5–6). This re-emphasis on class, according to Rutter, has led to some organizations, such as the NUT in their report *Opening Locked Doors: Educational Underachievement and White Working Class Young People* (2010), to argue for just one single ring-fenced fund to support all children experiencing unequal outcomes in education 'irrespective of their ethnic origins' (Rutter, 2010: 6). Even the Department for Children, Schools and Families (DCSF), before the 2010 election, began a consultation on the future of school funding and suggested that 'schools will be able to use monies previously used for ethnic minority pupils to target any under-performing pupil' (Rutter, 2010: 6).

At the same time, recent Local Authority research in Lambeth, London, (Demie, 2010), on ethnic groups and underachievement has begun to focus on White working-class under-achievement and this has gained national attention (Davies, 2010: 2). A conclusion reached through this research was that,

> What is needed from national policy makers is to commit new ring-fenced additional funding to target white working class pupils as a group without reducing current funding to minority ethnic groups. (Demie, 2010: 25)

It is noticeable here that White pupils are presented in terms of their class while all other pupils are only presented in terms of their 'race'/ethnicity. This is a concern expressed in the NUT report and by the National Association for Language Development in the Curriculum (NALDIC) about many current policy discussions (National Association for Language Development in the Curriculum, 2010: 26).

In the presentation of the Lambeth research it also states that, 'White working class people interviewed felt that no-one (was) listening or speaking for them' (Demie, 2010: 25). This is a view that is increasingly articulated. NALDIC cite as an example a recent article in the Times Educational Supplement (TES) and correctly point out that such views ignore the fact that White working-class pupils do receive support through targeted funding aimed at deprived areas (NALDIC, 2010: 26). Gillborn has been very articulate in condemning this turn to making the White working class the new 'victims' (see Gillborn, 2009: 1–2). In addition he argues that,

> . . . there is a very great danger at the moment that the focus on social class will be used to silence a concern with race equality and that the effect is that racism is effectively removed from the policy agenda. (Gillborn, 2009: 1)

It would certainly seem the case that the new coalition government's proposed 'Pupil Premium' in England and Wales, through which additional funding to support (economically) disadvantaged pupils will be allocated to schools, and the concurrent threat to the Ethnic Minority Achievement Grant, bears out this trend to focus on poverty and disadvantage and not the need to address racial disadvantage in the education system.

Conceptualizing national and local policy

While, as we have seen above, there is disagreement about the extent to which current government can be critiqued, there is agreement among commentators that government policy (at national and local level) can be understood as passing through different phases, founded upon different understandings or expectations about the relationship of minority ethnic groups to a notion of British society. Three phases are usually identified – assimilation, integration and cultural pluralism (Troyna and Carrington, 1990: 20, cited in Pilkington, 2003: 159) although there are overlaps between them and elements of each can be seen in operation at the same time in whichever period of education history considered.

Assimilation

As we have already seen above, in the 1960s the government expectation, or underlying philosophy, was that 'immigrants' and 'immigrant' children would assimilate. To this end English language programmes were offered as these children's lack of English was seen as the prime obstacle to this assimilation taking place. Once English had been acquired it was expected that 'immigrant' children would be 'absorbed within the overall school population' (Pilkington, 2003: 160). It was this expectation that also led to the policy of bussing in an attempt to disperse 'immigrant' children across a wide number of schools (and so prevent any school becoming 'predominantly immigrant in character' (Swann, 1985: 192, cited in Pilkington, 2003: 160) thereby aiding the assimilation of 'immigrant' children into the mainstream, majority society. As Pilkington argues, this approach, which prevailed throughout the 1960s, was based on a number of questionable assumptions, namely, that only a few changes were needed in the education system to cater for the needs of 'immigrant children', that the problems that 'immigrant' children might face in the education system were only caused by their lack of proficiency in English, and that assimilation, which expected 'immigrants' to change and to lose their languages, cultural practices and identities, was what was wanted and was achievable (Pilkington, 2003: 160–1). As Troyna and Carrington eloquently put it, such assimilationist approaches expected 'immigrant' children (and their families) to 'forget the culture of (their) parents, discard any affiliation to (their) ethnic background and blend in' (Troyna and Carrington, 1990: 2). Becoming British in terms of group membership and identity was an 'instead of' rather than a 'as well as' (Cashmore and Troyna, 1990: 8 cited in Troyna and Carrington, 1990: 2).

Integration

In the 1970s the underlying approach moved from assimilation to integration. The expectation was still that ethnic minority pupils and their families would become absorbed into British society but there was a shift towards recognizing the existence of cultural diversity and to an understanding that the educational support that ethnic minority pupils might need might be more that simply providing English lessons. There was a greater recognition of the benefits of cultural diversity and, as a result, multicultural education for all pupils became, as we have seen above, a policy approach. However, by the end of the 1970s it was becoming clear, through a recognition that certain ethnically defined pupil groups were seriously underperforming in the education system, that integrationism was also flawed as an approach. According to Pilkington, the setting up of a government inquiry into the causes of West Indian children's underachievement in 1977 (the Rampton Report and the subsequent Swann Report – see above) signalled the temporary end of the integrationist phase and the beginning of a phase of 'cultural pluralism' (Pilkington, 2003: 162).

Cultural pluralism

Cultural pluralism recognized that ethnic groups and communities could be assisted in 'maintaining their distinctive ethnic identities' while participating 'fully in shaping . . . society as a whole within a framework of commonly accepted values, practices and procedures' (Swann, 1985: 5, cited in Pilkington, 2003: 162). As noted above, the Rampton Report was the first to explicitly discuss racism as a factor in the schooling experiences of ethnic minority pupils and arising from both of the reports, during the 1980s, was a focus in local authority education policy on a multiculturalism that included elements of anti-racist education and which recognized and accepted a version of British society as a society made up of diverse groups. Cultural pluralism as a dominant understanding and approach did not, however, have the opportunity to flourish and develop for very long. As clashes emerged between multiculturalist and anti-racists (clashes that split school, education and Local Authority activists who were key to pushing forward policy and practice), the 'New Right' began to vociferously attack anti-racist policies and practices, and the notion of cultural pluralism. These attacks, which spilled over into the media, referred to advocates of such policies as the 'loony left'. At the same time the government began their introduction of education reform in the 1980s (culminating in the ERA 1988) that shifted the focus from equality of opportunity to one of standards and which removed power from LEAs and their ability to continue to develop policy based on a notion of cultural pluralism (Pilkington, 2003: 162–4). These educational reforms also heralded the introduction of a 'national curriculum', one which was to present a singular national identity based on 'the centrality of British history, . . . the English literary heritage, and the study of Christianity' (Nicholas Tate, 1966 quoted in Pilkington, 2003: 164) as well as the end of a cultural pluralist approach.

Alternative conceptualizations

Other commentators have come up with different conceptualizations to chronicle the shifts in government reaction and response. These include 'racially explicit' and 'racially inexplicit' government policy responses (Kirp, 1979, see Troyna and Carrington, 1990: 21–2) and 'deracialization' and 'racialization' processes (Reeves, 1983, developed by Troyna and Williams, 1986: 10) whereby government responses are understood as either 'deracialized' (in which policy 'deliberately eschews' overt references to race/'race' and ethnic minorities in its formulations and speaks of 'unraced' educational imperatives such as language tuition) or 'racialized' (in which explicit reference is made to 'race', such as in collecting data about ethnicity or the formulation of anti-racist education initiatives by LEAs). Racialized responses can be either benign or malevolent: benign responses would be those that focus on 'race' and racial categories for a good purpose (e.g. collecting recruitment data about ethnicity so that patterns of discrimination can be noticed and acted upon to ensure equality) while malevolent ones would be those that focused on 'race' for negative and discriminatory purposes (Troyna and Williams, 1986: 4). 'Deracialized' and 'racialized' seem useful concepts for discussing current policy shifts as outlined above.

School initiatives

In the above account we have considered some of the ways in which government, both national and local, responded to (or failed to respond to) racial disadvantage in education. In this section we will consider the actions taken in schools, and by activists in schools and further and higher education settings, in an attempt to respond to the needs of minority ethnic pupils, tackle racism and racial disadvantage and promote inclusion and social justice. This account will begin by looking in more depth at multicultural and anti-racist educational initiatives. These are understood by some to share similar characteristics and by others to be very distinct understandings and approaches.

Multicultural Education (MCE) and Anti-Racist Education (ARE):

Troyna and Williams (1986: 45) presented multicultural and anti-racist educational initiatives as distinct. Their description and definitions have been pulled together and presented in the table below as they clearly convey what they thought of as the differences between the initiatives. In reproducing their argument in this way it is possible to see clearly the main elements of multicultural and anti-racist initiatives as well as to consider one's own approach and practice. Although Troyna and Williams presented these descriptions as a way of delineating the differences between multiculturalism and anti-racism, the table can be used to explore the ways in which in our own practice and policies they also overlap. In some places what Troyna and Williams present has been added to. These comments do not have a page number so the fact that they are additions is clearly indicated.

Summary of Troyna and Williams's (1986: 29–30; 45–7) definitions and descriptions of the differences between multicultural and anti-racist education

	Multicultural Education	Anti-Racist Education
Key assumptions	–Learning about cultural/ethnic roots will improve the educational achievement of ethnic minority pupils (1986: 29). –Learning about culture and traditions will improve equality of opportunity (1986: 29). –'Learning about other cultures will reduce people's prejudice and discrimination towards ethnic minorities (1986: 29). Racism is an exceptional phenomenon and is irrational. Only individuals are racist, not institutions or structures.	–The formal and hidden curriculum in schools and other educational establishments needs to be critically explored in order to identify (and remedy) how racism and racist practices are produced and reproduced. –The focus should be on learning about the ethnic majority ('us') rather than ethnic minorities ('them') and exploring how practices, subject knowledge and materials in the classroom perpetuate racial disadvantage (as well as how these can be changed). –Learning about 'our' culture will reduce racism and challenge racist practices. –Racism does not arise simply from ignorance and is to be found operating through the structures and process of institutions as well as in wider society. It is a structural, institutional and societal issue and everyone is implicated in the reproduction of racial disadvantage.
Aims	Harmony and integration (1986: 47)	Racial equality and social justice (1986: 47)
Ways in which 'problem' conceptualized	–Presence of ethnic minorities is the problem (underachievement, lack of motivation, poor self-esteem, cultural differences) (1986: 46) ------------------------------------- –Ethnic minority pupils have identity problems (1986: 46). –Black families are not secure or stable enough (1986: 46).	–White racism is the problem (racist ideologies, racist practices, structural inequalities): the alienation of ethnic minority students is a result of racism (1986: 46). –'racism is an integral feature of the educational system' (1986: 46). ------------------------------------- –Anti-racists look at the origins and perpetuation of racism, the (re) production or racial inequality and institutional racism.

Contd.

	Multicultural Education	Anti-Racist Education
	–Ethnic minority culture is not respected or acknowledged in school (1986: 46).	
	–Families and pupils are materially deprived and disadvantaged (1986: 46).	
Remedial Policies	–Compensatory policies – remedying linguistic, cultural, identity deficits of ethnic minority pupils (1986: 47).	–Aim is for equality of outcome not access (1986: 47).
	–'development of a multicultural curriculum to increase students' motivation and commitment to achievement in school' and the re-education of White pupils out of prejudice (1986: 47).	–Policies are to change institutions not pupils (e.g. 'changes in the way pupils are assessed and allocated to ability streams', increase in the number of ethnic minority teachers, creation of school anti-racist policies that prevent/respond to racist incidents (1986: 47), the inclusion of ethnic minority parents and pupils in decision making).
		–Politicization of the curriculum so that all pupils (both White and Black) consider 'the origins and manifestations of racism' (1986: 47).
		–Curriculum used to challenge racial attitudes of staff and pupils (1986: 53)

Adapted from Troyna and Williams (1986), pp. 29–30 and pp. 45–7. Text that is not referenced are additions provided by the author.

Activity

Use the above chart to evaluate your own practice and your beliefs.

Do you find that you favour one approach over the other in your beliefs?

If you are a teacher, do you favour one approach over the other in your practice? What about your schools' policy and approach?

What is revealed by completing this activity? Are there any surprises?

Reflection activity

What action is required by a school in order to meet the needs of pupils living in a multi-ethnic society?

Multicultural education, as we have seen in the section above, emerged as a response to the perceived need to recognize and facilitate the integration of minority ethnic pupils into mainstream schooling and this was to be done through including and celebrating the cultures and practices of minority ethnic children present in the classroom. In this manner, the curriculum was to make some space for the recognition and celebration of the cultural diversity of the pupil group and of the British nation.

Reflection activity

What problems are raised by a multicultural approach in relation to:
- **culture?**
- **difference?**
- **racism?**
- **activities undertaken in the classroom?**
- **power?**

One of the major critiques of multicultural education arises from its conceptualization of culture (Troyna and Carrington, 1990: 2) which is presented as something fixed and unchanging and belonging to specific, and specified, cultural groups. As well as a tendency to veer into stereotyping, such a conceptualization ignores differences between people perceived to belong to the same culture, for example differences caused by social class, and ignores changing cultural identifications that people make, the multiple identities that they are able to call on in their everyday lives (see Chapter 1). Such a view obscures the way in which social categories are constructed. At the same time, multiculturalist approaches present racism as an individual prejudice born of ignorance which can be challenged and ended through this exposure to and celebration in schools of other cultures and lives (Troyna and Carrington, 1990: 1–2).

In contrast, for anti-racists, racism is not a problem of one or two individuals and their actions (the 'bad apple' theory) but something that is much wider and more pervasive and that 'is lodged squarely in the policies, structures, practices and beliefs of everyday life' (Thomas, 1984: 24 quoted in Troyna and Carrington, 1990: 3). Thus those taking an anti-racist approach place the focus of their activities very much on 'us' and 'the development of strategies which help children, and schools, to probe and challenge 'the manner in which racism rationalises and helps maintain injustice and the differential power accorded to groups in society' (Troyna, 1989: 182 quoted in Troyna and Carrington, 1990: 3).

Troyna and Carrington thus argue that anti-racist education 'refers to a wide range of organizational, curricular and pedagogical strategies which aim to promote racial equality and to eliminate attendant forms of discrimination and oppression, both individual and institutional' (Troyna and Carrington, 1990: 1). They present multicultural education as a response that had assimilationist roots, that arose from the understandings of White, middle-class professionals and which left unchanged the power relationship between Black and

White citizens (Troyna and Carrington, 1990: 20). Troyna and Williams famously described the curriculum outcomes of multicultural initiatives as 'the three Ss approach', namely, 'Saris, Samosas and Steel bands' (Troyna and Williams, 1986: 24) in which 'there was a determination to ensure that the lifestyles of black pupils were reflected (and respected) in curriculum models and teaching materials' (Troyna and Carrington, 1990: 20) but which resulted in a danger of tokenism, of the exoticization of ethnic minority lives and cultures and of stereotyping. Such initiatives failed to consider the impact of racism on minority ethnic pupils' lives and learning experiences. Brandt went as far as to claim that multicultural approaches contributed to racism within schools as they allowed the structures and process of racism that depended on notions of difference to continue (Gillborn, 2004: 36). Anti-racist educational initiatives were founded upon this consideration and commitment to challenge racism.

Anti-racist education initiatives called for changes to the school curriculum so that explicit teaching about racism was included as well as the development of policies and strategies to deal with racist incidents in school, the recruitment of more minority ethnic teachers and the democratization of school decision-making processes so that minority ethnic parents were involved (Troyna and Carrington, 1990: 1).

Reflection activity

What problems do you think are raised by an anti-racist approach?

Like multicultural education, anti-racist education was subject to many critiques, this time from within the academy and from the media and politicians. According to Troyna and Carrington (1990: 6–10) criticisms were made of the application and mismanagement of anti-racist education initiatives and their principles and the relevance. In some cases, ARE initiatives were found to have been poorly conceptualized and implemented and as being too simplistic – this being one of the important findings of the MacDonald Inquiry in its investigation of the murder of Ahmed Iqbal Ullah in a Burnage High School playground by a White pupil in 1986. The popular press reported the Inquiry findings as proof that anti-racism was damaging and some went as far as to claim that Ullah was a victim of anti-racist education policies (Gillborn, 2004: 41). Others, including the then British Prime Minister Margaret Thatcher, claimed that ARE initiatives hindered a good education by distracting pupils and teachers from what needed to be taught. The most vociferous critiques of ARE came from the 'New Right' who claimed that racism was not an institutional, nor structural, problem in education (or in society) and that it was not the place of schools to act as 'instruments for equalising' (Troyna and Carrington, 1990: 9) and to waste time and resources tackling racism. A prominent 'New Right' proponent of these 'anti-anti-racist' views was Honeyford (see above).

In addition to these critiques from the 'New Right', which were picked up by the tabloid media and became a dominant, well-rehearsed critique of what schools and local authorities were trying to achieve through anti-racist educational initiatives in their schools (constant references to the 'loony left' and denunciations of what some schools were including in their lessons), there were also critiques of anti-racist education from academics known and respected for their work and commitment to work on racism and racial equality in education and the social world (see Gillborn, 1995: 73–90). These critiques arose out of what was perceived to be an oversimplification of 'race', ethnicity and identity by the advocates of anti-racist education. Gilroy, for example, critiqued LEA anti-racist educational initiatives for what he termed their 'coat of paint' theorization of racism, i.e. racism that was something on the surface of social life that could be simply addressed and removed. His theorization placed 'race' and 'racism' at the heart of society, implicated in all aspects of social and political life, and thus not to be addressed as a blot or blemish on the surface of things (Gilroy, 1990: 73–74 cited in Gillborn, 1995: 77). Gilroy also critiqued the very notions of 'race' and racism and the dangers of an oversimplified notion of 'culture' that could and frequently did underlie anti-racist approaches to understanding and tackling racism. Gilroy argued for an understanding of 'race', ethnicity and racism that recognized the manner in which these means of categorization and social action were changeable and changing over time and how they depended on context for their meaning. He argued that anti-racist initiatives simplified too much what racism was, putting forward one idea, understanding or definition of racism rather than seeing racism as something contingent on the context (Gilroy, 1990: 72), and because of this making the mistake that there was a blue print or just one plan that needed to be called upon in order to tackle racism. He also argued that notions of culture were too simplified and that anti-racist initiatives were implicated in defining minority ethnic people as located within one unchanging culture and as all the same as each other as if there was 'some innate quality that characterizes the essence of a particular 'racial'/cultural group' (Gillborn, 1995: 78). He felt that such a theorization of culture and race reinforced majority notions about fixed differences between groups of ethnically/racially defined people and, at the same time, reduced minority ethnic peoples' lives to being always and only a response to racism, no other identity or social experience being allowed (Gilroy, 1990: 81).

Donald and Rattansi (1992) also critiqued anti-racist education initiatives for their too simplistic understanding of 'race' and culture and called for a more sophisticated notion of culture to be utilized. Modood criticized anti-racism for its focus on colour rather than culture, pointing out, in his writing about the experiences of South Asian people in Britain, that the use of the category of 'Black' in anti-racist initiatives excluded those, like the majority of British South Asians, who saw their identity (in relation to how it was defined and experienced as 'different' to that of White British people) in terms of culture rather than colour (Gillborn, 1995: 74–6).

Gillborn, in his commentary on these critiques (from what might be termed 'The New Left') reminds us that none of the above commentators wanted to see the abandonment of anti-racism per se in education (Gillborn, 1995: 83). What they were arguing against was what they perceived as a 'racial dualism' situated at the heart of many anti-racist initiatives. By 'racial dualism' is meant a view which sees the social world as divided neatly into Black and White. Many anti-racist education initiatives had at their heart a view of education and society in which people were either Black (and victims) or White (and perpetrators of racism). For our 'New Left' critics this was a serious weakness that needed to be abandoned. At the same time, critics like Gilroy and Donald and Rattansi were warning that steps had to be taken to guard against 'ethnicism' (Gillborn, 1995: 83) whereby ethnicity and culture are seen as an essentialized category and in which 'cultural needs are defined largely as independent of other social experiences centred around class, gender, racism or sexuality. This means that a group identified as culturally different is assumed to be internally homogeneous'(Brah, 1992: 129 cited in Gillborn, 1995: 84) and that other perceived differences between people based on class, gender and sexuality are ignored. In the work of Gilroy, Donald and Rattansi, this avoidance of essentialized identities is to be achieved through 'foregrounding the dynamic and fluid nature of contemporary cultures' (Gillborn, 1995: 84) and by recognizing the interlocking, criss-crossing or intermeshing of gender, class, 'race'/ethnicity and sexuality in everyday identities (as we have seen in the work of Youdell – see Chapter 3). Here we can make a link back to the discussion of theory in Chapter 1. What has been outlined is, as we recognize, located very much within the understandings and theorization of postmodern or post-structural understanding of the social world and 'race'and ethnicity, namely that the categories and ways that people are grouped are always being constructed and constituted, that they depend on context and that people do not have just one identity but many depending on context, time and place, and the social interactions taking place in that place. This is the view that culture, 'race', and racism are always changing, shifting and that people have multiple identities, rather than singular identities: there is no one dominant subjectivity. What is being argued here is that there is, and was, a need for any anti-racist initiatives to work with these more sophisticated theorizations while maintaining a recognition that the material realities of racism and power continue to exist and affect people's lives.

Actions taken by schools, teachers and teaching unions

A lot of the focus above has been on describing the distinctive qualities of multicultural and antiracist education initiatives and the critiques of such initiatives; however, it is worth noting that these initiatives, whether multicultural or antiracist, originally grew from the work of teachers who were concerned about and committed to doing something about racism in their schools and in society. It was only in the 1980s that LEAs began to consider this issue important enough to begin to devise and implement policies (Troyna and Williams, 1986: 2).

There have been a number of research studies that have focused on the development of anti-racist policies and practices in schools. Gillborn directs us to: Siraj Blatchford, 1994 (early years); Epstein, 1993; Connolly, 1994 (primary); Troyna, 1988; Gillborn, 1995 (secondary); Troyna and Selman, 1991; Neal, 1998 (Further and Higher Education) (all from Gillborn, 2004: 42). According to Gillborn one of the key issues to arise out of these studies is the complexity of developing anti-racist policies and the need for them to be context specific: there can be no blueprint for school change (Gillborn, 2004: 42).

Since the 1970s, the key role that teachers have in leading change and promoting initiatives that allow all pupils to challenge racism and/or prepare to live in a multiethnic society has been continually acknowledged. In the Rampton Report it was stated that teachers needed to lead the way in challenging racism (Epstein, 1993). Tomlinson has also described teachers as 'crucial agents' with a key role in 'educating the majority towards knowledge, understanding and acceptance of ethnic minorities' (Tomlinson, 2008: 37).

It is certainly the case that teachers have been active in developing a wealth of good practice in their schools as well as documentation and guides to multicultural and anti-racist education initiatives (see for example work of Dadzie, 2000; Knowles and Ridley, 2006). A great deal of work was accomplished through changing and developing the curriculum offered in school so that it included other cultures and experiences and/or included a focus on racism, its origins and how to challenge it (see Tomlinson, 1990: 17–21). This was done through teachers working individually in their schools and in groups and organizations across schools. One such organization, the National Association for Multiracial Education (NAME) developed from a small group of practitioners in the early 1970s to an active, influential group by the 1980s (Tomlinson, 2008: 66).

At the same time, during the 1980s, many LEAs were responding to the need to prepare all pupils for life in an ethnically diverse society and to challenge racism by developing and adopting multicultural and anti-racist policies and by appointing advisors to support schools in implementing them (Gaine, 1995: 48). Training, such as Race Awareness Training, was also provided to schools (Dadzie, 2000: xv). Some of this work continues today, although curtailed in many respects by changes in national policy (see above). This kind of work is also likely to be curtailed by recent public spending cuts and by the shift we have identified above from a focus on 'race'/ethnicity to a focus for funding purposes on disadvantage and poverty. In addition the proposed introduction of 'free schools' and the encouragement of a greater diversity of schools in England at the same time as a declining role for LEAs limits the possibilities and opportunities for this kind of training.

Teachers' unions have also been involved in developing and disseminating multicultural and anti-racist initiatives. In 1992 the NUT published guidelines for an anti-racist curriculum, while the Association of Teachers and Lecturers published *Multicultural Education in White Schools* in the same year. Since the 1990s teacher unions have continued to publish guidelines and support for teachers, for example: NUT (2003), *Racism, Antiracism and Islamophobia: Issues for Teachers and Schools*; NASUWT (National Association of

Schoolmasters/Union for Women Teachers) (2003), *Islamophobia*; NASUWT (2009), *The Race Relations Act and the Duty to Promote Race Equality, Implications for Schools and Colleges*. However a recent publication from the NUT (2010), *Opening Locked Doors* would appear to be part of the shift from focusing on race equality to focusing once again on disadvantage.

Examples of research: ESG Projects 1985–1986

The work of teachers, schools and LEAs in 'mainly White areas' can also be seen in the range of Educational Support Grant (ESG) projects that were initiated from 1985. These grants were funded by the DES (following the Swann Report) and LEAs had to work with schools in order to bid for project money. Tomlinson (1990) gives a detailed account of the projects and the initiatives that were developed in schools as a result of this funding.

The range of the projects and their focus can be seen in the following examples:
Birmingham: Promotion of Racial Equality in Secondary Education
Trafford: Twinning Schools with High and Low Percentage of Ethnic Minority Pupils
Kirklees: Team to Support Initiatives in Countering Racial Harassment
Rotherham: Establishment of Multi-Cultural Education Centre
Derbyshire: Team to Assist Schools in Raising Pupil Awareness of Ethnic Diversity
Kent: Development of Multicultural Resource Centre
(see Tomlinson, 1990: 106–9)

Gaine (1995) claims that this work did have some positive effects in that over 4000 teachers were directly involved in the work. Epstein's research was of an ESG project and her study claimed that there was a significant change in practice within the school as a result of the project. (see Gaine, 1995: 144–6)

According to Gillborn, 'advances in anti-racist education were easier' when there was:

- wide institutional support (locally and nationally) for anti-racist initiatives and support within the school from the headteacher.
- the involvement of pupils, the feeder communities and the school staff. (The involvement of pupils to include genuine democratic participation.)
- genuine links with the community.
- a recognition of the need to see beyond 'race labels' as a way of considering pupils and a need to 'engage with (the) cross-cutting realities of gender, sexuality and class' (Gillborn, 2004: 42–3).

The above account presents a positive view of action taken by teachers, schools, LEAs and teacher unions. However, there is another side to a consideration of how teachers and schools responded to a need to tackle racial inequality and racism in schools. In the first place, there were a number of constraints that prevented committed teachers from developing their work:

- the reaction of White parents who objected to multicultural initiatives in their children's classrooms (e.g. in Cleveland, the High Court found in favour of a White parent who objected to her primary-aged child being taught Asian language songs at school – Dadzie, 2000: xvi);
- the introduction of the ERA (1988) and the subsequent centralization of control over the curriculum (a 'national' curriculum with a new emphasis on a notion of national identity) so that teachers felt that they had much less control over what they could teach;
- the reduction in the power and influence of LEAs (Gill et al., 1992: vii);
- the influence of the media and critiques from the 'New Right' about 'loony left wing' policies and teachers.

In this respect then we can see that teachers were not always free in choosing how they wanted to move forward with anti-racist or multicultural education initiatives. The decline in the role of the LEA in supporting schools and teachers may also remove support from teachers who wish to challenge racial inequality and racism in their schools.

At the same time, a number of commentators have noted that while there were, and are, many teachers who worked tirelessly to challenge racism and racial inequality in the classroom there has been a tendency for teachers to be more comfortable with multicultural approaches in the classroom and to shy away from tackling racism (e.g. Dadzie, 2000: xv; Epstein, 1993). Epstein has written about how many teachers at the time of her research claimed that they could not do anything about racism as it was something that the children experienced and brought with them from outside school, yet, as Epstein points out, the same teachers were comfortable with banning toy guns from school in an effort to not promote violence (Epstein, 1993: 102). She has also written about how teachers had changed their practice by introducing artefacts from other cultural practices into their classrooms but describes how this approach ignored racism, was potentially superficial, led to exoticization and presented culture as something static and belonging only to ethnic minority people (Epstein, 1993: 102–3). This is the critique of multicultural approaches that we have come across before.

Gaine has written about teachers in mainly White areas and how they may ignore race issues even though national policy directs them to prepare pupils for living in a culturally diverse society (Gaine, 1995: 13). In discussing this he claims that it is easy to see why teachers in these contexts avoid racial issues as it is a 'difficult and sensitive territory' (Gaine, 1995: 11).

At the same time, as Tomlinson and Epstein point out, many teachers themselves hold unexamined views about race and/or inappropriate beliefs which impact their practice. For example, Tomlinson notes that research shows that teachers have lower expectations of Black pupils (Tomlinson, 2008: 38). Tomlinson goes on to make the point that teachers are let down by a lack of attention to these issues in teacher training (Tomlinson, 2008: 38) and by the lack of a clearly stated policy by national government (Tomlinson, 2008: 180). Teacher training courses have since the 1980s recognized that student teachers need to be prepared for teaching about, in and for a multiracial society (see Tomlinson,

1990: 17–18) but even in 2000 Blair and Cole were arguing that teacher education needed a radical re-examination (Blair and Cole, 2000: 71) and since the Initial Teacher Education (ITE) reforms starting in 1993, such courses have nearly all disappeared (Tomlinson, 2008: 122).

Epstein discusses how the presence of 'New Right' discourses and agendas in school staff-rooms in the 1980s, through regular columns in the TES by 'New Right' writers (Epstein, 1993: 26–27), and in the popular media, made it easy for many teachers opposed to anti-racist initiatives to opt out of, or voice opposition to, anti-racist and multicultural initiatives in their schools and classrooms by claiming that these were part of the 'loony left' (Epstein, 1993: 31).

There are of course racist teachers in teaching. Knowles and Ridley provide evidence of the fact that ITE students often hold racist views (Knowles and Ridley, 2006: 1)and that while in mainly White areas there is a belief that there is very little racism 'under the surface may be prejudiced attitudes that grow unchallenged'. In Cumbria, they report, 75 per cent of the population admit to being prejudiced against at least one minority group (Knowles and Ridley, 2006: 1) while Tomlinson discusses the inappropriate beliefs and attitudes held by teachers in *Multicultural Education in White Schools* (1990, Chapter 2).

Parents and pupils

Parents

Minority ethnic parents have been instrumental in many of the initiatives in education that have supported their children.

From the 1960s minority ethnic parents have voiced concerns over the underachievement and disadvantage they have seen their children experience in mainstream schools (Epstein, 1993: 32). By the end of the 1960s some migrant parents were becoming vocal about the disadvantage they felt their children were experiencing in the education system and protest groups developed. Concerns were expressed by minority ethnic parents about exclusions, underachievement and the failure of mainstream schools to take account of their children's cultural, linguistic and religious needs (Dadzie, 2000: xvii). While parent groups did not necessarily want curriculum change they did want equal opportunities for their children and valued educational qualifications. Black parents were more likely to want to see some reflection of their history and background in the mainstream curriculum while Asian parents were more likely to want to see account taken of their cultural and religious practices (Tomlinson, 2008: 65). A number of parent and community pressure groups emerged in the 1970s. The discontent of Black parents led to the setting up of the Committee of Inquiry that became the Rampton Report and then the Swann Report (Epstein, 1993: 32). As Mirza notes, the Black parents' movement of this time was an important response to the disregard of their children (Mirza, 2006: 148). In the late 1980s, with the introduction of the ERA, minority ethnic parents voiced concerns about the introduction of a National Curriculum, fearing that it would undermine many of the hard won gains of the 1980s in terms of inclusion in the curriculum of some recognition of minority ethnic lives, backgrounds and histories (Dadzie, 2000: xvii). There were also concerns expressed regarding the introduction of increasing school choice for parents (a key plank of the ERA legislation) from a number of commentators who saw this as increased school choice for majority, White, middle-class parents and not for minority ethnic parents (see Epstein, 1993: 34; Tomlinson, 2008: 113; Wright et al., 2000: 98).

Another course of action taken by minority ethnic parents was the setting up and running of supplementary schools to teach either the language(s), religion and/or cultural practices of their community. Some of the schools, particularly those in the Black community were set up as study schools to support children's progress in mainstream education. Mirza writes eloquently about these schools (2006) referring to them as 'amazing places' set up by and for the Black community to supplement the education system that fails their children and as more than a response to mainstream education. She describes such schools as 'spaces of hope and transcendence' and as places 'where whiteness is displaced and Blackness becomes the norm' (Mirza, 2006: 143). By the 1970s hundreds of supplementary schools were well established. These schools continue to this day but there is still a wide gulf between these schools and mainstream schools with supplementary schools remaining invisible and undervalued by the mainstream.

Black parents have continued to be vocal and active in challenging the over-exclusion of African-Caribbean boys from mainstream secondary schools. Many Muslim parents have been active in campaigning for Muslim faith schools to be financed and supported by the state in the same way that Church of England and Catholic schools are.

Pupils

We have considered above how various groups have responded to and taken action around racial inequality in education. One group that is often left out of these discussions is minority ethnic pupils themselves. While there is not very much information available about how young minority ethnic pupils have taken action within schools or organized themselves within schools in order to challenge racial inequality, there have been a number of research studies that describe how minority ethnic pupils resist the minority statuses that they are offered within school (e.g. Mac an Ghaill, 1988; Mirza, 1992; Sewell, 1997; Shain, 2003; Wright et al., 2000. For an account of all of these research studies see Chapter 3.). Resistance is a viable and powerful response to racial inequality and to positionings that can lead to disadvantage and low status. Some of the actions and identities adopted by the young people in these research studies result in their lack of access to successful educational outcomes while others do provide access to educational success.

Chapter summary

In this chapter we have considered the actions that have been taken by official 'majority' organizations and institutions (government, LEAs and schools) and by minorities themselves in order to address racial disadvantage in education. We have seen that government actions have never really, to quote Pilkington, 'been underpinned by a clearly formulated, coherent policy' (2003: 159) and how they have been subject to a great deal of critique. We have looked at the kinds of actions the government and LEAs took in the 1960s (the use of bussing, Section 11 grants, the teaching of English and the provision of language centres) and how the political context and talk of immigrants 'swamping' British society in the 1970s led, according to Tomlinson (2008), to a lack of overt action. We considered the increasing recognition of racial disadvantage in the 1980s, expressed through both the Rampton and Swann reports, and the subsequent view that education should prepare young people for life in a multi-ethnic society as well as the opposition that was expressed to these views. This opposition was increasingly articulated through a version of Britishness that excluded non-White people. We have also considered claims that the restructuring of education in the 1980s, with the increasing centralization of education and emphasis on choice and competition, and the continuation of this into the 1990s, increased inequalities for minority ethnic pupils while a concomitant switch to speaking of culture, religion, language and nationhood, instead of racism, removed race equality from the agenda (Gillborn, 1995: 29).

We then considered how the murder of Stephen Lawrence, and the report and inquiry that followed, forced a political and public recognition of racism in British society, made central the concept of 'institutional racism' and led to the government introducing the Race Relations Amendment Act in 2000. This made it a statutory duty for all public institutions, including schools, to develop race equality schemes. We noted that by the end of the century there was an increasingly articulated commitment in government to the principles of social and racial equality. However, we also discussed the many critiques of government policy that were made. The general feeling of these critiques was that policy was increasing or ignoring racial inequalities rather than challenging them. We ended this section of the chapter by considering the twenty-first century and how recent political changes and spending cuts are likely to weaken initiatives introduced into schools to tackle racial inequality as well as LEA support for teachers wishing to take on anti-racist initiatives. In addition we noted the shift from a focus on 'race'/ethnicity back to 'disadvantage' and poverty in policy initiatives and funding formulae.

In the rest of the chapter we have considered how commentators have tended to see government policy as either assimilationist, integrationist or culturally pluralistic and what these terms mean as well as the differences and similarities between multicultural education and anti-racist education and what these initiatives might have looked like, and might still look like, in schools. We have considered in some depth critiques of both approaches as well as looked briefly at the particular actions that schools and teachers have taken in challenging racial inequality. Finally, we have looked at how minority ethnic parents and pupils have responded to and taken action against racial inequality in education.

Further reading

The best account of government action and policy is to be found in Tomlinson (2008), *Race and Education: Policy and Politics in Britain*. See also Gillborn (1995), *Racism and Antiracism in Real Schools: Theory, Policy, Practice* and Pilkington (2003), *Racial Disadvantage and Ethnic Diversity in Britain*.

Good critiques of government policy can be found in Gillborn (2008), *Racism and Education: Confidence or Conspiracy* and Gillborn and Youdell (2000), *Rationing Education: Policy, Practice, Reform and Equity*.

For a commentary on critiques of anti-racism from the 'The New Left' see Gillborn, (1995), *Racism and Antiracism in Real Schools: Theory, Policy, Practice*: 73–90.

For a detailed discussion of the Honeyford Affair see Tomlinson (2008), *Race and Education: Policy and Politics in Britain*: 89.

Troyna gives a detailed account of the history and background to Rampton and Swann in *Racism and Education* (1993b): 61–71.

For a further discussion of 'racialized' and 'deracialized' policy see Troyna and Williams (1986), *Racism, Education and the State*: 3–5; Troyna and Carrington (1990), *Education, Racism and Reform*: 23–4.

Connolly in the chapter 'Reconsidering multicultural/anti-racist strategies in education: Articulations of 'race' and gender in primary school' in M. Griffiths and B. Troyna's edited book *Anti-Racism, Culture and Social Justice in Education* (1995) looks at multicultural and anti-racist strategies utilized in one primary school and draws attention to the need for such initiatives to be fully grounded in an understanding of the 'complex nature of racism' and of other systems of inequality such as gender.

There are a number of good accounts of actions taken by schools and teachers. See Epstein (1993), *Changing Classroom Cultures: Anti-Racism, Politics and Schools* and Gillborn (1995), *Racism and Antiracism in Real Schools: Theory, Policy, Practice*

Other accounts of school change and anti-racist initiatives can be found in:

Dadzie (2000), *Toolkit for Tackling Racism in Schools*; Knowles and Ridley (2006), *Another Spanner in the Works: Challenging Prejudice and Racism in Mainly White Schools* and Blair and Bourne (1998), *Making the Difference*. The later is a research report which looks at parent and pupil perspectives, the importance of leadership, ethos and monitoring. It includes Gypsy Traveller and refugee/asylum pupils in its account as well as case studies of five different schools.

Gaine and Weiner's (2005) edited book *Kids in Cyberspace: Teaching Anti-Racism Using the Internet in Britain, Spain and Sweden* covers the use of the internet in anti-racist work with young people.

Making EMAG Work (2001) edited by Jones and Wallace provides a collection of essays that look at good practice in schools. It also includes a history of Section 11 and EMAG.

Anti-racist initiatives in Scotland are outlined in *Strategies for the Implementation of Effective Anti Racist Policies in Education (RRR No. 4)* (2003) and can be found on the website www.gara.org.uk as can *Education of Minority Ethnic Groups in Scotland* (1988) by the University of Glasgow.

For accounts of such work in 'mainly White' schools see Gaine (1987) *No Problem Here*; (1995) *Still No Problem Here* and (2005) *We're All White Thanks: The Persisting Myth about 'White' Schools*.

Gaine writes in more detail about the history of ITE in relation to 'race' – see Gaine, (1995) *Still No Problem Here*: 115–39.

Tomlinson in Chapter 2 of (1990) *Multicultural Education in White Schools* discusses the inappropriate beliefs and attitudes held by teachers.

For actions taken by parents, activists and academics see Richardson, B. (2005), *Tell It Like It Is: How Our Schools Fail Black Children*. This book reprints a famous, highly influential text by Bernard Coard ('How the West Indian Child is Made Educationally Subnormal in the British School System' first published in 1971) alongside a number of new essays. These make the case that Black children are still experiencing racism and being denied equal opportunities with the education system and explore how this occurs. The book also includes a section of essays on what can be done and describes a number of successful projects.

Majors's edited volume (2001), *Educating Our Black Children: New Directions and Radical Approaches* contains a chapter by Majors, Gillborn and Sewell, 'The exclusion of Black children: Implications for a racialised perspective', pp. 105–9, which provides examples of actual approaches and programmes to address Black exclusion. The book also has chapters by Blair on why some schools do better than others in educating Black children and by Reay and Mirza on Black supplementary schools.

Richardson and Miles book *Racist Incidents and Bullying in School: How to Prevent Them and How to Respond When They Happen* (2008) looks at a number of initiatives at national, local and institutional level as does their book *Equality Stories* (2003), which shares experiences of using funding for race equality work.

For accounts and information about supplementary schools see:

Arthur (2003), '"Baro afkaago hooyo!" A case study of Somali literacy teaching in Liverpool', in *The International Journal of Bilingual Education and Bilingualism*, 6 (3–4);

Creese and Martin (2006), 'Interaction in complementary school contexts: developing identities of choice – an introduction', in *Language and Education*, 20 (1);

Hall et al. (2002), '"This is our school": Provision, purpose and pedagogy of supplementary schooling in Leeds and Oslo', in *British Educational Research Journal*, 28 (3);

Khan and Kabir (1999), 'Mother-tongue education among Bangladeshi children in Swansea: An exploration', in *Language Learning Journal*, 20;

Martin et al. (2006), 'Managing bilingual interaction in a Gujerati complementary school in Leicester', in *Language and Education*, 20 (1);

Mau (2007), *Politics and Pedagogy: Understanding the Population and Practices of Chinese Complementary Schools*;

Rashid and Gregory (1997), 'Learning to read, reading to learn: The importance of siblings in the language development of young bilingual children', in Eve Gregory's edited book *One Child, Many Worlds: Early Learning in Multicultural Communities*;

Rutter (2004) web article 'Community Schools and Refugee Children' available at www.multiverse.ac.uk;

Sewell (1996), 'United front to preserve cultural practices', in the *Times Educational Supplement*, October (no. 4191);

Sneddon (2003), 'Every teacher has a story to tell: A pilot study of teachers in supplementary and mother tongue schools', also available from www.multiverse.ac.uk;

Strand (2007a), 'Surveying the views of pupils attending supplementary schools in England', in *Educational Research*, 49 (1);

Walters (2011), 'Provision, purpose and pedagogy in a Bengali supplementary school' in *Language Learning Journal*, 39 (2);

Wei (2006), 'Complementary schools, past, present and future', in *Language and Education*, 20 (1); and

Wu (2006), 'Look who's talking: Language choices and culture of learning in UK Chinese classrooms', in *Language and Education*, 20 (1).

For research accounts of pupil resistance see:

Mac an Ghail (1988), *Young, Gifted and Black: Student Teacher Relations in the Schooling of Black Youth*; Mirza (1992), *Young, Female and Black*; Sewell (1997), *Black Masculinities and Schooling: How Black Boys Survive Modern Schooling*; Shain (2003), *The Schooling and Identity of Asian Girls*; Wright et al.(2000), *'Race', Class and Gender in Exclusion from School*.

The Runnymede Trust (see website below) provides many publications of interest including: *'Race' Policy in Education*; *Black and Ethnic Minority Young People and Educational Disadvantage*; *Black Parents and Their Children's Education*; *Complementing Teachers* (A Practical Guide to Promoting Race Equality in Schools); *Failure By Any Other*

Name?; *Right to Divide* (Faith Schools and Community Cohesion); *School Choice and Ethnic Segregation* (Educational Decision-Making Among Black and Minority-Ethnic Parents).

The RoutledgeFalmer Reader in Multicultural Education (2004) is also a very useful resource as is Gill et al.'s edited (1992) book *Racism and Education: Structures and Strategies* for their chapters on various policy issues.

The journals *Race, Equality and Teaching* and *Multicultural Teaching* are worth consulting.

An excellent guide to government policy resources is *Narrowing the Gaps: Resources to Support the Achievement of Black and Minority Ethnic, Disadvantaged and Gifted and Talented Pupils* put together by the DCSF in 2009.

Useful websites

www.runnymedetrust.org (Publications: Education and Young People)

Runnymede Trust

http://egfl.net/equalities/index.html

Edinburgh Grid for Learning: Equalities

www.continyou.org.uk

Supplementary Schools

www.scotlandagainstracism.com

Scotland Against Racism

www.britkid.org

Britkid, a website about race, racism and life . . . as seen through the eyes of Britkids

www.gara.org.uk

Glasgow Anti-Racist Alliance about to become Coalition for Racial Equality and Rights (CRER)

www.underfives.co.uk/CWGEYRacism.html

For an excellent resource list for early years education

www.ltscotland.org.uk/supportinglearners/positivelearningenvironments/inclusionandequality/antiracism

Learning and Teaching Scotland's Race Equality web pages

www.measuringdiversity.org.uk

Measuring Diversity website – provides information on ethnic segregation in schools.

www.multiverse.ac.uk

Multiverse – a website for teacher educators and student teachers.

www.srtrc.org

Show Racism the Red Card – Resources for Challenging Racism

Conclusions

In the introduction to this book three questions were posed:

Do 'race' and ethnicity make a difference to our experience of education?

Does our 'race' and ethnicity make a difference to our achievement in school?

Does education reproduce ethnic differences and racial inequalities or can it challenge and change them?

The intervening chapters have attempted to provide a 'road map' of the research, debates and issues that have been at the centre of work on 'race', ethnicity and education over the past 30 years in order to provide answers to, or at least insights into, these questions.

The 'road map' has been an attempt to represent what other people have said and written in order to present a picture of what the 'story' is that has emerged and evolved over these 30 years: what the key concerns, findings and actions have been but also the history of this 'story'. Each chapter has aimed to introduce you to what people have said, claimed and argued over, what they have agreed on and disagreed about, and also to give an account that brings together and represents the key work and the 'stuff' that makes up current accounts of the relationship between 'race', ethnicity and education. To speak of what is presented in the preceding chapters as a 'story' is not to deny or minimize the importance, nor materiality, of 'race' and ethnicity in education, and in everyday lives, nor the importance of taking these issues seriously and taking action around these issues. 'Race', racism and racial inequalities are serious issues that need to be challenged and addressed. It is hoped that the book gives you, its readers, a very sound, solid basis from which to take action, either as educational professionals, school governors, student teachers, undergraduate or postgraduate learners or researchers, in the field of education.

To answer the three questions that we began with it is clear that the answer to the first two, as revealed by the research reports that we have looked at, is a 'yes'. 'Race'/ethnicity seems to make a difference to educational performance and achievement as evidenced in the statistical studies we looked at in Chapter 2 with some, ethnically defined, groups of pupils achieving more highly than others. Statistical analysis revealed that this difference could not all be explained away by socio-economic status or any other singular social factor. Qualitative studies that also considered achievement in school also found that 'race' and ethnicity certainly had a role to play in positioning pupils as achieving or underachieving pupils. 'Race' and ethnicity also make a difference to our experiences of school: our interactions and relationships with teachers and peers, our sense of identity, our placement in the mainstream or in Special Educational Needs provision and our journeys through the educational world. However, what we have also discussed and discovered is that 'race' and ethnicity cannot be considered as solitary factors that affect experience and achievement but that 'race' and ethnicity must be considered first, as we saw in Chapter 3, as complexly intermeshed with other social factors like class and gender, framing identity, informing interactions and creating opportunities for achievement and underachievement and secondly, as we saw in Chapter 1, as dynamic and evolving, defined and created in context. We have gained, it is hoped, a nuanced understanding of what 'race' and ethnicity are and their dynamic, fluid, context-bound natures as well as how they intermesh with other social factors in complex ways in educational settings to provide differing opportunities and positionings for minority ethnic pupils, parents and teachers. Both have implications for the actions that we can take. We have seen the impossibility, or at least the dangers, of working with a simplistic notion of 'race', racism and ethnicity, that maintain and perpetuate tightly bounded, defined categories of people, based on spurious notions of a shared and static biology or culture, as we either work to challenge racism and racial inequalities in schools, or, as we saw in Chapter 4, as we research 'race' issues in educational settings.

It is through a consideration of educational experiences in Chapter 3 that we came to some of the insights that have been provided by research regarding how and why 'race' and ethnicity make a difference to achievement. We have seen that teacher responses to pupils, and expectations of pupils, frequently call on assumptions and ideas about particular ethnic practices and attributes that are unquestioningly ascribed to pupils and their families thereby limiting (or increasing) the identities, resources and opportunities that are open to particular ethnically defined pupil groups. We have also seen how particular institutional and policy processes, despite their sometimes progressive intentions, also limit (or increase) opportunities for different ethnically defined groups. In addition, we have seen how pupils can themselves choose to take up resistant positions to institutional and classroom norms that they experience as demeaning, racist or unhelpful and how this 'resistance' strategy can often position such pupils outside of the possibility of being an 'ideal learner' and achieving well in school. Achievement and underachievement are also enmeshed with minority and majority ethnic parents' experiences of schools and teachers' responses to and expectations of parents.

We are already some way to answering the third question. It would indeed appear that the education system does reproduce ethnic differences and inequalities, although, as we have seen, not in a simplistic, straightforward way. It would also appear to be the case that it does possess some capacity for challenging and changing them. We can see that different ethnically defined groups of pupils have been afforded opportunities by the education system and that the relative achievement of different pupil groups has changed over the years: Bangladeshi pupils in England for example, have improved their achievement over the past 7 years to such an extent that they have ceased to be one of the lowest achieving groups and are now achieving alongside White and Mixed Heritage pupils at the end of compulsory schooling. In this respect we can say that education can challenge and change patterns of inequality. However, at another level, as we have seen, the education system and educational processes continue to operate with firmly entrenched racial and ethnic categories that are reproduced within classrooms, playgrounds, at policy level and in research – and that these categories, and the assumptions and expectations that accompany them, work, particularly within the classroom, to the detriment of certain groups of pupils. Racism continues to exist even for those pupils who achieve well. David Gillborn goes as far as to claim that education policy making, and therefore the education system, knowingly and deliberately perpetuates racial inequalities. The answer to this question is then 'yes' and 'yes'.

Finally, in considering these questions and in presenting a 'road map' it has been possible to show something of the developments that have occurred in theorizing and understanding 'race', ethnicity and racism in educational settings and the methodological issues that have accompanied research work in this area. These have been important aspects of 'what we know' as they touch on 'how we know' and how we go about questioning and reflecting on our own assumptions, actions and understandings: how we might begin to challenge the reproduction of racial inequalities. Together with the presentation of the research, debates and issues that have formed the substance of this book, it is hoped that you are able to use what has been presented as a platform upon which to reflect, discuss and take action in your own particular setting and practice and feel confident that it is based on an informed understanding of what we currently know.

References

Abbas, T. (2004), *The Education of British South Asians*. London: Palgrave Macmillan.

Afitska, O., Conteh, J., Jones, A. E., Leung, C. and Wallace, C. (2010), 'EAL practice and experience: Issues from current research'. *Naldic Quarterly*, 7: 35–8.

Amin, K., Drew, D., Fosam, D., Gillborn, D. and Demack, S. (1997), *Black and Ethnicity Minority Young People and Educational Disadvantage*. London: The Runnymede Trust.

Archer, L. (2003), *Race, Masculinity and Schooling*. Maidenhead: Open University Press.

Archer, L. and Francis, B. (2007), *Understanding Minority Ethnic Achievement*. Abingdon: Routledge.

Arshad, R., Diniz, F., Kelly, E., O'Hara, P., Sharp, S. and Syed, R. (2005), *Minority Ethnic Pupils' Experiences of School in Scotland*. Edinburgh: Scottish Executive Education Department.

Arthur, J. (2003), '"Baro afkaago hooyo!" A case study of Somali literacy teaching in Liverpool'. *The International Journal of Bilingual Education and Bilingualism*, 6 (3–4): 253–66.

Association of Teachers and Lecturers (1992), *Multicultural Education in White Schools*. London: Association of Teachers and Lecturers.

Back, L. (1996), *New Ethnicities and Urban Culture*. London: UCL Press.

Ball, S., Reay, D. and David, M. (2002), '"Ethnic choosing": Minority ethnic students, social class and higher education choice'. *Race, Ethnicity and Education*, 5 (4): 333–57.

Barot, R., Bradley, H. and Fenton, S. (1999), *Ethnicity, Gender and Social Change*. Basingstoke and London: Macmillan.

Barth, F. (1969), 'Introduction', in F. Barth (ed.), *Ethnic Groups and Boundaries*. London: George Allen & Unwin, pp. 9–37.

Becker, H. (1967), 'Whose side are we on?' *Social Problems*, 14: 239–47.

Bhattacharyya, G., Gabriel, J. and Small, S. (2002), *Race and Power: Global Racism in the Twenty-First Century*. London: Routledge.

Bhattacharyya, G., Ison, L. and Blair, M. (2003), *Minority Ethnic Attainment and Participation in Education and Training: The Evidence*. London: DfES.

Bhatti, G. (1999), *Asian Children at Home and at School: An Ethnographic Study*. London: Routledge.

— (2007), 'The irresistible attraction of ICT: Experiences of trainee teachers from minority ethnic backgrounds', in G. Bhatti, C. Gaine, F. Gobbo and Y. Leeman (eds), *Social Justice and Intercultural Education: An Open Ended Dialogue*. Stoke-on-Trent: Trentham, pp. 33–47.

Bhavnani, R., Mirza, H. and Meetoo, V. (2005), *Tackling the Roots of Racism*. Bristol: Policy Press.

Birmingham City Council (1994), Report of the Chief Executive Officer: Education Services Committee: National Curriculum Assessment 1994: Key Stage One Results. Birmingham: Birmingham City Council.

— (1995), Report of the Chief Executive Officer: Education Services Committee: 14th November 1995: Examination Results 1995. Birmingham: Birmingham City Council.

Blackledge, A. (2000), *Literacy, Power and Social Justice*. Stoke-on-Trent: Trentham.

Blair, M. (1992), 'Review of policy and practice in multicultural antiracist education'. *European Journal of Intercultural Studies*, 2: 63–64.

— (2001), *Why Pick On Me? School Exclusion and Black Youth*. Stoke-on-Trent: Trentham.

Blair, M. and Bourne, J. (1998), *Making the Difference: Teaching and Learning Strategies in Successful Multiethnic Schools*. London: DfES.

Blair, M. and Cole, M. (2000), 'Racism and education', in M. Cole (ed.), *Education, Equality and Human Rights*. London: Routledge Falmer, pp. 70–88.

Bloch, A. (2002), *Refugees' Opportunities and Barriers in Employment and Training*. London: Department for Work and Pensions.

Bourne, J., Bridges, L. and Searle, C. (1994), *How Schools Exclude Black Children*. London: Institute of Race Relations.

Brent (1994), *Report Summarising the Analysis of the 1993 GCSE Results*. London: Policy Studies Institute.

Brooker, L. (2003), 'Learning how to learn: Parental ethnotheories and young children's preparation for school'. *International Journal of Early Years Education*, 11 (2): 117–28.

Bullock, A. (1975), *A Language for Life*. London: HMSO.

Camden (1995), Analysis of 1994 London Reading Test and GCSE Results by Ethnic Group: Report of the Director of Education to the Education (Strategy) Sub-Committee. London: London Borough of Camden.

— (1996), Raising the Achievement of Bangladeshi Pupils in Camden Schools. London: London Borough of Camden.

Carrington, B. and Wood, E. (1983), 'Body talk'. *Multiracial Education*, 11,(2): 29–38.

Centre for Bangladeshi Studies (2001), *Routes and beyond*. Surrey: Centre for Bangladeshi Studies.

Chitty, C. (2007), *Eugenics, Race and Intelligence in Education*. London: Continuum.

Cline, T., de Abrue, G., Fihosy, C., Gray, H., Lambert, H. and Neale, J. (2002), *Minority Ethnic Pupils in Mainly White Schools*. London: DfES.

Coard, B. (1971), *How the West Indian Child is Made Educationally Subnormal in the British School System: The Scandal of the Black Child in Schools in Britain*. London: New Beacon for the Caribbean Education and Community Workers' Association.

Cole, M. (2007), '"Racism" is about more than colour', *Times Higher Education Supplement*. 23 November 2007

— (2009), *Critical Race Theory and Education*. Basingstoke: Palgrave Macmillan.

Commission for Racial Equality (1986), Teaching English as a Second Language: Report of Formal Investigation in Calderdale LEA. London: Commission for Racial Equality.

Connolly, P. (1992), 'Playing it by the rules: The politics of research in 'race' and racism: the limits of research and policy'. *British Educational Research Journal*, 18 (2): 133–48.

— (1994), '"All lads together?: Racism masculinity and multicultural/anti-racist strategies in a primary school'. *International Studies in the Sociology of Education*, 4 (2): 191–211.

— (1995), 'Racism, masculine peer group relations and the schooling of African-Caribbean infant boys'. *British Journal of Sociology of Education*, 16 (1): 75–92.

— (1998), *Racism, Gender Identities and Young Children*. London: Routledge.

— (2006a), 'Summary statistics, educational achievement gaps and the ecological fallacy'. *Oxford Review of Education*, 32 (2): 235–52.

— (2006b), 'Keeping a sense of proportion but loosing all perspective: A critique of Gorard's notion of the "politician's error"'. *British Journal of Education Studies*, 54 (1): 73–88.

Connolly, P. and Keenan, M. (2002), 'Racist harassment in the white hinterlands: Minority ethnic children and parents' experiences of schooling in Northern Ireland'. *British Journal of Sociology of Education*, 23 (3): 341–55.

Connolly, P. and Troyna, B. (eds) (1998), *Researching Racism in Education: Politics, Theory and Practice*. Buckingham: Open University Press.

Craft, M. and Craft, A. (1983), 'The participation of ethnic minority pupils in further and higher education'. *Educational Research*, 25: 10–19.

Creese, A. and Martin, P. (2006), 'Interaction in complementary school contexts: Developing identities of choice – an introduction'. *Language and Education*, 20 (1): 1–4.

Crozier, G. (2004), Parents, Children and the School Experience: Asian Families' Perspectives. End of Award Report. ESRC Ref no. R000239671. London: ESRC.

Dadzie, S. (2000), *Toolkit for Tackling Racism in Schools*. Stoke-on-Trent: Trentham.

Davies, N. (2010), 'View from the Chair'. *Naldic Quarterly Spring 2010*, 7 (3): 3–4.

Demack, S., Drew, D. and Grimsley, M. (2000), 'Minding the gap: Ethnic, gender and social class differences in attainment at 16, 1988–95'. *Race, Ethnicity and Education*, 3 (2): 117–43.

Demie, F. (2001), 'Ethnic and gender differences in educational achievement and implications for school improvement strategies'. *Educational Research*, 43: 91–106.

— (2010), 'White working class: New research highlights barriers and successful strategies to raise achievement (Research Brief: 27 January 2010)'. *Naldic Quarterly Spring 2010*, 7 (3): 25.

Department for Children, Schools and Families (2009), *Narrowing The Gaps: Resources To Support the Achievement of Black and Minority Ethnic, Disadvantaged and Gifted and Talented Pupils*. London: Department for Children, Schools and Families.

— (2010a), *Identifying Components of Attainment Gaps*. London: Department for Children, Schools and Families.

— (2010b), 'Parental Involvement'. www.standards.dcsf.gov.uk/parentinvolvment/pwp

Department for Education (2010), *Youth Cohort Study and Longitudinal Study of Young People in England: The Activities and Experiences of 18 Year Olds: England 2009*. London: Department for Education.

Department for Education and Skills (2002), *Removing the Barriers: Raising Achievement Levels for Minority Ethnic Pupils*. London: Department for Education and Skills.

— (2003), *Raising the Achievement of Gypsy Traveller Pupils – A Guide to Good Practice*. London: Department for Education and Skills.

— (2004), *Aiming High: Guidance on Supporting the Education of Asylum Seeking and Refugee Children*. London: Department for Education and Skills.

— (2004), *Aiming High: Supporting Effective Use of EMAG*. London: Department for Education and Skills

— (2004), *Aiming High: Understanding the Educational Needs of Minority Ethnic Pupils in Mainly White Schools*. London: Department for Education and Skills.

— (2005), *Ethnicity and Education: The Evidence on Minority Ethnic Pupils*. London: Department for Education and Skills.

— (2006), *Evaluation of Aiming High: African Caribbean Achievement Project*. London: Department for Education and Skills.

— (2006), *Pupils Learning English as an Additional Language*. London: Department for Education and Skills.

— (2006), *Special Educational Needs and Ethnicity: Issues of Over and Under-Representation*. London: Department for Education and Skills.

Department of Education (2010), 'Qualifications and Destinations of Northern Ireland School Leavers 2008/09 Statistical Press Release'. www.deni.gov.uk/sls0809.pdf.

Department of Education and Science (1981), *West Indian Children in Our Schools: A Report from the Committee of Enquiry into the Education of Children from Ethnic Minorities (The Rampton Report)*. London: HMSO.

— (1985), *Education for All: Report of the Committee of Enquiry into the Education of Children from Minority Groups (The Swann Report)*. London: HMSO.

Derbyshire, H. (1994), *Not in Norfolk*. Norwich: Norwich and Norfolk Race Equality Council.

Derrington, C. and Kendall, S. (2007), 'Still at school at 16? Gypsy traveller students in English secondary schools', in G. Bhatti, C. Gaine, F. Gobbo and Y. Leeman, (eds), *Social Justice and Intercultural Education: An Open Ended Dialogue*. Stoke-on-Trent: Trentham, pp. 17–31.

Donald, J. and Rattansi, A. (1992), *Race, Culture and Difference*. London: Sage.

Drew, D. (1995), *'Race', Education and Work: The Statistics of Inequality*. Aldershot: Avebury.

Drew, D. and Gray, J. (1990), 'The fifth year examination achievements of Black young people in England and Wales'. *Educational Research*, 32: 107–16.

Dyer, R. (1988), 'White'. *Screen*, 29: 44–65.

Edwards, R. (1990), 'Connecting method and epistemology: A white woman interviewing black women'. *Women's Studies International Forum*, 13: 477–90.

Elton-Chalcraft, S. (2009), *'Its Not Just about Black and White Miss': Children's Awareness of Race*. Stoke-on-Trent: Trentham.

Epstein, D. (1993), *Changing Classroom Cultures: Anti-Racism, Politics and Schools*. Stoke-on-Trent: Trentham.

Fenton, S. (1999), *Ethnicity: Racism, Class and Culture*. Basingstoke and London: Macmillan.

— (2003), *Ethnicity*. Cambridge, UK: Polity Press.

Fine, M. (1994), 'Working the hyphens: Reinventing self and other in qualitative research', in N. Denzin and Y. Lincoln, (eds), *Handbook of Qualitative Research*. London: Sage, pp 70–82.

Foster, P. (1990a), *Policy and Practice in Multicultural and Anti-Racist Education*. London: Routledge.

— (1990b), 'Cases not proven: Evaluation of two studies of teacher racism'. *British Educational Research Journal* 16 (4): 335–49.

— (1991), 'Cases still not proven: A reply to Cecile Wright'. *British Educational Research Journal*, 17 (2): 165–70.

— (1992a), 'Equal treatment and cultural difference in multi-ethnic schools: A critique of teacher ethnocentrism theory'. *International Studies in the Sociology of Education*, 2 (1): 89–103.

— (1992b), 'Teacher attitudes and Afro-Caribbean achievement'. *Oxford Review of Education*, 18 (3): 269–81.

— (1993a), 'Some problems in establishing equality of treatment in multi-ethnic schools'. *British Journal of Sociology*, 44 (3): 519–35.

— (1993b), '"Methodological purism" or "a defence against hype"? Critical readership in research in "race" and education'. *New Community*, 19 (3): 547–52.

— (1994), 'The uses of "ethnic data" in education'. *New Community*, 20 (43): 647–54.

Foster, P., Hammersley, M. and Gomm, R. (1996), *Constructing Educational Inequality*. London: Falmer.

Gaine, C. (1987), *No Problem Here*. London: Hutchinson.

— (1995), *Still No Problem Here*. Stoke-on-Trent: Trentham.

Gaine, C. and Burch, K. (2004), 'Self-Identification and Ethnicity: "You Can't Be An English Pakistani"'. European Conference on Educational Research, University of Crete.

Gaine, C. and George, R. (1999), *Gender, 'Race' and Class in Schooling: A New Introduction*. London: RoutledgeFalmer.

Gaine, C. and Weiner, G., (eds). (2005), *Kids in Cyberspace: Teaching Anti-Racism Using the Internet in Britain, Spain and Sweden*. Didcot: Symposium.

Gardner, H. (1995), 'Cracking open the IQ box', in S. Fraser, (ed.), *The Bell Curve Wars*. New York: Basic Books, pp. 23–35.

General Register Office (2010), '2011 Census'. www.gro-scotland.gov.uk/census/censushm2011. Last accessed on 23 October 2010.

Gill, D., Mayor, B. and M. Blair (eds). (1992), *Racism and Education: Structures and Strategies*. London: OUP/Sage.

Gillborn, D. (1990), *'Race', Ethnicity and Education: Teaching and Learning in Multi-Ethnic Schools*. London: Unwin Hyman.

— (1995), *Racism and Antiracism in Real Schools: Theory, Policy, Practice*. Buckingham: Open University Press.

— (1997), 'Young, black and failed by school'. *International Journal of Inclusive Education*, 1 (1): 1–23.

— (2004), 'Anti-racism: From policy to praxis', in G. Ladson-Billings and D. Gillborn, (eds), *The Routledge Falmer Reader in Multicultural Education*. Abingdon: Routledge Falmer, pp. 35–48.

— (2008), *Racism and Education: Coincidence or Conspiracy?* Abingdon: Routledge.

— (2009). 'Whatever happened to institutional racism? How the "White working class" were made into the new race victims.' National Arts Learning Network Annual Conference 'What now for Widening Participation in the Arts'. Keynote Speech available at http://ukadia.ac.uk/en/naln-migrate/conference/previous-conferences/conference-2009/keynote-presentations/index.cfm. Last accessed on 5 November 2010.

Gillborn, D. and Drew, D. (1992), '"Race", class and school effects'. *New Community*, 18 (4): 551–65.

Gillborn, D. and Gipps, C. (1996), *Recent Research on the Achievements of Ethnic Minority Pupils*. London: HMSO.

Gillborn, D. and Mirza, H. S. (2000), *Educational Inequality: Mapping Race, Class and Gender: A Synthesis of Research Evidence*. London: OFSTED.

Gillborn, D. and Youdell, D. (2000), *Rationing Education: Policy, Practice, Reform and Equity*. Buckingham: OUP.

Gilroy, P. (1990), 'The end of anti-racism'. *New Community*, 17 (1): 71–83.

Goldstein, H. (2000), 'School Effectiveness Research' (Seminar Paper presented at the Oxford University Department of Educational Studies). November, 2000.

Gomm, R. (1993), 'Figuring out ethnic equity: A response to Troyna'. *British Educational Research Journal*, 19 (2): 147–63.

— (1995), 'Strong claims, weak evidence: A response to Troyna's "Ethnicity and the organisation of learning groups"'. *Educational Research*, 37 (1): 79–86.

Gorard, S. (1999), 'Keeping a sense of proportion: The 'politician's error' in analysing school outcomes'. *British Journal of Education Studies*, 47 (3): 235–46.

Green, P. (1985), Multi-Ethnic Teaching and the Pupils' Self Concepts. in Department of Education and Science Education for All: Report of the Committee of Enquiry into the Education of Children from Minority Groups (The Swann Report). London: HMSO, pp. 46–56.

Griffiths, M. and Troyna, B., (eds). (1995), *Antiracism, Culture and Social Justice in Education*. Stoke-on-Trent: Trentham.

Hall, K. (1995), '"There's a time to act English and a time to act Indian": The politics of identity among British-Sikh teenagers', in S. Stephens, (ed.), *Children and the Politics of Culture*. Princeton, NJ: Princeton University Press, pp. 242–62.

Hall, K., Ozerk, K., Zulfiqar, M. and Tan, J. (2002), '"This is our school": Provision, purpose and pedagogy of supplementary schooling in Leeds and Oslo'. *British Educational Research Journal*, 28 (3): 399–418.

Hall, S. (1992), 'New ethnicities', in A. Rattansi and J. Donald (eds), *Race, Culture and Difference*. London: Sage, pp. 252–59.

Halstead, M. (1988), *Education, Justice and Cultural Diversity: An Examination of the Honeyford Affair 1984–85*. London: Falmer Press.

Hammersley, M. (1991), *Reading Ethnographic Research*. London: Longman.

— (1992a), 'A response to Barry Troyna's 'Children, 'race' and racism': The limits of research and policy'. *British Journal of Education Studies*, 40 (2): 174–77.

— (1992b), *What's Wrong with Ethnography*. London: Routledge.

— (1993a), 'On methodological purism: A response to Barry Troyna'. *British Educational Research Journal*, 19 (4): 339–41.

— (1993b), 'Research and "anti-racism": The case of Peter Foster and his critics'. *British Journal of Sociology*, 44 (3): 429–48.

— (1995), *The Politics of Social Research*. London: Sage.

Hammersley, M. and Gomm, R. (1993), 'A response to Gillborn and Drew on "'Race', class and school effects"'. *New Community*, 19 (2): 348–53.

Haque, Z. (1999), 'Exploring the Validity and Possible Causes of the Apparently Poor Performances of Bangladeshi Students in British Secondary Schools'. Unpublished PhD thesis. Cambridge: University of Cambridge.

Harris, R. (2001), 'Keynote Speech', NALDIC General Council Meeting, 7 July.

Hatcher, R. (1995), 'Racism and children's cultures', in M. Griffiths and B. Troyna, (eds), *Antiracism, Culture and Social Justice in Education*. Stoke-on-Trent: Trentham.

Haw, K. (1996), 'Explaining the educational experiences of Muslim girls: Tales told to tourists – should the white researcher stay at home?' *British Educational Research Journal*, 22: 319–30.

— (1998), *Educating Muslim Girls: Shifting Discourses*. Buckingham: Open University Press.

Haynes, J., Tikly, L. and Caballero, C. (2006), 'The barriers to achievement for White/Black Caribbean pupils in English schools'. *British Journal of Sociology of Education*, 27 (5): 569–83.

Hegarty, S. and Lucas, D. (1978), *Able to Learn: The Pursuit of Culture-Fair Assessment*. Windsor: National Federation for Educational Research.

Hernstein, R. and Murray, C. (1994), *The Bell Curve: Intelligence and Class Structure in American Life*. New York: Free Press.

House of Commons (1987), *Home Affairs First Report 1986–1987: Bangladeshis in Britain*. London: HMSO (House of Commons).

Inner London Education Authority (1990), *Differences in Examination Performances*. London: ILEA Research and Statistics Branch.

Juy, E. (1992), *Keep Them in Birmingham: Challenging Racism in South West England*. London: CRE.

Jeffcoate, R. (1984), *Ethnic Minorities and Education*. London: Harper and Row.

Jones, C. and Wallace, C. (2001), *Making EMAG Work*. Stoke-on-Trent: Trentham.

Karner, C. (2007), *Ethnicity and Everyday Life*. London: Routledge.

Keith, M. (1993), *Race, Riots and Policing: Lore and Disorder in a Multi-Racist Society*. London: UCL Press.

Kendall, L., Rutt, S. and Schagen, I. (2005), *Minority Ethnic Pupils and Excellence in Cities: Final Report*. Windsor: National Foundation for Educational Research

Khan, N. A. and Kabir, M. A. (1999), 'Mother-tongue education among Bangladeshi children in Swansea: an exploration'. *Language Learning Journal*, 20: 20–6.

Kivi, M. (1991), 'Lies, damn lies and GCSE results'. *Education*, 177 (20): 401.

Knowles, E. and Ridley, W. (2006), *Another Spanner in the Works: Challenging Prejudice and Racism in Mainly White Schools*. Stoke-on-Trent: Trentham.

Kysel, F. (1988), 'Ethnic background and examination results'. *Educational Research*, 30: 83–9.

Ladner, J. (1975), 'Introduction', in J. Ladner, (ed.), The Death of White Sociology. New York: Vintage Books, pp. xix–xxix

Lambeth (1994), *Summer 1993 Examination Achievement at GCSE: Report by the Director of Education*. London: London Borough of Lambeth.

Lather, P. (1986), 'Research as praxis'. *Harvard Educational Review*, 56 (3): 257–77.

Leech, K. (1989), *A Question in Dispute: The Debate About An 'Ethnic' Question in the Census*. London: The Runnymede Trust.

Little, A. (1975), 'Performance of children from ethnic minority backgrounds in primary school'. *Oxford Review of Education*, 1 (2): 117–35.

Mabey, C. (1981), 'Black British literacy: a study of the reading attainment of London Black children from 8–15 years'. *Educational Research*, 23 (2): 83–95.

— (1985), 'Achievement of Black Pupils: Reading Competence as a Predictor of Examination Success Among Afro-Caribbean Pupils in London'. Unpublished PhD thesis. London: University of London.

— (1986), 'Black pupils' achievement in inner London'. *Educational Research*, 28 (3): 163–73.

Mac an Ghaill, M. (1988), *Young, Gifted and Black: Student Teacher Relations in the Schooling of Black Youth*. Buckingham: Open University Press.

— (1992), 'Coming of age in 1980s England: Reconceptualizing black students' schooling experiences', in D. Gill, B. Mayor and M. Blair (eds), *Racism and Education: Structures and Strategies*. London: Sage, pp 42–58.

Macpherson, W. (1999), *The Stephen Lawrence Inquiry*. London: The Stationery Office.

Majors, R. (2001), *Educating Our Black Children: New Directions and Radical Approaches*. London: Routledge.

Martin, P., Bhatt, A., Bhojani, N. and Creese, A. (2006), 'Managing bilingual interaction in a Gujerati complementary school in Leicester'. *Language and Education*, 20 (1): 5–22.

Mau, A. (2007), 'Politics and Pedagogy: Understanding the Population and Practices of Chinese Complementary Schools'. British Educational Research Association Conference, Institute of Education, University of London.

Merriam, S. (1988), *Case Study Research in Education: A Qualitative Approach*. San Francisco: Jossey-Bass.

Miles, R. (1989), *Racism*. London: Routledge.

Mirza, H. S. (1992), *Young, Female and Black*. London: Routledge.

— (1997), 'Black women in education: A collective movement for social change', in H. S. Mirza, (ed.), *Black British Feminism: A Reader*. London: Routledge, pp. 269–77.

— (1998), 'Race, gender and IQ: The social consequence of pseudo-scientific discourse'. *Race, Ethnicity and Education*, 1 (1): 109–26.

— (2006), ' "Race", gender and educational desire'. *Race, Ethnicity and Education*, 9 (2): 137–58.

Modood, T. and Berthoud, R. et al. (1997), *Ethnic Minorities in Britain*. London: Policy Studies Institute.

Mortimore, P., Sammons, P., Stoll, L., Lewis, D. and Ecob, R. (1988), *School Matters: The Junior Years*. Wells: Open Books.

National Association for Language Development in the Curriculum (2010) 'NUT argues for a new ringed fenced grant'. *NALDIC Quarterly*, 7 (26) Spring 2010.

National Association of Schoolmasters and Union of Women Teachers (2003), *Tackling Islamophobia: Advice for Schools and Colleges*. Birmingham: National Association of Schoolmasters and Union of Women Teachers.

— (2009), *The Race Relations Act and the Duty to Promote Race Equality: Implications for Schools and Colleges*. Birmingham: National Association of Schoolmasters and Union of Women Teachers.

National Curriculum Council (1990a), *Curriculum Guidance 3: The Whole Curriculum*. London: DES.

— (1990b), *Curriculum Guidance 8: Education for Citizenship*. York: NCC.

National Union of Teachers (1992), *Anti-Racist Curriculum Guidelines*. London: National Union of Teachers.

— (2003), *Racism, Antiracism and Islamophobia: Issues for Teachers and Schools*. London: National Union of Teachers.

— (2010), Opening Locked Doors: Educational Underachievement and White Working Class Young People. London: National Union of Teachers.

Neal, S. (1998), *The Making of Equal Opportunities Policies in Universities*. Buckingham: Open University Press.

Newham (1995), *Newham ELS GCSE Monitoring Report*. London: Newham LEA.

Northern Ireland Statistics and Research Agency (2010), 'Census 2011'. www.nisranew.nisra.gov/uk/census. Last accessed on 13 October 2010.

Office for National Statistics (2009a), 'Final Recommended Questions for 2011 Census in England and Wales: Ethnic Group'. www.ons.gov.uk/census/2011-census/2011-census-questionnaire-content. Last accessed on 13 October 2010.

— (2009b), 'Final Recommended Questions for 2011 Census in England and Wales: Language'. www.ons.gov.uk/census/2011-census/2011-census-questionnaire-content. Last accessed on 13 October 2010.

— (2009c), 'Final Recommended Questions for 2011 Census in England and Wales: Migration'. www.ons.gov.uk/census/2011-census/2011-census-questionnaire-content. Last accessed on 13 October 2010.

— (2009d), 'Final Recommended Questions for 2011 Census in England and Wales: National Identity'. www.ons.gov.uk/census/2011-census/2011-census-questionnaire-content. Last accessed on 13 October 2010.

— (2009e), 'Final Recommended Questions for the 2011 Census in England and Wales: Religion'. www.ons.gov.uk/census/2011-census/2011-census-questionnaire-content. Last accessed on 13 October 2010.

Office for Standards in Education (1999), *Raising the Attainment of Minority Ethnic Pupils: School and LEA Responses*. London: Office for Standards in Education.

— (2001), *Managing Support for the Attainment of Pupils from Ethnic Minority Groups*. London: Office for Standards in Education.

— (2002), *Achievement of Black Caribbean Pupils*. London: Office for Standards in Education.

— (2002), *Support for Minority Ethnic Achievement: Continuing Professional Development*. London: Office for Standards in Education.

— (2002), *Unlocking Potential: Raising Ethnic Minority Attainment at Key Stage 3*. London: Office for Standards in Education.

— (2003), *The Education of Asylum-Seeker Pupils*. London: Office for Standards in Education.

— (2004), *Achievement of Bangladeshi Heritage Pupils*. London: Office for Standards in Education

— (2004), *Managing the Ethnic Minority Achievement Grant: Good Practice in Primary Schools*. London: Office for Standards in Education.

— (2004), *Managing the Ethnic Minority Achievement Grant: Good Practice in Secondary Schools*. London: Office for Standards in Education.

Open University (2010a). 'Diversity and Difference in Communication 2.6: "Racialisation" and Racism.' Open University Open Learn. http://openlearn.open.ac.uk/mod/oucontent/view. Last accessed on 23 July 2010.

— (2010b). 'Diversity and Difference in Communication: 2.5 Ethnic Categories Open University Open Learn. Health and Social Care: K205_1'. http://openlearn.open.ac.uk/mod/oucontent/view. Last accessed on 27 July 2010.

Osler, A. (1997), *The Education and Careers of Black Teachers: Changing Identities, Changing Lives*. Buckingham: OUP.

Pathak, S. (2000), *Race Research for the Future: Ethnicity in Education, Training and the Labour Market*. London: DfEE.

Phillips, C. J. (1979), 'Educational underachievement in different ethnic groups'. *Educational Research*, 21 (2): 116–30.

Pilkington, A. (1999), 'Racism in schools and ethnic differentials in educational achievement: A brief comment on a recent debate'. *British Journal of Sociology of Education*, 20 (3): 441–17.

— (2003), *Racial Disadvantage and Ethnic Diversity in Britain*. Basingstoke: Palgrave Macmillan.

Plewis, I. (1991), 'Pupils' progress in reading and mathematics during primary school: Associations with ethnic group and sex'. *Educational Research*, 33 (2): 133–40.

Ramji, H. (2009), *Researching Race: Theory, Methods and Analysis*. Maidenhead: Open University Press.

Rashid, N. and Gregory, E. (1997), 'Learning to read, reading to learn: The importance of siblings in the language development of young bilingual children', in E. Gregory (ed.), *One Child, Many Worlds: Early Learning in Multicultural Communities*. London: David Fulton, pp. 107–23.

Rattansi, A. (1994), '"Western" racisms, ethnicities and identities in a "postmodern" frame', in S. Westwood and A. Rattansi (eds), *Racism, Modernity and Identity on the Western Front*. Cambridge: Polity Press, pp. 1–23.

Reay, D. and Mirza, H. S. (1997), 'Uncovering genealogies of the margins: Black supplementary schooling'. *British Journal of Sociology of Education*, 18 (4): 477–99.

Richards, S. (2008), *The Way We See It*. Stoke-on-Trent: Trentham.

Richardson, B. (ed.) (2005), *Tell It Like It Is: How Our Schools Fail Black Children*. London: Bookmarks.

Richardson, R. (2010), 'The Equality Act 2010, some of the implications for schools'. *Naldic Quarterly Spring 2010*, 7 (3): 10–13.

Richardson, R. and Miles, B. (2003), *Equality Stories: Recognition, Respect and Raising Achievement*. Stoke-on-Trent: Trentham.

— (2008), *Racist Incidents and Bullying in Schools: How To Prevent Them and How To Respond When They Happen*. Stoke-on-Trent: Trentham.

Richardson, R. and Wood, A. (2000), *Inclusive Schools, Inclusive Society: Race and Identity on the Agenda*. Stoke-on-Trent: Trentham.

Runnymede Trust (1997), *Islamophobia: A Challenge for Us All*. London: The Runnymede Trust.

— (1994), *Multi-Ethnic Britain: Facts and Trends*. London: The Runnymede Trust.

Rutter, J. (2004), 'Community Schools and Refugee Children'. www.multiverse.ac.uk/ViewArticle2. Last accessed on 7 November 2007.

— (2010), 'Lobbying for our future'. *Naldic Quarterly Spring 2010*, 7 (3): 5–7.

Sammons, P. (1994), 'Gender, Ethnic and Socio-Economic Differences in Attainment and Progress: A Longitudinal Analysis of Student Achievement Over Nine Years'. Paper prepared for the Symposium Equity Issues in Performance Assessment. Annual Meeting of the American Educational Research Association, New Orleans.

— (1995), 'Gender, ethnic and socio-economic differences in attainment and progress: A longitudinal analysis of student achievement over nine years'. *British Educational Research Journal*, 21 (4): 465–85.

Sammons, P. and Hind, A. (1997), 'Accounting for variation in pupil attainment at the end of Key Stage One'. *British Educational Research Journal*, 23 (4): 489–508.

Scottish Government (2009), *Destination of Leavers From Scottish Schools: 2008–2009*. Edinburgh: Scottish Government.

— (2010a), *SQA Attainment and School Leaver Qualifications in Scotland: 2008–2009*. Edinburgh: Scottish Government.

— (2010b), *Exclusions From School, 2008–2009*. Edinburgh: Scottish Government.

Scourfield, J., Evans, J., Shah, W. and Beynon, H. (2005), 'The negotiation of minority ethnic identities in virtually all-white communities: Research with children and their families in the South Wales valleys'. *Children and Society*, 19: 211–24.

Sewell, T. (1996), 'United front to preserve cultural practices'. *Times Educational Supplement*. October no. 4191.

— (1997), *Black Masculinities and Schooling: How Black Boys Survive Modern Schooling*. Stoke-on-Trent: Trentham.

Shain, F. (2003), *The Schooling and Identity of Asian Girls*. Stoke-on-Trent: Trentham.

Shiner, M. and Modood, T. (2002), 'Help or hindrance? Higher education and the route to ethnic equality'. *British Journal of Sociology of Education*, 23 (2): 209–32.

Siraj Blatchford, I. (1994), *The Early Years: Laying the Foundations for Racial Equality*. Stoke-on-Trent: Trentham.

Smith, D. and Tomlinson, S. (1989), *The School Effect: A Study of Multi-Racial Comprehensives*. London: Policy Studies Institute.

Smith, E. (2003), 'Failing boys and moral panics: Perspectives on the underachievement debate'. *British Journal of Education Studies*, 51 (3): 282–95.

— (2005), *Analysing Underachievement in Schools*. London: Continuum.

Sneddon, R. (2003) 'Every Teacher Has a Story to Tell: A Pilot Study of Teachers in Supplementary and Mother Tongue Schools'. www.multiverse.ac.uk/ViewArticle2

Solomos, J. and Back, L. (2000), 'Introduction: Theorising race and racism', in J. Solomos and L. Back, (eds), *Theories of Race and Racism: A Reader*. London: Routledge, pp. 1–32.

Southwark (1994), *Educational Statistics 1993–1994*. London: London Borough of Southwark.

Stanley, L. and Wise, S. (1990), 'Method, methodology and epistemology in feminist research processes', in L. Stanley, (ed.), *Feminist Praxis: Research, Theory and Epistemology in Feminist Sociology*. London: Routledge, pp. 20–60.

Stevens, P. (2009), 'Pupils' perspectives on racism and differential treatment by teachers: On stragglers, the ill and being deviant'. *British Educational Research Journal*, 35 (3): 413–30.

Strand, S. (1997), 'Pupil progress during Key Stage 1: A value added analysis of school effects'. *British Educational Research Journal*, 23 (4): 471–87.

— (1999), 'Ethnic group, sex and economic disadvantage: Associations with pupils' educational progress from Baseline to the end of Key Stage 1'. *British Educational Research Journal*, 25 (2): 179–200.

— (2007a), 'Surveying the views of pupils attending supplementary schools in England'. *Educational Research*, 49 (1): 1–19.

— (2007b), *Minority Ethnic Pupils in the Longitudinal Study of Young People in England*. London: Department for Children, Schools and Families.

— (2008), *Minority Ethnic Pupils in the Longitudinal Study of Young People in England: Extension Report on Performance in Public Examinations at Age 16*. London: Department for Children, Schools and Families.

Tanna, K. (1990), 'Excellence, equality and educational reform: The myth of South Asian achievement levels'. *New Community*, 16: 349–68.

Thomas, S. and Mortimore, P. (1994), *Report on Value Added Analysis of 1993 GCSE Examination Results in Lancashire*. London: University of London, Institute of Education.

Thomas, W. P. and Collier, V. (1997), *School Effectiveness for Language Minority Students*. Washington: National Clearing House for Bilingual Education.

Tikley, L., Chamion, C. and Haynes, J. (2004), *Understanding the Educational Needs of Mixed Heritage Pupils*. Birmingham: Department for Education and Skills.

Tizard, B., Blatchford, P., Burke, J., Farquar, C. and Plewis, I. (1988), *Young Children at School in the Inner City*. Hove: Lawrence Erlbaum.

Tomlinson, S. (1980), 'The educational performance of ethnic minority children'. *New Community*, 8: 213–35.

— (1983), *Ethnic Minorities in British Schools: A Review of the Literature 1960–82*. London: Heinemann.

— (1986), *Ethnic Minority Achievement and Equality of Opportunity*. Nottingham: University of Nottingham School of Education.

— (1990), *Multicultural Education in White Schools*. London: Batsford.

— (1993), 'Ethnic minorities: Involved partners or problem partners?', in P. Munn (ed.), *Parents and Schools, Customers, Managers or Partners?* London: Routledge, pp. 131–47.

— (2008), *Race and Education: Policy and Politics in Britain*. Maidenhead: Open University/McGrawHill Education.

Tomlinson, S. and Hutchinson, S. (1991), *Bangladeshi Parents and Education in Tower Hamlets: An ACE-University of Lancaster Research Project*. Lancaster: University of Lancaster.

TowerHamlets (1994), *Analysis of 1994 GCSE Results*. London: London Borough of Tower Hamlets.

Troyna, B. (1984), 'Fact or artefact? The 'educational underachievement' of Black pupils'. *British Journal of Sociology of Education*, 5 (2): 153–66.

— (1988), 'The career of an anti-racist education school policy: Some observations on the mismanagement of change', in A. G. Green and S. J. Ball (eds), *Progress and Inequality in Comprehensive Education*. London and New York: Routledge, pp. 158–78.

— (1991a), 'Children, 'race' and racism: The limitations of research and policy'. *British Journal of Education Studies*, 39 (4): 425–36.

— (1991b), 'Underachievers or underrated? The experiences of pupils of South Asian origin in secondary schools'. *British Educational Research Journal*, 17 (4): 361–76.

— (1992), 'Ethnicity and the organisation of learning groups: A case study'. *Educational Research*, 34 (1): 45–55.

— (1993a), 'Underachiever or misunderstood? A reply to Roger Gomm'. *British Educational Research Journal*, 19 (2): 167–74.

— (1993b), *Racism and Education*. Buckingham: Open University Press.

— (1995), 'Beyond reasonable doubt? Researching "race" in educational settings'. *Oxford Review of Education*, 21 (4): 395–408.

— (ed.) (1987), *Racial Inequality in Education*. London: Tavistock.

Troyna, B. and Carrington, B. (1989), 'Whose side are we on? Ethical dilemmas in research on 'race' and education', in R. Burgess (ed.), *The Ethics of Education Research*. London: Falmer, pp. 205–23.

— (1990), *Education, Racism and Reform*. London: Routledge.

Troyna, B. and Hatcher, R. (1992), *Racism in Children's Lives: A Study of Mainly-White Primary Schools*. London: Routledge.

Troyna, B. and Williams, J. (1986), *Racism, Education and the State*. Beckenham: Croom Helm.

Vincent, C. (2000), *Including Parents? Education, Citizenship and Parental Agency*. Buckingham: Open University Press.

Walters, S. (2001), 'Researching "Bangladeshi Underachievement": A Pilot Study'. Unpublished MSc Dissertation, Oxford University.

— (2003), 'Bangladeshi Pupils: Experiences, Identity and Achievement'. Unpublished DPhil thesis. Oxford University Department of Educational Studies.

— (2004), '"I don't think she knew I couldn't do it" Bangladeshi pupils and learning to read in the Year 3 classroom', in B. Jeffrey and G. Walford (eds), *Ethnographies of Educational and Cultural Conflicts: Strategies and Resolutions*. Amsterdam: Elsevier, pp. 107–28.

— (2007), '"How do you know that he's bright but lazy?" Teachers' assessments of Bangladeshi English as an additional language pupils in two Year Three classrooms'. *Oxford Review of Education*, 33 (1): 87–101.

— (2011), 'Provision, purpose and pedagogy in a Bengali Supplementary School'. *Language Learning Journal*, 39 (2): 163–75.

Wandsworth Education Department (1994), *Key Stage One Assessment Results: Research Report REU 40.49*. London: London Borough of Wandsworth.

Weedon, E., McCluskey, G., Riddell, S. and Ahlgren, L. (forthcoming), 'Muslim Pupils' Educational Experiences in England and Scotland: Policy and Practice in Scotland'. Edinburgh: Moray House School of Education, The University of Edinburgh.

Wei, L. (2006), 'Complementary schools, past, present and future'. *Language and Education*, 20 (1): 76–83.

Welsh Assembly Government (2003), 'The Achievement of Ethnic Minority Pupils in Wales'. http://wales.gov.uk/topics/educationalskills/publications/reports. Last accessed on 25 August 2010.

— (2009a), 'Schools in Wales: General Statistics 2009'. www.wales.gov.uk/topics/statistics/publications/schoolsgen09/?lang=en. Last accessed on 25 August 2010.

— (2009b), 'Schools in Wales: Examination Performance 2008'. www.wales.gov.uk/topics/statistics. Last accessed on 25 August 2010.

— (2009c), 'National Curriculum Assessments of 7, 11 and 14 Year Olds, 2009. www.wales.gov.uk/topics/statistics. Last accessed on 25 August 2010.

— (2009d), 'GCSE/GNVQ and GCE 'A', 'AS' and AVCE Results', 2009. www.wales.gov.uk/topics/statistics. Last accessed on 25 August 2010.

— (2010), 'Statistical Bulletin: Academic Achievement by Pupil Characteristics 2007–2009. http://wales.gov.uk/doc/statistics/2010. Last accessed on 25 August 2010.

Whalley, M. and Team, T. P. G. C. (2001), *Involving Parents in Their Children's Learning*. London: Paul Chapman.

Wright, C. (1986), 'School processes: An ethnographic study', in J. Egglestone, D. Dunn and M. Anjali (eds), *Education For Some*. Stoke-on-Trent: Trentham, pp. 127–79.

— (1987), 'Black students – white teachers', in B. Troyna, (ed.), *Racial Inequality in Education*. London: Tavistock, pp. 109–26.

— (1990), 'Comments in reply to the article by P. Foser: "Cases not proven: an evaluation of two studies of teacher racism"'. *British Educational Research Journal*, 16 (4): 351–55.

— (1992), *Race Relations in the Primary School*. London: David Fulton.

Wright, C., Weekes, D. and McGlaughlin, A. (2000), *'Race', Class and Gender in Exclusion from School*. London: Falmer.

Wu, C. J. (2006), 'Look who's talking: Language choices and culture of learning in UK Chinese classrooms'. *Language and Education*, 20 (1): 62–75.

Youdell, D. (2003), 'Identity traps or how Black students fail: The interactions between biographical, sub-cultural and learner identities'. *British Journal of Sociology of Education*, 24 (1): 3–20.

— (2006), *Impossible Bodies, Impossible Selves: Exclusions and Student Subjectivities*. Dordrecht, Netherlands: Springer.

Index